ENGLISH/THAI
อังกฤษ/ไทย

THE OXFORD
Picture
Dictionary

NORMA SHAPIRO AND JAYME ADELSON-GOLDSTEIN

Translated by Dr. Nisai Kaewsanchai

Oxford University Press

Oxford University Press
198 Madison Avenue, New York, NY 10016 USA
Great Clarendon Street, Oxford OX2 6DP England

Oxford New York

*Athens Auckland Bangkok Bogotá Buenos Aires
Cape Town Chennai Dar es Salaam Delhi Florence Hong Kong
Istanbul Karachi Kolkata Kuala Lumpur Madrid
Melbourne Mexico City Mumbai Nairobi Paris São Paulo
Shanghai Singapore Taipei Tokyo Toronto Warsaw*

*And associated companies in
Berlin Ibadan*

OXFORD is a trademark of Oxford University Press.

Editorial Manager: Janet Aitchison
Art Director: Lynn Luchetti
Senior Editor: Eliza Jensen
Senior Designer: Susan P. Brorein
Senior Production Editor: Robyn F. Clemente
Art Buyer: Tracy A. Hammond
Cover Design Production: Brett Sonnenschein
Translation Reviewed by: Karam S. Tannous
Cover design by Silver Editions
Translation in Thai by: Dr. Nisai Kaewsanchai

Printing (last digit): 10 9 8 7 6 5 4 3 2 1

Printed in Thailand.

Distributed by D.K. Today Co.,Ltd.

Illustrations by: David Aikins, Doug Archer, Craig Attebery,
Garin Baker, Sally Bensusen, Eliot Bergman, Mark Bischel, Dan
Brown / Artworks NY, Roy Douglas Buchman, George Burgos /
Larry Dodge, Rob Burman, Carl Cassler, Mary Chandler, Robert
Crawford, Jim Delapine, Judy Francis, Graphic Chart and Map
Co., Dale Gustafson, Biruta Akerbergs Hansen, Marcia
Hartsock, C.M.I., David Hildebrand, The Ivy League of Artists,
Inc. / Judy Degraffenreid, The Ivy League of Artists, Inc. / Tom
Powers, The Ivy League of Artists, Inc. / John Rice, Pam
Johnson, Ed Kurtzman, Narda Lebo, Scott A. MacNeill /
MACNEILL & MACINTOSH, Andy Lendway / Deborah Wolfe
Ltd., Jeffrey Mangiat, Suzanne Mogensen, Mohammad
Mansoor, Tom Newsom, Melodye Benson Rosales, Stacey
Schuett, Rob Schuster, James Seward, Larry Taugher, Bill
Thomson, Anna Veltfort, Nina Wallace, Wendy Wassink-
Ackison, Michael Wepplo, Don Wieland
Thanks to Mike Mikos for his preliminary architectural sketches
of several pieces.

References
Boyer, Paul S., Clifford E. Clark, Jr., Joseph F. Kett, Thomas L.
Purvis, Harvard Sitkoff, Nancy Woloch *The Enduring Vision: A
History of the American People*, Lexington, Massachusettes:
D.C. Heath and Co., 1990.

Grun, Bernard, *The Timetables of History: A Horizontal Linkage
of People and Events,* (based on Werner Stein's Kulturfahrplan)
New York: A Touchstone Book, Simon and Schuster, 1946,
1963, 1975, 1979.

Statistical Abstract of the United States: 1996, 116th Edition,
Washington, DC: US Bureau of the Census, 1996.

The World Book Encyclopedia, Chicago: World Book Inc., a
Scott Fetzer Co., 1988 Edition.

Toff, Nancy, Editor-in-Chief, *The People of North America*
(Series), New York: Chelsea House Publishers, Main Line
Books, 1988.

Trager, James, *The People's Chronology, A Year-by-Year Record
of Human Events from Prehistory to the Present,* New York:
Henry Holt Reference Book, 1992.

Acknowledgments

The publisher and authors would like to thank the following people for reviewing the manuscript and/or participating in focus groups as the book was being developed:

Ana Maria Aguilera, Lubie Alatriste, Ann Albarelli, Margaret Albers, Sherry Allen, Fiona Armstrong, Ted Auerbach, Steve Austen, Jean Barlow, Sally Bates, Sharon Batson, Myra Baum, Mary Beauparlant, Gretchen Bitterlin, Margrajean Bonilla, Mike Bostwick, Shirley Brod, Lihn Brown, Trish Brys-Overeem, Lynn Bundy, Chris Bunn, Carol Carvel, Leslie Crucil, Jill DeLa Llata, Robert Denheim, Joshua Denk, Kay Devonshire, Thomas Dougherty, Gudrun Draper, Sara Eisen, Lynda Elkins, Ed Ende, Michelle Epstein, Beth Fatemi, Andra R. Fawcett, Alice Fiedler, Harriet Fisher, James Fitzgerald, Mary Fitzsimmons, Scott Ford, Barbara Gaines, Elizabeth Garcia Grenados, Maria T. Gerdes, Penny Giacalone, Elliott Glazer, Jill Gluck de la Llata, Javier Gomez, Pura Gonzales, Carole Goodman, Joyce Grabowski, Maggie Grennan, Joanie Griffin, Sally Hansen, Fotini Haritos, Alice Hartley, Fernando Herrera, Ann Hillborn, Mary Hopkins, Lori Howard, Leann Howard, Pamela Howard, Rebecca Hubner, Jan Jarrell, Vicki Johnson, Michele Kagan, Nanette Kaska, Gena Katsaros, Evelyn Kay, Greg Keech, Cliff Ker, Gwen Kerner-Mayer, Marilou Kessler, Patty King, Linda Kiperman, Joyce Klapp, Susan Knutson, Sandy Kobrine, Marinna Kolaitis, Donna Korol, Lorraine Krampe, Karen Kuser, Andrea Lang, Nancy Lebow, Tay Lesley, Gale Lichter, Sandie Linn, Rosario Lorenzano, Louise Louie, Cheryl Lucas, Ronna Magy, Juanita Maltese, Mary Marquardsen, Carmen Marques Rivera, Susan McDowell, Alma McGee, Jerry McLeroy, Kevin McLure, Joan Meier, Patsy Mills, Judy Montague, Vicki Moore, Eneida Morales, Glenn Nadelbach, Elizabeth Neblett, Kathleen Newton, Yvonne Nishio, Afra Nobay, Rosa Elena Ochoa, Jean Owensby, Jim Park, John Perkins, Jane Pers, Laura Peskin, Maria Pick, Percy Pleasant, Selma Porter, Kathy Quinones, Susan Ritter, Martha Robledo, Maureen Rooney, Jean Rose, David Ross, Julietta Ruppert, Lorraine Ruston, Susan Ryan, Frederico Salas, Leslie Salmon, Jim Sandifer, Linda Sasser, Lisa Schreiber, Mary Segovia, Abe Shames, Debra Shaw, Stephanie Shipp, Pat Singh, Mary Sklavos, Donna Stark, Claire Cocoran Stehling, Lynn Sweeden, Joy Tesh, Sue Thompson, Christine Tierney, Laura Topete, Carmen Villanueva, Laura Webber, Renée Weiss, Beth Winningham, Cindy Wislofsky, Judy Wood, Paula Yerman.

A special thanks to Marna Shulberg and the students of the Saticoy Branch of Van Nuys Community Adult School.

We would also like to thank the following individuals and organizations who provided their expertise:

Carl Abato, Alan Goldman, Dr. Larry Falk, Caroll Gray, Henry Haskell, Susan Haskell, Los Angeles Fire Department, Malcolm Loeb, Barbara Lozano, Lorne Dubin, United Farm Workers.

Authors' Acknowledgments

Throughout our careers as English language teachers, we have found inspiration in many places—in the classroom with our remarkable students, at schools, conferences, and workshops with our fellow teachers, and with our colleagues at the ESL Teacher Institute. We are grateful to be part of this international community.

We would like to sincerely thank and acknowledge Eliza Jensen, the project's Senior Editor. Without Eliza, this book would not have been possible. Her indomitable spirit, commitment to clarity, and unwavering advocacy allowed us to realize the book we envisioned.

Creating this dictionary was a collaborative effort and it has been our privilege to work with an exceptionally talented group of individuals who, along with Eliza Jensen, make up the Oxford Picture Dictionary team. We deeply appreciate the contributions of the following people:

Lynn Luchetti, Art Director, whose aesthetic sense and sensibility guided the art direction of this book,

Susan Brorein, Senior Designer, who carefully considered the design of each and every page,

Klaus Jekeli, Production Editor, who pored over both manuscript and art to ensure consistency and accuracy, and

Tracy Hammond, Art Buyer, who skillfully managed thousands of pieces of art and reference material.

We also want to thank Susan Mazer, the talented artist who was by our side for the initial problem-solving and Mary Chandler who also lent her expertise to the project.

We have learned much working with Marjorie Fuchs, Lori Howard, and Renée Weiss, authors of the dictionary's ancillary materials. We thank them for their on-going contributions to the dictionary program.

We must make special mention of Susan Lanzano, Editorial Manager, whose invaluable advice, insights, and queries were an integral part of the writing process.

This book is dedicated to my husband, Neil Reichline, who has encouraged me to take the road less traveled, and to my sons, Eli and Alex, who have allowed me to sit at their baseball games with my yellow notepad. —NS

This book is lovingly dedicated to my husband, Gary and my daughter, Emily Rose, both of whom hugged me tight and let me work into the night. —JAG

A Letter to the Teacher จดหมายถึงคุณครู

หนังสือเล่มนี้เป็นแหล่งข้อมูลทางด้านคำศัพท์ที่กว้างขวางมาก สำหรับคุณครูและนักเรียนของท่านไว้ค้นคว้ามากกว่า 3,700 คำ โดยแต่ละคำมีภาพประกอบที่สวยงามและนำเสนอในบริบทที่เต็มไปด้วยความหมายชัดเจน The Oxford Picture Dictionary สามารถทำให้นักเรียนของท่านเรียนและใช้ภาษาอังกฤษในทุกแง่ทุกมุมของชีวิตประจำวัน หัวเรื่องต่างๆ ถึง 140 หัวเรื่องครอบคลุมไปถึงเรื่องบ้านและครอบครัว สถานที่ทำงาน ชุมชน สุขภาพอนามัย และสาขาวิชาการต่างๆ มากมาย หัวข้อต่างๆ ถูกจัดให้อยู่ใน 12 หมวดใหญ่ๆ ซึ่งอยู่บนพื้นฐานของหลักสูตรภาษาอังกฤษขั้นเริ่มเรียนและระดับต้นๆ บัญชีคำศัพท์ของพจนานุกรมมีทั้งคำศัพท์เดี่ยวๆ และคำศัพท์ที่เป็นกริยาวลี คำบุพบท และคำคุณศัพท์จำนวนมาก ก็ถูกนำเสนอในรูปของวลีเช่นกัน และการสาธิตการใช้คำเหล่านี้ก็จะอยู่ในลักษณะใช้ร่วมกัน

The Oxford Picture Dictionary ใช้รูปแบบหลากหลายในการนำเสนอเพื่อให้เหมาะสมกับหัวเรื่องนั้นๆ ในบางกรณีคำศัพท์ต่างๆ จะถูกจัดให้เป็นหมวดหมู่และหน้ากระดาษก็จัดให้เป็นสัดส่วน เพื่อเปิดโอกาสให้ท่านช่วยนักเรียนของท่านให้เน้นความสนใจเป็นเรื่องๆ ไป

ภายในบัญชีคำศัพท์

• คำนาม คำคุณศัพท์ คำบุพบท และคำวิเศษณ์ต่างๆ จะมีเลขกำกับข้างหน้า

• คำกริยาจะพิมพ์ด้วยตัวหนาและมีตัวอักษรนำหน้า

• คำบุพบทและคำคุณศัพท์ที่เป็นจุดเน้นในวลีต่างๆ จะพิมพ์ด้วยตัวหนา

พจนานุกรมเล่มนี้ได้รวบรวมแบบฝึกหัดหลากหลายชนิดและเครื่องมือในการศึกษาด้วยตนเองเพื่อนำไปสู่การใช้คำใหม่อย่างถูกต้องและคล่องแคล่ว

• แบบฝึกหัดข้างท้ายของหน้าช่วยให้นักเรียนพัฒนาคำศัพท์โดยการฝึกที่ใช้กระสวนประโยคและประยุกต์ภาษาที่เรียนใหม่ๆ เข้ากับหัวข้อเรื่องอื่นๆ ตลอดจนคำถามที่เป็นเรื่องส่วนตัว

• การเรียงคำตามลำดับตัวอักษรในดัชนีจะช่วยให้นักเรียนค้นหาคำทั้งหมดและหัวเรื่องได้รวดเร็ว

• สัทอักษรที่กำกับต่างๆในดัชนีจะช่วยแนะนำให้นักเรียนออกเสียงได้ถูกต้อง

• คำกริยาทั้งหมดในดัชนีที่นำเสนอในพจนานุกรมฉบับนี้ให้ข้อมูลแก่นักเรียนเกี่ยวกับรูปแบบ present past และ past participle อีกด้วย

การสอนคำศัพท์

ความต้องการของนักเรียนของท่านและปรัชญาในการสอนของท่านเป็นสิ่งที่จะบอกให้ทราบว่าท่านจะใช้หนังสือ The Oxford Picture Dictionary กับนักเรียนของท่านอย่างไร ข้อแนะนำต่อไปนี้ อาจช่วยให้ท่าน

ดัดแปลงเนื้อหาต่างๆ ให้เหมาะสมกับวิชาและนักเรียนที่ท่านกำลังสอน (สำหรับข้อแนะนำที่เป็นลักษณะเฉพาะและที่เป็นขั้นเป็นตอนในการจัดกิจกรรม ในการนำเสนอและฝึกคำศัพท์ ให้ท่านกรุณาศึกษาจากคู่มือครู)

ปริทัศน์เกี่ยวกับหัวเรื่อง

เริ่มต้นบทเรียนที่ดีคือการพูดคุยกับนักเรียนเพื่อที่จะทำให้ทราบว่านักเรียนเขามีความรู้เกี่ยวกับหัวเรื่องหรืออยังวิธีการที่จะทำกิจกรรมนี้อีกหลายวิธี เช่น

• ถามคำถามที่จะไปเกี่ยวข้องกับหัวเรื่อง

• ให้นักเรียนระดมพลังสมองช่วยกันบอกคำที่เขาทราบแล้วจากหัวเรื่องที่จะเรียน

• ถามคำถามเกี่ยวกับรูปภาพที่ปรากฏอยู่ในหน้านั้นๆ

การนำเสนอคำศัพท์

เมื่อท่านค้นพบว่าคำศัพท์ใดที่นักเรียนของท่านทราบแล้วท่านก็พร้อมที่จะเน้นความสนใจไปที่การนำเสนอคำที่นักเรียนจำเป็นต้องเรียนรู้ การแนะนำคำใหม่ 10-15 คำ ในแต่ละบทเรียนจะทำให้นักเรียนเกิดการเรียนรู้อย่างจริงจัง ในหน้าที่มีคำศัพท์มากๆ และนักเรียนยังไม่รู้จักคำเหล่านั้น ท่านอาจจะนำเสนอคำเป็นหมวดหมู่ก่อนหรืออาจจะเลือกคำที่ท่านต้องการจะสอนก็ได้

ต่อไปนี้เป็นเทคนิค 4 แบบ ในการนำเสนอการสอนคำศัพท์ เทคนิคที่ท่านเลือกใช้นั้นจะขึ้นอยู่กับหัวข้อที่กำลังเรียนและระดับความรู้ของนักเรียนของท่าน

• พูดคำใหม่และบรรยายหรือให้คำนิยามโดยอาศัยบริบทของรูปภาพนั้นๆ

• สาธิตหรือแสดงท่าทางของคำกริยาต่างๆ ให้นักเรียนดูและให้นักเรียนอาสาสมัครออกมาแสดงท่าทางของกริยานั้นๆ ตามคำที่ท่านพูด

• ใช้วิธีของ TPR คือ Total Physical Response เพื่อเพิ่มความเข้าใจในคำศัพท์มากยิ่งขึ้น TPR คือการที่ครูออกคำสั่งและให้นักเรียนปฏิบัติตาม เช่น Put the pencil on your book. Put it on your notebook. Put it on your desk.

• ถามคำถาม 2-3 คำถามเพื่อเสริมสร้างความเข้าใจยิ่งขึ้นและให้โอกาสแก่นักเรียนพูดคำศัพท์ใหม่ๆ เหล่านั้น ตัวอย่างเช่น

➤ เริ่มต้นด้วยคำถามประเภท "yes/no" เช่น
Is # 16 chalk? (yes)

➤ แล้วดำเนินต่อด้วยคำถามประเภท "or" เช่น
Is # 16 chalk or marker? (chalk)

➤ สุดท้ายถามคำถามประเภท "Wh" เช่น
What can I use to write on this paper? (a marker/use a marker)

ตรวจสอบความเข้าใจ (Check comprehension)

ก่อนที่เริ่มสอนขั้นฝึก (practice stage) นั้นคุณครูควรมีความแน่ใจว่านักเรียนทั้งหมดเข้าใจคำศัพท์ที่เรียน มีหลายสิ่งหลายอย่างที่ท่านสามารถทำได้ในการเช็คว่านักเรียนเข้าใจหรือไม่ ต่อไปนี้เป็น 2 กิจกรรมที่น่าลองทำดู

- บอกให้นักเรียนเปิดหนังสือและให้ชี้ไปที่ภาพที่ท่านขอดู ให้ท่านพูดคำศัพท์ที่เรียนแบบชนิดสุ่มตัวอย่าง คือสลับไปมาหรือคละกันและให้ท่านเดินไปรอบๆ ห้อง ขณะที่พูดคำศัพท์เหล่านั้นไปและดูว่านักเรียนชี้ภาพเหล่านั้นถูกต้องหรือไม่

- สร้างข้อความที่ถูกหรือผิด (true/false) ขึ้นมาเกี่ยวกับคำศัพท์ที่เรียนให้นักเรียนชู 2 นิ้ว ถ้าข้อความนั้นถูกต้อง ให้ชู 3 นิ้วถ้าข้อความนั้นผิด เช่น

> You can write with a marker. (นักเรียนชู 2 นิ้ว)
>
> You raise your notebook to talk to the teacher. (นักเรียนชู 3 นิ้ว)

ให้คุณครูใช้เวลาอีกเล็กน้อยทบทวนดูว่าคำใดบ้างที่นักเรียนยังมีปัญหาอยู่ก่อนที่จะเริ่มให้ทำกิจกรรมการฝึกต่อไป

การฝึกคำศัพท์ (Practice the vocabulary)

กิจกรรมที่เสนอแนะไว้ให้แล้วนั้นจะช่วยให้นักเรียนมีโอกาสใช้คำศัพท์ใหม่ในการสื่อสารที่มีความหมาย แบบฝึกหัดที่อยู่ด้านท้ายของหน้ามากมายเป็นแหล่งของกิจกรรมที่เสนอแนะสำหรับฝึกให้คล่อง

- **Talk about.....(การพูดเกี่ยวกับ....)**

กิจกรรมนี้จะทำให้นักเรียนมีโอกาสฝึกคำศัพท์ต่างๆ โดยวิธีการนำประโยคหนึ่งเป็นประโยคเริ่มต้น แล้วนักเรียนก็พูดประโยคที่สองแทนที่ประโยคที่หนึ่ง และประโยคที่สามแทนที่ประโยคที่สองไปเรื่อยๆ ประโยคที่นำมาฝึกเป็นประโยคที่มีความหมายตามหัวข้อเรื่องที่เรียนด้วย เช่น

- **Practice asking for things in the dinning room.** (ฝึกการขอร้องเพื่อต้องการบางสิ่งบางอย่างในห้องรับประทานอาหาร)

> *Please pass <u>the platter</u>.*
>
> *May I have <u>the creamer</u>?*
>
> *Could I have a <u>fork please</u>?*

- **Use the new language. (การใช้ภาษาใหม่)**

กิจกรรมนี้ให้นักเรียนได้มีโอกาสระดมกำลังสมอง (brainstorm) ช่วยกันบอกคำศัพท์จากหมวดหมู่ต่างๆ หรืออาจให้นักเรียนประยุกต์คำศัพท์ที่ได้เรียนไปแล้วใช้กับคำศัพท์ในหมวดหมู่อื่นๆ เช่น เรื่องสีต่างๆ ที่อยู่หน้า 12 ครูให้นักเรียนเปิดไปดูหมวดเสื้อผ้า I (clothing) หน้า 64-65 แล้วให้นักเรียนบอกสีของเสื้อผ้าที่พบเห็นในหน้านั้นๆ

- **Share your answer. (แลกเปลี่ยนคำตอบ)**

คำถามเหล่านี้จะช่วยให้นักเรียนมีโอกาสขยายการใช้คำศัพท์ที่เรียนให้กว้างขวางขึ้นและอยู่ในรูปของการสนทนาอภิปรายในเรื่องส่วนตัวมากขึ้น นักเรียนสามารถที่จะถามและตอบคำถามในลักษณะเป็นการอภิปรายทั้งห้องก็ได้ เป็นคู่ก็ได้ หรือเป็นกลุ่มย่อยก็ได้หรือนักเรียนอาจจะเขียนคำตอบในลักษณะเป็นบันทึกก็ได้

สำหรับแบบฝึกหัดต่างๆ ที่เป็นลักษณะการสื่อสารท่านจะพบได้อีกมากจากหนังสือคู่มือครู Oxford Picture Dictionary Activities ส่วนหนังสือ The oxford Picture Dictionary Beginning and Intermediate Work books และหนังสือ the Oxford Picture Dictionary Readers ให้นักเรียนของท่านมีโอกาสฝึกฝนแบบฝึกหัดในการอ่านและเขียนที่เป็นลักษณะการสื่อสารอีกด้วย โดยยังอยู่ในรูปแบบของการควบคุมโครงสร้างทางภาษาอยู่ (controlled)

เราขอสนับสนุนให้ท่านดัดแปลงเนื้อหาในเล่มนี้เพื่อให้เข้ากับความเหมาะสมและความต้องการของชั้นเรียนของท่านและเรายินดีรับฟังข้อคิดเห็นและข้อเสนอแนะจากท่านเสมอโปรดเขียนมาถึงเราที่

Oxford University Press
ESL Department
198 Madison Avenue
New York, N.Y. 10016

Jayme Adelson-Goldstein

Norma Shapiro

A Letter to the Student

Dear Student of English,

Welcome to *The Oxford Picture Dictionary.* The more than 3,700 words in this book will help you as you study English.

Each page in this dictionary teaches about a specific topic. The topics are grouped together in units. All pages in a unit have the same color and symbol. For example, each page in the Food unit has this symbol:

On each page you will see pictures and words. The pictures have numbers or letters that match the numbers or letters in the word lists. Verbs (action words) are identified by letters and all other words are identified by numbers.

How to find words in this book

- Use the Table of Contents, pages vii–ix.
  Look up the general topic you want to learn about.

- Use the Index, pages 173–205.
  Look up individual words in alphabetical (A–Z) order.

- Go topic by topic.
  Look through the book until you find something that interests you.

How to use the Index

When you look for a word in the index this is what you will see:

the word   the number (or letter) in the word list

apples [apəlz] 50–4

the pronunciation   the page number

If the word is on one of the maps, pages 122–125, you will find it in the Geographical Index on pages 206–208.

How to use the Verb Guide

When you want to know the past form of a verb or its past participle form, look up the verb in the verb guide. The regular verbs and their spelling changes are listed on pages 170–171. The simple form, past form, and past participle form of irregular verbs are listed on page 172.

Workbooks

There are two workbooks to help you practice the new words:
The Oxford Picture Dictionary Beginning and *Intermediate Workbooks.*

As authors and teachers we both know how difficult English can be (and we're native speakers!). When we wrote this book, we asked teachers and students from the U.S. and other countries for their help and ideas. We hope their ideas and ours will help you. Please write to us with your comments or questions at:

Oxford University Press
ESL Department
198 Madison Avenue
New York, NY 10016

We wish you success!

Jayme Adelson-Goldstein   *Norma Shapiro*

สวัสดีนักเรียนที่กำลังเรียนภาษาอังกฤษ

ยินดีต้อนรับสู่ The Oxford Picture Dictionary คำที่มีมากกว่า 3700 คำในหนังสือเล่มนี้จะช่วยนักเรียนขณะเรียนภาษาอังกฤษ

แต่ละหน้าในพจนานุกรมนี้จะให้ความรู้เกี่ยวกับหัวข้อเรื่องเฉพาะเจาะจง หัวเรื่องต่างๆ ถูกจัดเป็นกลุ่มเข้าด้วยกันในแต่ละบทเรียน หน้าทุกหน้าในแต่ละบทจะมีสัญลักษณ์เดียวกันและสีเดียวกันทั้งหมด ตัวอย่างเช่นในแต่ละหน้าของหมวดที่เป็นอาหารจะมีสัญลักษณ์นี้

ในแต่ละหน้านักเรียนจะเห็นภาพและคำต่างๆ ภาพต่างๆ จะมีตัวเลขหรือตัวอักษรที่จับคู่ตรงกับตัวเลขหรืออักษรในบัญชีคำ คำกริยา จะนำหน้าด้วยตัวอักษรส่วนคำอื่นๆ ทั้งหมดจะนำหน้าด้วยตัวเลข

วิธีการหาคำในหนังสือเล่มนี้ (How to find words in this book)

- ใช้ตารางสารบัญหน้า VII - IX มองหาหัวข้อทั่วไปที่นักเรียนต้องการจะศึกษา
- ใช้ดัชนีที่อยู่ในหน้า 173-205 ค้นหาคำแต่ละคำในลักษณะที่เป็นการเรียงลำดับตัวอักษร (A-Z)
- หาตามลักษณะหัวข้อเรื่อง ค้นดูตลอดทั้งเล่มจนกระทั่งนักเรียนพบสิ่งที่น่าสนใจ

วิธีการใช้ดัชนี (How to use the index)

เมื่อนักเรียนค้นหาคำในดัชนีนักเรียนจะเห็นสิ่งเหล่านี้

the word   the number (or letter) in the word list

apples [apəlz] 50 – 4

the pronunciation   the page number

ถ้าคำอยู่ในแผนที่หน้า 122-125 นักเรียนจะค้นพบคำเหล่านั้นได้ในดัชนีที่เกี่ยวกับภูมิศาสตร์ (Geographical Index อยู่หน้า 206-208)

วิธีการใช้คำแนะนำเกี่ยวกับคำกริยา

เมื่อนักเรียนต้องการจะทราบว่า past form หรือ past participle form ของกริยาให้ค้นหาคำกริยาในหน้า verb guide คำกริยาที่เป็น regular verbs และการเปลี่ยนแปลงการสะกดคำของกริยาเหล่านี้อยู่ในหน้า 170-171 ส่วน simple form, past from และ past participle form ของกริยาที่เป็น irregular verbs จะอยู่ในหน้า 172

หนังสือแบบฝึกหัด (Workbooks)

มีหนังสือแบบฝึกหัดอยู่ 2 เล่ม ที่จะช่วยนักเรียนฝึกคำใหม่ๆ

The Oxford Picture Dictionary Beginning and Intermediate workbooks

ในฐานะที่เป็นผู้เขียนหนังสือและในฐานะที่เป็นครูเราทั้งสองทราบดีว่า ภาษาอังกฤษยากเพียงใดแม้เราซึ่งเป็นเจ้าของภาษาด้วยซ้ำ

เมื่อเราเขียนหนังสือเล่มนี้เราขอความร่วมมือไปยังครูและนักเรียนจากประเทศสหรัฐและประเทศอื่นสำหรับความช่วยเหลือและความเชื่อต่างๆ เราหวังว่าความคิดของท่านเหล่านั้นและความคิดของเราจะช่วยนักเรียนทุกคน โปรดเขียนมาถึงเราแสดงข้อคิดเห็นหรือคำถามมายัง

Oxford University Press
ESL Department
198 Madison Avenue
New York, N.Y. 10016

ขอให้นักเรียนจงประสบความสำเร็จ

Jayme Adelson-Goldstein   *Norma Shapiro*

Contents สารบัญ

1. Everyday Language ภาษาที่ใช้ในชีวิตประจำวัน

2. People ผู้คน

3. Housing บ้านเรือน

4. Food อาหาร

Contents สารบัญ

10. Plants and Animals พืชและสัตว์

11. Work งาน

12. Recreation การพักผ่อนหย่อนใจ

1. chalkboard
กระดานดำ

2. screen
ฉาก, จอ

3. student
นักเรียน

4. overhead projector
เครื่องฉายภาพข้ามศีรษะ

5. teacher
ครู

6. desk
โต๊ะเรียน

7. chair / seat
เก้าอี้ / ที่นั่ง

A. Raise your hand.
ยกมือขึ้น

B. Talk to the teacher.
พูดกับครู

C. Listen to a cassette.
ฟังเทป

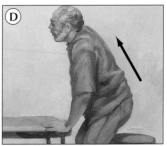

D. Stand up.
ยืนขึ้น

E. Sit down. / Take a seat.
นั่งลง

F. Point to the picture.
ชี้รูปภาพ

G. Write on the board.
เขียนกระดาน

H. Erase the board.
ลบกระดาน

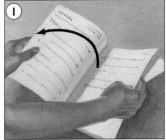

I. Open your book.
เปิดหนังสือ

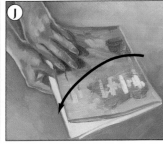

J. Close your book.
ปิดหนังสือ

K. Take out your pencil.
หยิบดินสอออกมา

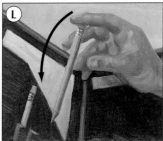

L. Put away your pencil.
เก็บดินสอ

8. bookcase
ชั้นวางหนังสือ

9. globe
ลูกโลก

10. clock
นาฬิกา

11. cassette player
เครื่องเล่นเทป

12. map
แผนที่

13. pencil sharpener
เครื่องเหลาดินสอ

14. bulletin board
กระดานติดประกาศ

15. computer
คอมพิวเตอร์

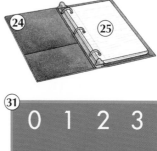

16. chalk
ชอล์กเขียนกระดาน

17. chalkboard eraser
แปรงลบกระดาน

18. pen
ปากกา

19. marker
ปากกาสำหรับทำเครื่องหมาย

20. pencil
ดินสอ

21. pencil eraser
ยางลบดินสอ

22. textbook
ตำรา

23. workbook
หนังสือแบบฝึกหัด

24. binder/notebook
แฟ้มเอกสาร / สมุดจด

25. notebook paper
กระดาษบันทึกข้อความ

26. spiral notebook
สมุดจดที่มีสันเป็นเกลียว

27. ruler
ไม้บรรทัด

28. dictionary
พจนานุกรม

29. picture dictionary
พจนานุกรมภาพ

30. the alphabet
ตัวอักษร

31. numbers
ตัวเลข

Use the new language. ใช้ภาษาใหม่

1. Name three things you can open.
2. Name three things you can put away.
3. Name three things you can write with.

Share your answers. แลกเปลี่ยนคำตอบ

1. Do you like to raise your hand?
2. Do you ever listen to cassettes in class?
3. Do you ever write on the board?

① SAM B. LARSON ② ③ ④

⑤ PINE AVE 446

⑥ 10

⑦ NEW YORK → Queens

⑧ NEW YORK

⑨ To: Sam B. Larson 446 Pine Ave. Queens, N.Y. → 11364

(718) 555-6314 ⑩ ② ⑪ 4 5 6 7 8 9 * 0 #

⑫ ⑬ ⑭

⑮ SOCIAL SECURITY 914-00-0000 OF HEALTH & HU... THIS NUMBER HAS BEEN ESTABLISHED FOR SAM B. LARSON Sam B. Larson SIGNATURE

⑯ MAY 1972
S M T W T F S
1 2 3 4 5 6
7 8 9 10 11 12 13
14 15 16 17 18 19 20
21 22 23 24 25 26 27
28 29 30 31

⑰ CANADA Ottawa ★

⑱ Sam B. Larson

School Registration Form
แบบฟอร์มการลงทะเบียนเข้าโรงเรียน

1. name _____

2. first name
ชื่อตัว

3. middle initial
ชื่อย่อตรงกลาง

4. last name
นามสกุล

5. address _____
ที่อยู่

6. apt. # * _____
หมายเลขอพาร์ตเม้นต์

7. city _____
เมือง

8. state _____
รัฐ

9. ZIP code _____
รหัสไปรษณีย์

( )
___ ___ ___

10. area code
รหัสทางไกล

11. telephone number
หมายเลขโทรศัพท์

12. sex:
เพศ

13. ☐ male
ชาย

14. ☐ female
หญิง

15. Social Security number
หมายเลขประกันสังคม

16. date of birth _____
วันที่เกิด (month) (date) (year)
เดือน วัน ปี

17. place of birth _____
สถานที่เกิด

18. signature _____
ลายมือชื่อ

* apt. # = apartment number หมายเลขอพาร์ตเม้นต์

Ⓐ L-A-R-S-O-N

Ⓑ 3. middle initial 7. city Queens 8. sta...
6. apt. # * 10
(718) 555-6314 11. telephone number
9. area code
15. Social Security number
17. place of birth
18. signature

Ⓒ SAM B. LARSON

Ⓓ Sam B. Larson

A. Spell your name.
สะกดชื่อของคุณ

B. Fill out a form.
กรอกแบบฟอร์ม

C. Print your name.
เขียนชื่อคุณด้วยตัวบรรจง

D. Sign your name.
เซ็นชื่อของคุณ

Talk about yourself. พูดเกี่ยวกับตัวคุณ

My first name is Sam.

My last name is spelled L-A-R-S-O-N.

I come from Ottawa.

Share your answers. แลกเปลี่ยนคำตอบ

1. Do you like your first name?

2. Is your last name from your mother? father? husband?

3. What is your middle name?

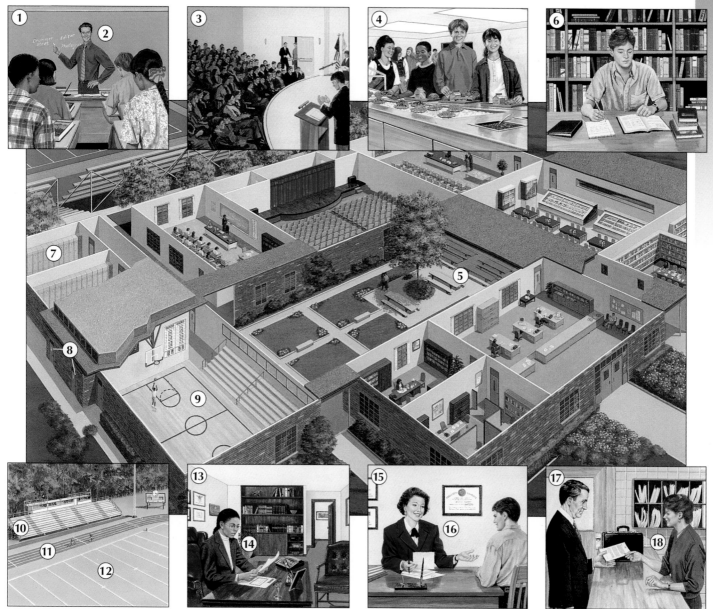

1. classroom
ห้องเรียน

2. teacher
ครู

3. auditorium
ห้องประชุม

4. cafeteria
โรงอาหาร

5. lunch benches
ม้านั่งตอนกลางวัน

6. library
ห้องสมุด

7. lockers
ตู้ใส่ของ

8. rest rooms
ห้องน้ำ

9. gym
โรงพลศึกษา

10. bleachers
อัฒจันทร์

11. track
ลู่วิ่งแข่ง

12. field
สนาม

13. principal's office
ห้องพักอาจารย์ใหญ่

14. principal
อาจารย์ใหญ่

15. counselor's office
ห้องพักอาจารย์แนะแนว

16. counselor
อาจารย์แนะแนว

17. main office
สำนักงานใหญ่

18. clerk
เสมียน/เจ้าหน้าที่

More vocabulary คำศัพท์เพิ่มเติม

instructor: teacher

coach: gym teacher

administrator: principal or other school supervisor

Share your answers. แลกเปลี่ยนคำตอบ

1. Do you ever talk to the principal of your school?

2. Is there a place for you to eat at your school?

3. Does your school look the same as or different from the one in the picture?

Dictionary work การใช้พจนานุกรม

A. Look up a word.
ค้นหาคำ

B. Read the word.
อ่านคำ

C. Say the word.
ออกเสียงคำ

D. Repeat the word.
พูดคำซ้ำ

E. Spell the word.
สะกดคำ

F. Copy the word.
คัดลอกคำ

Work with a partner ทำงานเป็นคู่

G. Ask a question.
ถามคำถาม

H. Answer a question.
ตอบคำถาม

I. Share a book.
ใช้/ดูหนังสือด้วยกัน

J. Help your partner.
ช่วยคู่ของคุณ

Work in a group ทำงานเป็นกลุ่ม

K. Brainstorm a list.
ระดมพลังสมอง

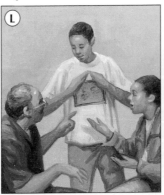

L. Discuss the list.
อภิปราย

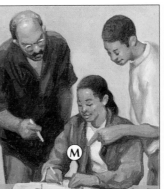

M. Draw a picture.
วาดรูป

N. Dictate a sentence.
บอกประโยคให้เขียนตาม

Class work งานที่ครูทำในห้องเรียน

O. Pass out the papers.
แจกกระดาษ

P. Talk with each other.
พูดคุยกับคนอื่นๆ

Q. Collect the papers.
รวบรวมกระดาษคืน

Follow directions ปฏิบัติตามคำสั่ง

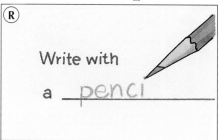

R. Fill in the blank.
เติมในช่องว่าง

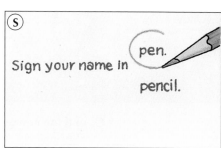

S. Circle the answer.
ทำวงกลมคำตอบ

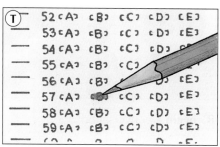

T. Mark the answer sheet.
ทำเครื่องหมายในกระดาษคำตอบ

U. Cross out the word.
ขีดฆ่าคำ

V. Underline the word.
ขีดเส้นใต้คำ

W. Put the words **in order**.
เรียงลำดับคำ

X. Match the items.
จับคู่คำ

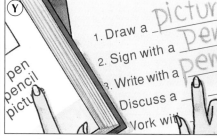

Y. Check your work.
ตรวจงาน

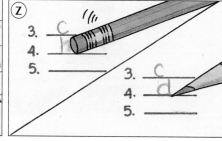

Z. Correct the mistake.
แก้ไขข้อผิด

Share your answers. แลกเปลี่ยนคำตอบ

1. Do you like to work in groups?
2. Do you like to share books?
3. Do you like to answer questions?
4. Is it easy for you to talk with your classmates?
5. Do you always check your work?
6. Do you cross out your mistakes or erase them?

A. greet someone
ทักทาย

B. begin a conversation
เริ่มต้นการสนทนา

C. end the conversation
จบการสนทนา

D. introduce yourself
แนะนำตัวเอง

E. make sure you **understand**
แน่ใจว่าคุณเข้าใจ

F. introduce your friend
แนะนำเพื่อนของคุณ

G. compliment your friend
ชมเพื่อนของคุณ

H. thank your friend
ขอบคุณเพื่อน

I. apologize
ขอโทษ

Practice introductions. ฝึกการพูดแนะนำ

Hi, I'm Sam Jones and this is my friend, Pat Green.

Nice to meet you. I'm Tomas Garcia.

Practice giving compliments. ฝึกการให้คำชมเชย

That's a great sweater, Tomas.

Thanks Pat. I like your shoes.

Look at **Clothing I,** pages **64–65** for more ideas.

 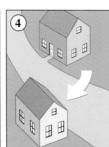  

 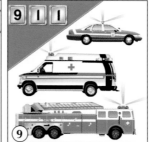 

1. telephone/phone
   โทรศัพท์

2. receiver
   หูโทรศัพท์

3. cord
   สายโทรศัพท์

4. local call
   โทรในพื้นที่

5. long-distance call
   โทรทางไกล

6. international call
   โทรระหว่างประเทศ

7. operator
   พนักงานรับโทรศัพท์

8. directory assistance (411)
   พนักงานบริการข้อมูลทางโทรศัพท์

9. emergency service (911)
   บริการฉุกเฉิน

10. phone card
    บัตรโทรศัพท์

11. pay phone
    โทรศัพท์หยอดเหรียญ

12. cordless phone
    โทรศัพท์ไร้สาย

13. cellular phone
    โทรศัพท์มือถือ

14. answering machine
    เครื่องตอบรับ

15. telephone book
    สมุดโทรศัพท์

16. pager
    เพจเจอร์ / วิทยุติดตามตัว

Using a pay phone การใช้โทรศัพท์หยอดเหรียญ

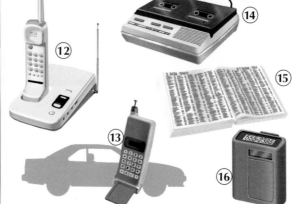

A. **Pick up** the receiver.
   ยกหูโทรศัพท์

B. **Listen** for the dial tone.
   ฟังเสียงสัญญาณ

C. **Deposit** coins.
   หยอดเหรียญ

D. **Dial** the number.
   กดหมายเลขโทรศัพท์

E. **Leave** a message.
   ฝากข้อความ

F. **Hang up** the receiver.
   วางหูโทรศัพท์

More vocabulary คำศัพท์เพิ่มเติม

When you get a person or place that you didn't want to call, we say you have the **wrong number**.

Share your answers. แลกเปลี่ยนคำตอบ

1. What kinds of calls do you make?
2. How much does it cost to call your country?
3. Do you like to talk on the telephone?

Temperature
อุณหภูมิ

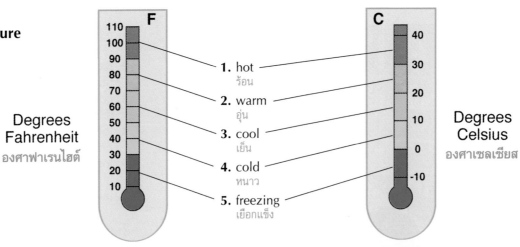

Degrees Fahrenheit
องศาฟาเรนไฮต์

Degrees Celsius
องศาเซลเซียส

F
110 100 90 80 70 60 50 40 30 20 10

C
40 30 20 10 0 -10

1. hot
ร้อน
2. warm
อุ่น
3. cool
เย็น
4. cold
หนาว
5. freezing
เยือกแข็ง

6. sunny/clear
แดดร้อน/ฟ้าโปร่ง

7. cloudy
มีเมฆมาก

8. raining
ฝนตก

9. snowing
หิมะตก

10. windy
ลมแรง

11. foggy
หมอกลงจัด

12. humid
ร้อนชื้น

13. icy
เป็นน้ำแข็ง

14. smoggy
มีหมอกควัน

15. heat wave
คลื่นความร้อน

16. thunderstorm
พายุฝนฟ้าคะนอง

17. lightning
ฟ้าแลบ

18. hailstorm
พายุลูกเห็บ

19. hail
ลูกเห็บ

20. snowstorm
พายุหิมะ

21. dust storm
พายุฝุ่น

Language note: *it is, there is* ข้อสังเกตุทางภาษา

For **1–14** we use,   *It's cloudy.*

For **15–21** we use,   *There's a heat wave.*

There's lightning.

Talk about the weather. พูดเกี่ยวกับสภาพอากาศ

Today it's hot. It's 98 degrees.

Yesterday it was warm. It was 85 degrees.

1. **little** hand
   มือเล็ก
2. **big** hand
   มือใหญ่

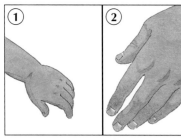

3. **fast** driver
   คนขับรถเร็ว
4. **slow** driver
   คนขับรถช้า

5. **hard** chair
   เก้าอี้แข็ง
6. **soft** chair
   เก้าอี้นุ่ม

7. **thick** book/
   fat book
   หนังสือเล่มหนา
8. **thin** book
   หนังสือเล่มบาง

9. **full** glass
   แก้วมีน้ำเต็ม
10. **empty** glass
    แก้วเปล่า

11. **noisy** children/
    loud children
    เด็กเสียงดัง
12. **quiet** children
    เด็กเงียบ

13. **heavy** box
    กล่องหนัก
14. **light** box
    กล่องเบา

15. **neat** closet
    ตู้เสื้อผ้าที่เป็นระเบียบ
16. **messy** closet
    ตู้เสื้อผ้าที่รก

17. **good** dog
    สุนัขนิสัยดี
18. **bad** dog
    สุนัขนิสัยไม่ดี

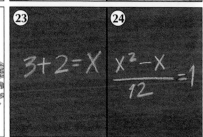

19. **expensive** ring
    แหวนราคาแพง
20. **cheap** ring
    แหวนราคาถูก

21. **beautiful** view
    ทัศนียภาพที่สวยงาม
22. **ugly** view
    ทัศนียภาพที่ไม่น่าดู

23. **easy** problem
    โจทย์ง่าย
24. **difficult** problem/
    hard problem
    โจทย์ยาก

Use the new language. ใช้ภาษาใหม่
1. Name three things that are thick.
2. Name three things that are soft.
3. Name three things that are heavy.

Share your answers. แลกเปลี่ยนคำตอบ
1. Are you a slow driver or a fast driver?
2. Do you have a neat closet or a messy closet?
3. Do you like loud or quiet parties?

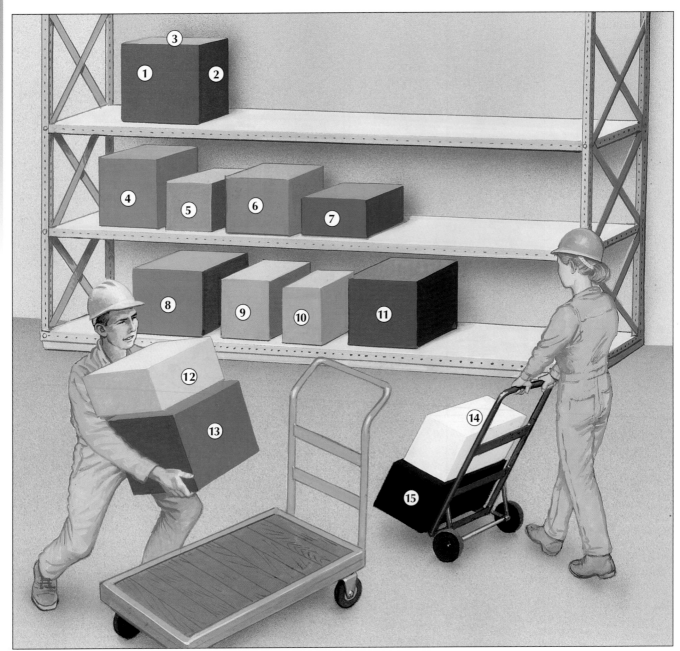

1. blue สีน้ำเงิน	**6.** orange สีส้ม	**11.** brown สีน้ำตาล
2. dark blue สีน้ำเงินเข้ม	**7.** purple สีม่วง	**12.** yellow สีเหลือง
3. light blue สีฟ้า	**8.** green สีเขียว	**13.** red สีแดง
4. turquoise สีเขียวขุ่น	**9.** beige สีน้ำตาลอ่อน	**14.** white สีขาว
5. gray สีเทา	**10.** pink สีชมพู	**15.** black สีดำ

Use the new language. ใช้ภาษาใหม่

Look at **Clothing I,** pages **64–65.**

Name the colors of the clothing you see.

That's a dark blue suit.

Share your answers. แลกเปลี่ยนคำตอบ

1. What colors are you wearing today?

2. What colors do you like?

3. Is there a color you don't like? What is it?

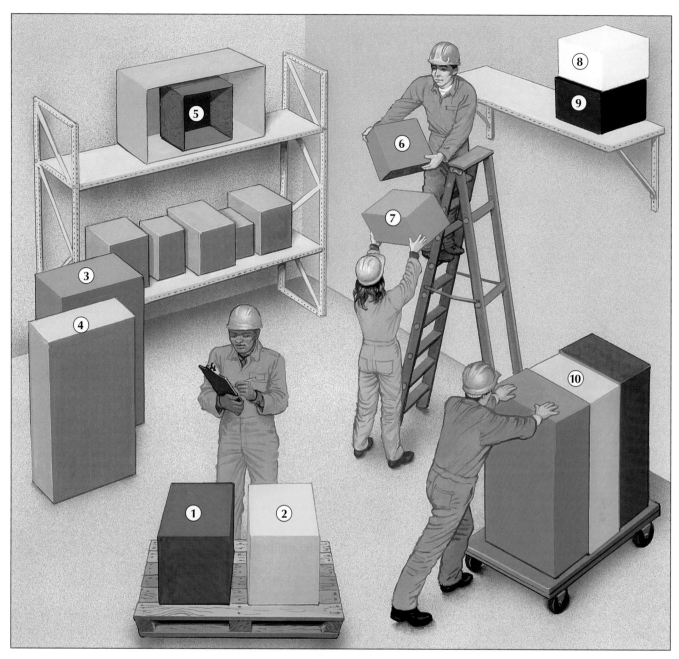

1. The red box is **next to** the yellow box, **on the left.**
   กล่องสีแดง**อยู่ถัดจาก**กล่องสีเหลือง**ทางด้านซ้าย**

2. The yellow box is **next to** the red box, **on the right.**
   กล่องสีเหลือง**อยู่ถัดจาก**กล่องสีแดง**ทางด้านขวา**

3. The turquoise box is **behind** the gray box.
   กล่องสีเขียวขุ่น**อยู่ด้านหลัง**กล่องสีเทา

4. The gray box is **in front of** the turquoise box.
   กล่องสีเทา**อยู่ด้านหน้า**กล่องสีเขียวขุ่น

5. The dark blue box is **in** the beige box.
   กล่องสีน้ำเงินเข้ม**อยู่ใน**กล่องสีน้ำตาลอ่อน

6. The green box is **above** the orange box.
   กล่องสีเขียว**อยู่ด้านบน**กล่องสีส้ม

7. The orange box is **below** the green box.
   กล่องสีส้ม**อยู่ด้านล่าง**กล่องสีเขียว

8. The white box is **on** the black box.
   กล่องสีขาว**อยู่บน**กล่องสีดำ

9. The black box is **under** the white box.
   กล่องสีดำ**อยู่ใต้**กล่องสีขาว

10. The pink box is **between** the purple box and the brown box.
    กล่องสีชมพู**อยู่ระหว่าง**กล่องสีม่วงและกล่องสีน้ำตาล

More vocabulary คำศัพท์เพิ่มเติม

near: in the same area
*The white box is **near** the black box.*

far from: not near
*The red box is **far from** the black box.*

HOME **1 8**
VISITOR **2 2**

SAN DIEGO
235 miles

Cardinals ตัวเลขจำนวนนับ

0 zero ศูนย์	11 eleven สิบเอ็ด	21 twenty-one ยี่สิบเอ็ด
1 one หนึ่ง	12 twelve สิบสอง	22 twenty-two ยี่สิบสอง
2 two สอง	13 thirteen สิบสาม	30 thirty สามสิบ
3 three สาม	14 fourteen สิบสี่	40 forty สี่สิบ
4 four สี่	15 fifteen สิบห้า	50 fifty ห้าสิบ
5 five ห้า	16 sixteen สิบหก	60 sixty หกสิบ
6 six หก	17 seventeen สิบเจ็ด	70 seventy เจ็ดสิบ
7 seven เจ็ด	18 eighteen สิบแปด	80 eighty แปดสิบ
8 eight แปด	19 nineteen สิบเก้า	90 ninety เก้าสิบ
9 nine เก้า	20 twenty ยี่สิบ	100 one hundred หนึ่งร้อย
10 ten สิบ		

101
one hundred one
หนึ่งร้อยหนึ่ง

1,000
one thousand
หนึ่งพัน

1,001
one thousand one
หนึ่งพันหนึ่ง

10,000
ten thousand
หนึ่งหมื่น

100,000
one hundred thousand
หนึ่งแสน

1,000,000
one million
หนึ่งล้าน

1,000,000,000
one billion
หนึ่งพันล้าน

Ordinals เลขบอกลำดับที่

1st first ที่หนึ่ง	8th eighth ที่แปด	15th fifteenth ที่สิบห้า
2nd second ที่สอง	9th ninth ที่เก้า	16th sixteenth ที่สิบหก
3rd third ที่สาม	10th tenth ที่สิบ	17th seventeenth ที่สิบเจ็ด
4th fourth ที่สี่	11th eleventh ที่สิบเอ็ด	18th eighteenth ที่สิบแปด
5th fifth ที่ห้า	12th twelfth ที่สิบสอง	19th nineteenth ที่สิบเก้า
6th sixth ที่หก	13th thirteenth ที่สิบสาม	20th twentieth ที่ยี่สิบ
7th seventh ที่เจ็ด	14th fourteenth ที่สิบสี่	

Roman numerals ตัวเลขโรมัน

I	= 1	VII	= 7	XXX	= 30
II	= 2	VIII	= 8	XL	= 40
III	= 3	IX	= 9	L	= 50
IV	= 4	X	= 10	C	= 100
V	= 5	XV	= 15	D	= 500
VI	= 6	XX	= 20	M	= 1,000

Fractions เศษส่วน

1. 1/8 one-eighth
หนึ่งในแปด

2. 1/4 one-fourth
หนึ่งในสี่

3. 1/3 one-third
หนึ่งในสาม

4. 1/2 one-half
หนึ่งในสอง/ครึ่งหนึ่ง

5. 3/4 three-fourths
สามในสี่

6. 1 whole
ทั้งหมด

1 cup
หนึ่งถ้วย
3/4
2/3
1/2
1/3
1/4

Percents เปอร์เซ็นต์

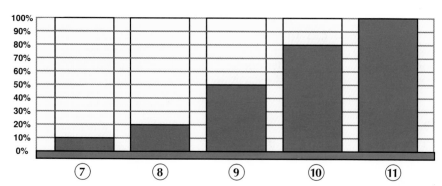

7. 10% ten percent
สิบเปอร์เซ็นต์

8. 20% twenty percent
ยี่สิบเปอร์เซ็นต์

9. 50% fifty percent
ห้าสิบเปอร์เซ็นต์

10. 80% eighty percent
แปดสิบเปอร์เซ็นต์

11. 100% one hundred percent
หนึ่งร้อยเปอร์เซ็นต์

Dimensions มิติ

Measurement การวัด

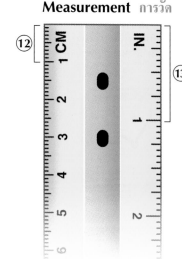

12. centimeter [cm]
เซนติเมตร

13. inch [in.]
นิ้ว

Equivalencies การเทียบ

1 inch = 2.54 centimeters
นิ้ว   เซนติเมตร
1 yard =   .91 meters
หลา   เมตร
1 mile = 1.6 kilometers
ไมล์   กิโลเมตร
12 inches   = 1 foot
นิ้ว   ฟุต
3 feet   = 1 yard
ฟุต   หลา
1,760 yards = 1 mile
หลา   ไมล์

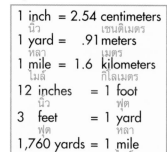

14. height
ความสูง

15. depth
ความลึก

16. length
ความยาว

17. width
ความกว้าง

More vocabulary คำศัพท์เพิ่มเติม

measure: to find the size or amount of something

count: to find the total number of something

Share your answers. แลกเปลี่ยนคำตอบ

1. How many students are in class today?

2. Who was the first person in class today?

3. How far is it from your home to your school?

1. second
เข็มวินาที

2. minute
เข็มนาที

3. hour
เข็มชั่วโมง

A.M.
ตั้งแต่เที่ยงคืนถึง
11 นาฬิกา
59 นาที

P.M.
ตั้งแต่เที่ยงวันถึง
23 นาฬิกา
59 นาที

4. 1:00
one o'clock
หนึ่งนาฬิกา

5. 1:05
one-oh-five
five after one
หนึ่งนาฬิกาห้านาที

6. 1:10
one-ten
ten after one
หนึ่งนาฬิกาสิบนาที

7. 1:15
one-fifteen
a quarter after one
หนึ่งนาฬิกาสิบห้านาที

8. 1:20
one-twenty
twenty after one
หนึ่งนาฬิกายี่สิบนาที

9. 1:25
one twenty-five
twenty-five after one
หนึ่งนาฬิกายี่สิบห้านาที

10. 1:30
one-thirty
half past one
หนึ่งนาฬิกาสามสิบนาที

11. 1:35
one thirty-five
twenty-five to two
หนึ่งนาฬิกาสามสิบห้านาที

12. 1:40
one-forty
twenty to two
หนึ่งนาฬิกาสี่สิบนาที

13. 1:45
one forty-five
a quarter to two
หนึ่งนาฬิกาสี่สิบห้านาที

14. 1:50
one-fifty
ten to two
หนึ่งนาฬิกาห้าสิบนาที

15. 1:55
one fifty-five
five to two
หนึ่งนาฬิกาห้าสิบห้านาที

Talk about the time. พูดเกี่ยวกับเวลา

What time is it? It's 10:00 a.m.

What time do you wake up on weekdays? At 6:30 a.m.

What time do you wake up on weekends? At 9:30 a.m.

Share your answers. แลกเปลี่ยนคำตอบ

1. How many hours a day do you study English?

2. You are meeting friends at 1:00. How long will you
   wait for them if they are late?

16. morning
ตอนเช้า

17. noon
เที่ยงวัน

18. afternoon
ตอนบ่าย

19. evening
ตอนเย็น

20. night
กลางคืน

21. midnight
เที่ยงคืน

22. early
มาก่อนเวลา

23. late
มาสาย

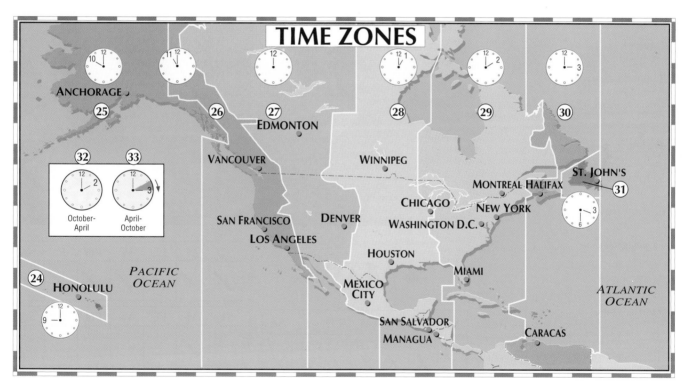

TIME ZONES

24. Hawaii-Aleutian time
เวลาฮาวายอิ-อลูเซิน

25. Alaska time
เวลาอลาสก้า

26. Pacific time
เวลาแปซิฟิค

27. mountain time
เวลาด้านภูเขา

28. central time
เวลาพื้นที่ตอนกลาง

29. eastern time
เวลาซีกตะวันออก

30. Atlantic time
เวลาแอตแลนติก

31. Newfoundland time
เวลานิวฟาวน์แลนด์

32. standard time
เวลามาตรฐาน

33. daylight saving time
เวลาที่ปรับใหม่เพื่อขยายเวลา
กลางวัน

More vocabulary คำศัพท์เพิ่มเติม

on time: not early and not late

He's **on time.**

Share your answers. แลกเปลี่ยนคำตอบ

1. When do you watch television? study?
do housework?

2. Do you come to class on time? early? late?

Days of the week วันต่าง ๆ

1. Sunday
   วันอาทิตย์

2. Monday
   วันจันทร์

3. Tuesday
   วันอังคาร

4. Wednesday
   วันพุธ

5. Thursday
   วันพฤหัสบดี

6. Friday
   วันศุกร์

7. Saturday
   วันเสาร์

8. year
   ปี

9. month
   เดือน

10. day
    วัน

11. week
    สัปดาห์

12. weekdays
    วันทำงาน

13. weekend
    วันสุดสัปดาห์

14. date
    วันที่

15. today
    วันนี้

16. tomorrow
    วันพรุ่งนี้

17. yesterday
    เมื่อวานนี้

18. last week
    สัปดาห์ที่แล้ว

19. this week
    สัปดาห์นี้

20. next week
    สัปดาห์หน้า

21. every day
    ทุกวัน

22. once a week
    หนึ่งครั้งต่อสัปดาห์

23. twice a week
    สองครั้งต่อสัปดาห์

24. three times a week
    สามครั้งต่อสัปดาห์

Talk about the calendar. พูดเกี่ยวกับปฏิทิน

What's today's date? It's <u>*March 10th*</u>.

What day is it? It's <u>*Tuesday*</u>.

What day was yesterday? It was <u>*Monday*</u>.

Share your answers. แลกเปลี่ยนคำตอบ

1. How often do you come to school?

2. How long have you been in this school?

2001

JAN ㉕
SUN	MON	TUE	WED	THU	FRI	SAT
	1	2	3	4	5	6
7	8	9	10	11	12	13
14	15	16	17	18	19	20
21	22	23	24	25	26	27
28	29	30	31			

FEB ㉖
SUN	MON	TUE	WED	THU	FRI	SAT
				1	2	3
4	5	6	7	8	9	10
11	12	13	14	15	16	17
18	19	20	21	22	23	24
25	26	27	28			

MAR ㉗
SUN	MON	TUE	WED	THU	FRI	SAT
				1	2	3
4	5	6	7	8	9	10
11	12	13	14	15	16	17
18	19	20	21	22	23	24
25	26	27	28	29	30	31

APR ㉘
SUN	MON	TUE	WED	THU	FRI	SAT
1	2	3	4	5	6	7
8	9	10	11	12	13	14
15	16	17	18	19	20	21
22	23	24	25	26	27	28
29	30					

MAY ㉙
SUN	MON	TUE	WED	THU	FRI	SAT
		1	2	3	4	5
6	7	8	9	10	11	12
13	14	15	16	17	18	19
20	21	22	23	24	25	26
27	28	29	30	31		

JUN ㉚
SUN	MON	TUE	WED	THU	FRI	SAT
					1	2
3	4	5	6	7	8	9
10	11	12	13	14	15	16
17	18	19	20	21	22	23
24	25	26	27	28	29	30

JUL ㉛
SUN	MON	TUE	WED	THU	FRI	SAT
1	2	3	4	5	6	7
8	9	10	11	12	13	14
15	16	17	18	19	20	21
22	23	24	25	26	27	28
29	30	31				

AUG ㉜
SUN	MON	TUE	WED	THU	FRI	SAT
			1	2	3	4
5	6	7	8	9	10	11
12	13	14	15	16	17	18
19	20	21	22	23	24	25
26	27	28	29	30	31	

SEP ㉝
SUN	MON	TUE	WED	THU	FRI	SAT
						1
2	3	4	5	6	7	8
9	10	11	12	13	14	15
16	17	18	19	20	21	22
23/30	24	25	26	27	28	29

OCT ㉞
SUN	MON	TUE	WED	THU	FRI	SAT
	1	2	3	4	5	6
7	8	9	10	11	12	13
14	15	16	17	18	19	20
21	22	23	24	25	26	27
28	29	30	31			

NOV ㉟
SUN	MON	TUE	WED	THU	FRI	SAT
				1	2	3
4	5	6	7	8	9	10
11	12	13	14	15	16	17
18	19	20	21	22	23	24
25	26	27	28	29	30	

DEC ㊱
SUN	MON	TUE	WED	THU	FRI	SAT
						1
2	3	4	5	6	7	8
9	10	11	12	13	14	15
16	17	18	19	20	21	22
23/30	24/31	25	26	27	28	29

Months of the year
เดือนต่าง ๆ

25. January
เดือนมกราคม

26. February
เดือนกุมภาพันธ์

27. March
เดือนมีนาคม

28. April
เดือนเมษายน

29. May
เดือนพฤษภาคม

30. June
เดือนมิถุนายน

31. July
เดือนกรกฎาคม

32. August
เดือนสิงหาคม

33. September
เดือนกันยายน

34. October
เดือนตุลาคม

35. November
เดือนพฤศจิกายน

36. December
เดือนธันวาคม

Seasons ฤดูกาล

37. spring
ฤดูใบไม้ผลิ

38. summer
ฤดูร้อน

39. fall
ฤดูใบไม้ร่วง

40. winter
ฤดูหนาว

41. birthday
วันเกิด

42. anniversary
วันครบรอบปี

43. legal holiday
วันหยุดตามที่กฎหมายกำหนด

44. religious holiday
วันหยุดทางศาสนา

45. appointment
การนัดหมาย

46. vacation
วันหยุดพักผ่อน

MARCH 21 — 37
JUNE 21 — 38
SEPT. 21 — 39
DEC. 21 — 40

JUNE 5 TIM! — 41
MARCH 2 ANNIVERSARY — 42

JULY 4 INDEPENDENCE DAY — STATE BANK — CLOSED-JULY 4 — 43

APRIL 4 EASTER SUNDAY — 44

MAY 17 DOCTOR 4:30 — 45
AUGUST — 46

Use the new language. ใช้ภาษาใหม่
Look at the **ordinal numbers** on page **14.**
Use ordinal numbers to say the date.
It's June 5th. It's the fifth.

Talk about your birthday. พูดเกี่ยวกับวันเกิดของคุณ
My birthday is in the winter.
My birthday is in January.
My birthday is on January twenty-sixth.

Coins เหรียญ

1. $.01 = 1¢
a penny/1 cent
หนึ่งเพนนี / หนึ่งเซ็นต์

2. $.05 = 5¢
a nickel/5 cents
หนึ่งนิคเกิล / ห้าเซ็นต์

3. $.10 = 10¢
a dime/10 cents
หนึ่งไดม์ / สิบเซ็นต์

4. $.25 = 25¢
a quarter/25 cents
หนึ่งควอเตอร์ / ยี่สิบห้าเซ็นต์

5. $.50 = 50¢
a half dollar
ครึ่งดอลล่าร์

6. $1.00
a silver dollar
หนึ่งดอลล่าร์

Bills ธนบัตร

7. $1.00
a dollar
หนึ่งดอลล่าร์

8. $5.00
five dollars
ห้าดอลล่าร์

9. $10.00
ten dollars
สิบดอลล่าร์

10. $20.00
twenty dollars
ยี่สิบดอลล่าร์

11. $50.00
fifty dollars
ห้าสิบดอลล่าร์

12. $100.00
one hundred dollars
หนึ่งร้อยดอลล่าร์

Ways to pay วิธีการจ่ายเงิน

13. cash
เงินสด

14. personal check
เช็คส่วนตัว

15. credit card
บัตรเครดิต

16. money order
ธนาณัติ

17. traveler's check
ตั๋วแลกเงินเดินทาง

More vocabulary คำศัพท์เพิ่มเติม

borrow: to get money from someone and return it later

lend: to give money to someone and get it back later

pay back: to return the money that you borrowed

Other ways to talk about money: วิธีอื่น ๆ ที่พูดเกี่ยวกับเงิน

a dollar bill or *a one*

a five-dollar bill or *a five*

a ten-dollar bill or *a ten*

a twenty-dollar bill or *a twenty*

A. shop for
ซื้อของ

B. sell
ขาย

C. pay for/**buy**
จ่ายเงิน/ซื้อ

D. give
ให้

E. keep
เก็บ

F. return
คืนสินค้า

G. exchange
แลกเปลี่ยน

1. price tag
ป้ายราคา

2. regular price
ราคาปกติ

3. sale price
ราคาลด

4. bar code
รหัสสินค้า

5. receipt
ใบเสร็จรับเงิน

6. price/cost
ราคาสินค้า

7. sales tax
ภาษีการขาย

8. total
ยอดสุทธิ

9. change
เงินทอน

More vocabulary คำศัพท์เพิ่มเติม

When you use a credit card to shop, you get a **bill** in the mail. Bills list, in writing, the items you bought and the total you have to pay.

Share your answers. แลกเปลี่ยนคำตอบ

1. Name three things you pay for every month.

2. Name one thing you will buy this week.

3. Where do you like to shop?

1. children
เด็ก

2. baby
ทารก

3. toddler
เด็กเพิ่งหัดเดิน

4. 6-year-old boy
เด็กผู้ชายอายุ 6 ขวบ

5. 10-year-old girl
เด็กผู้หญิงอายุ 10 ขวบ

6. teenagers
วัยรุ่น

7. 13-year-old boy
เด็กผู้ชายอายุ 13 ขวบ

8. 19-year-old girl
เด็กผู้หญิงอายุ 19 ขวบ

9. adults
ผู้ใหญ่

10. woman
ผู้หญิง

11. man
ผู้ชาย

12. senior citizen
ผู้สูงอายุ

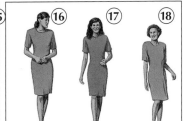
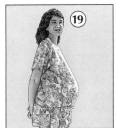

13. young
วัยหนุ่มสาว

14. middle-aged
วัยกลางคน

15. elderly
ผู้สูงอายุ

16. tall
สูง

17. average height
ความสูงโดยเฉลี่ย

18. short
เตี้ย

19. pregnant
ตั้งครรภ์

20. heavyset
มีร่างใหญ่

21. average weight
น้ำหนักปานกลาง

22. thin/slim
ผอม / บาง

23. attractive
น่าดึงดูดใจ / หน้าตาดี

24. cute
น่ารัก / น่าเอ็นดู

25. physically challenged
ท้าทายพละกำลัง

26. sight impaired/blind
ตาบอด

27. hearing impaired/deaf
หูหนวก

Talk about yourself and your teacher.
พูดเกี่ยวกับตัวคุณและครูของคุณ
I am young, average height, and average weight.
My teacher is a middle-aged, tall, thin man.

Use the new language. ใช้ภาษาใหม่
Turn to **Hobbies and Games**, pages **162–163.**
Describe each person on the page.
He's a heavy-set, short, senior citizen.

Trends Hair Salon
NO APPT. NECESSARY
SHAMPOO
BLOW DRY
CUT

 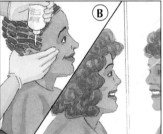  

1. short hair
ผมสั้น

2. shoulder-length hair
ผมยาวประบ่า

3. long hair
ผมยาว

4. part
แสกผม

5. mustache
หนวด

6. beard
เครา

7. sideburns
จอน

8. bangs
ผมม้า

9. straight hair
ผมตรง

10. wavy hair
ผมหยักศก

11. curly hair
ผมหยิก

12. bald
หัวล้าน

13. gray hair
ผมหงอก

14. red hair
ผมสีแดง

15. black hair
ผมสีดำ

16. blond hair
ผมสีทอง

17. brown hair
ผมสีน้ำตาล

18. brush
แปรง

19. scissors
กรรไกร

20. blow dryer
เครื่องเป่าผม

21. rollers
โรลม้วนผม

22. comb
หวี

A. cut hair
ตัดผม

B. perm hair
ตัดผม

C. set hair
ม้วนผมด้วยโรล

D. color hair/dye hair
ย้อมสีผม

More vocabulary คำศัพท์เพิ่มเติม

hair stylist: a person who cuts, sets, and perms hair

hair salon: the place where a hair stylist works

Talk about your hair. พูดเกี่ยวกับผมของคุณ

My hair is long, straight, and brown.

I have long, straight, brown hair.

When I was a child my hair was short, curly, and blond.

23

Tom Lee's Family
ครอบครัวของทอม ลี

1. grandparents
ปู่ ย่า ตา ยาย

Min

Lu

2. grandmother
ย่า, ยาย

3. grandfather
ปู่ ตา

4. parents
พ่อแม่

Rose

Chang

Helen

Daniel

Tom

5. mother
แม่

6. father
พ่อ

10. aunt
ป้า น้า

11. uncle
ลุง อา

Lily

Alex

Emily

8. sister
น้องสาว

9. brother
น้องชาย

12. cousin
ลูกพี่ลูกน้อง

7. (Min and Lu's)
grandson
หลานชาย
(ของปู่ย่าตายาย)

Berta

Mario

Ana Garcia's Family
ครอบครัวของ
แอนนา กาเชีย

13. mother-in-law
แม่ยาย

14. father-in-law
พ่อตา

Marta

Carlos

Tito

20. (Tito's) wife
ภรรยา

15. sister-in-law
พี่สะใภ้

16. brother-in-law
พี่เขย

19. husband
สามี

Alice

Eddie

Sara

Felix

17. niece
หลานสาว

18. nephew
หลานชาย

21. daughter
ลูกสาว

22. son
ลูกชาย

More vocabulary คำศัพท์เพิ่มเติม
Lily and Emily are Min and Lu's **granddaughters.**
Daniel is Min and Lu's **son-in-law.**
Ana is Berta and Mario's **daughter-in-law.**

Share your answers. แลกเปลี่ยนคำตอบ
1. How many brothers and sisters do you have?
2. What number son or daughter are you?
3. Do you have any children?

Lisa Smith's Family *ครอบครัวของลิซ่า สมิธ*

23. married
แต่งงานแล้ว

Carol   Dan

Lisa

24. divorced
หย่าร้าง

25. single mother
ครอบครัวที่มีแต่แม่

26. single father
ครอบครัวที่มีแต่พ่อ

Rick   Carol

27. remarried
สมรสใหม่

Dan   Sue

Rick   Carol

28. stepfather
พ่อเลี้ยง

David   Mary

29. half brother
น้องชายต่างบิดา

30. half sister
น้องสาวต่างบิดา

Lisa

Dan   Sue

31. stepmother
แม่เลี้ยง

Kim   Bill

32. stepsister
พี่สาวต่างมารดา

33. stepbrother
พี่ชายต่างมารดา

More vocabulary *คำศัพท์เพิ่มเติม*

Carol is Dan's **former wife**.

Sue is Dan's **wife**.

Dan is Carol's **former husband**.

Rick is Carol's **husband**.

Lisa is the **stepdaughter** of both Rick and Sue.

A. wake up
ตื่นนอน

B. get up
ลุกขึ้น

C. take a shower
อาบน้ำฝักบัว

D. get dressed
แต่งตัว

E. eat breakfast
รับประทานอาหารเช้า

F. make lunch
ทำอาหารกลางวัน

G. take the children to school
ส่งลูกไปโรงเรียน

H. take the bus to school
ขึ้นรถประจำทางไปโรงเรียน

I. drive to work/**go** to work
ขับรถไปทำงาน/ไปทำงาน

J. be in school
อยู่ที่โรงเรียน

K. work
ทำงาน

L. go to the market
ไปตลาด

M. leave work
เลิกงาน

Grammar point: 3rd person singular หลักไวยากรณ์ : เอกพจน์บุรุษที่ 3

For **he** and **she**, we add **-s** or **-es** to the verb.

He/She wakes up.

He/She watches TV.

These verbs are different (irregular):

be   *He/She **is** in school at 10:00 a.m.*

have   *He/She **has** dinner at 6:30 p.m.*

N. clean the house
ทำความสะอาดบ้าน

O. pick up the children
ไปรับลูก

P. cook dinner
ทำอาหารเย็น

Q. come home/**get** home
กลับถึงบ้าน

R. have dinner
รับประทานอาหารเย็น

S. watch TV
ดูโทรทัศน์

T. do homework
ทำการบ้าน

U. relax
พักผ่อน

V. read the paper
อ่านหนังสือพิมพ์

W. exercise
ออกกำลังกาย

X. go to bed
เข้านอน

Y. go to sleep
นอนหลับ

Talk about your daily routine. พูดเกี่ยวกับกิจวัตรประจำวันของคุณ

I take _a shower_ in _the morning_.
I go to _school_ in _the evening_.
I go to _bed_ at _11 o'clock_.

Share your answers. แลกเปลี่ยนคำตอบ

1. Who makes dinner in your family?
2. Who goes to the market?
3. Who goes to work?

27

Life Events เหตุการณ์ในชีวิต

A. be born
เกิด

B. start school
เข้าโรงเรียน

C. immigrate
ย้ายเข้าประเทศ

D. graduate
สำเร็จการศึกษา

E. learn to drive
เรียนขับรถ

F. join the army
เข้าเป็นทหาร

G. get a job
ได้งานทำ

H. become a citizen
เข้าเป็นพลเมือง

I. rent an apartment
เช่าอพาร์ตเม้นท์

J. go to college
เข้าเรียนวิทยาลัย

K. fall in love
มีความรัก

L. get married
แต่งงาน

Grammar point: past tense หลักไวยากรณ์

start		immigrate	
learn		graduate	
join	+ed	move	+d
rent		retire	
travel		die	

These verbs are different (irregular):

be	— was	have	— had
get	— got	buy	— bought
become	— became		
go	— went		
fall	— fell		

28

1960

1967

M. have a baby
มีลูก

N. travel
เดินทาง

1971

1971

O. buy a house
ซื้อบ้าน

P. move
ย้ายบ้าน

1985

1997

Q. have a grandchild
มีหลาน

R. die
ตาย

1. birth certificate
ใบสูติบัตร

2. diploma
วุฒิบัตร

3. Resident Alien card
บัตรคนต่างด้าว

4. driver's license
ใบขับขี่

5. Social Security card
บัตรประกันสังคม

6. Certificate of Naturalization
ใบรับรองการโอนสัญชาติ

7. college degree
ปริญญาบัตร

8. marriage license
ทะเบียนสมรส

9. passport
หนังสือเดินทาง

More vocabulary คำศัพท์เพิ่มเติม

When a husband dies, his wife becomes a **widow**.

When a wife dies, her husband becomes a **widower**.

When older people stop working, we say they **retire**.

Talk about yourself. พูดเกี่ยวกับตัวของคุณ

I was born in 1968.

I learned to drive in 1987.

I immigrated in 1990.

Feelings ความรู้สึก

1. hot
   ร้อน
2. thirsty
   กระหาย
3. sleepy
   ง่วง

4. cold
   หนาว
5. hungry
   หิว
6. full
   อิ่ม

7. comfortable
   สะดวกสบาย
8. uncomfortable
   ไม่สะดวกสบาย/อึดอัด
9. disgusted
   น่ารังเกียจ
10. calm
    สงบ, เงียบ
11. nervous
    กลัว/ตื่นเต้น

12. in pain
    เจ็บปวด
13. worried
    วิตกกังวล
14. sick
    ไม่สบาย
15. well
    สบายดี
16. relieved
    โล่งใจ

17. hurt
    เจ็บปวดใจ/เสียใจ
18. lonely
    ว้าเหว่
19. in love
    มีความรัก

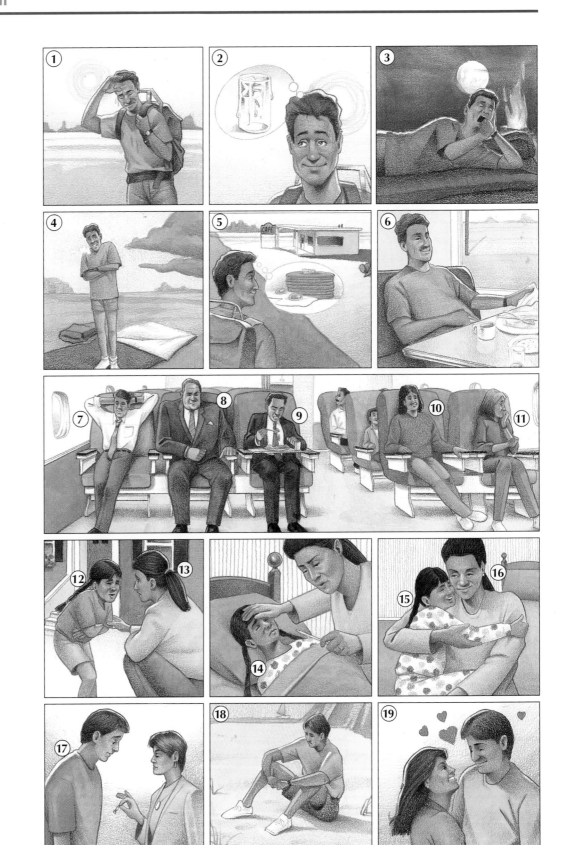

More vocabulary คำศัพท์เพิ่มเติม

furious: very angry

terrified: very scared

overjoyed: very happy

exhausted: very tired

starving: very hungry

humiliated: very embarrassed

Talk about your feelings.

พูดเกี่ยวกับความรู้สึกของคุณ

I feel <u>happy</u> when I see <u>my friends</u>.

I feel <u>homesick</u> when I think about <u>my family</u>.

20. sad
เศร้า

21. homesick
คิดถึงบ้าน

22. proud
ภูมิใจ

23. excited
ตื่นเต้น

24. scared
กลัว

25. embarrassed
อับอายขายหน้า

26. bored
เบื่อ

27. confused
สับสน/งง

28. frustrated
คับข้องใจ

29. angry
โกรธ

30. upset
ผิดหวัง

31. surprised
แปลกใจ

32. happy
มีความสุข

33. tired
เหนื่อย

Use the new language. ใช้ภาษาใหม่

Look at **Clothing I,** page **64,** and answer the questions.

1. How does the runner feel?

2. How does the man at the bus stop feel?

3. How does the woman at the bus stop feel?

4. How do the teenagers feel?

5. How does the little boy feel?

The Ceremony
พิธีรับปริญญา

1. graduating class ชั้นที่จบการศึกษา	**5. podium** แท่นสำหรับยืนพูด	**9. guest speaker** แขกปราศรัยรับเชิญ	**B. applaud / clap** ปรบมือ
2. gown เสื้อครุย	**6. graduate** บัณฑิต	**10. audience** ผู้เข้าร่วมพิธี	**C. cry** ร้องไห้
3. cap หมวกปริญญา	**7. diploma** วุฒิบัตร/ปริญญาบัตร	**11. photographer** ช่างถ่ายรูป	**D. take a picture** ถ่ายรูป
4. stage เวที	**8. valedictorian** ตัวแทนนักเรียนหรือนักศึกษาที่ กล่าวคำปราศรัยอำลา	**A. graduate** ได้รับปริญญา	**E. give a speech** กล่าวคำสุนทรพจน์

Talk about what the people in the pictures are doing. พูดเกี่ยวกับสิ่งที่คนในรูปภาพกำลังกระทำอยู่

She is	taking a picture. giving a speech. smiling. laughing.	*He is*	making a toast. clapping.	*They are*	graduating. hugging. kissing. applauding.

NEWS SCOOP EDITION • MARCH 17, 2006 • VOL. 11 • NO. 21

TIME
FOR KIDS

1995 10 YEARS 2005

Who Were the First Americans?

A 9,400-year-old skeleton gives new clues about our earliest history.

Early Man in America

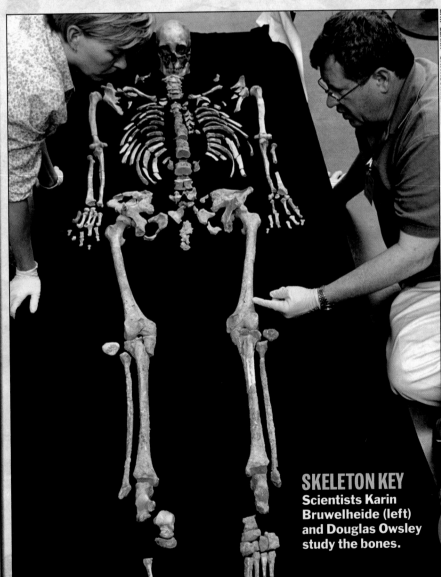

Two college students found the skull in 1996 along the bank of the Columbia River near Kennewick, Washington. Later, more bones were found. The bones looked old. Really old. Tests showed that the skeleton, now known as Kennewick Man, is 9,400 years old. Only about 50 skeletons that old or complete have ever been found in the Americas.

Scientists were **eager** to study the bones. But for about nine years, Indian tribes, the U.S. government and scientists could not agree on what to do with the bones. The Indian tribes wanted them treated with respect and reburied.

Last summer, scientists got to study the bones for 10 days. Now, the results are in.

Secrets of the Bones

Kennewick Man was about 38 years old. He had suffered many injuries, including a **spear** jab to his hip. "The injury looks healed," Douglas Owsley of the Smithsonian Institution told TIME.

The most surprising discovery: Others had taken the time to bury him. The bones hold many more secrets. Researchers say more tests may even show what the man ate.

The bones may also help **solve** mysteries about where the earliest Americans came from and when they got here (*see map*). Did they walk across an ancient land bridge between Russia and Alaska? Could they have traveled down the **coast** by boat? By studying Kennewick Man and other ancient people, scientists hope to answer such questions.

ASIA
ARCTIC OCEAN
BERING LAND BRIDGE
ICE SHEET
NORTH AMERICA
Kennewick, Washington
PACIFIC OCEAN

= What the coastline may have looked like about 12,000 years ago

CHIP CLARK—SMITHSONIAN

SKELETON KEY
Scientists Karin Bruwelheide (left) and Douglas Owsley study the bones.

WHAT'S THE SCOOP?

Should scientists study any bones they want to? Who should decide?

A Real People Person

When Marta Tienda was 10 years old, she spent the summer working on a farm with her family. Tienda's father, Toribio, was from Mexico. Like many **migrants,** he worked long hours at low-paying jobs to support his family.

Today, Marta Tienda is a **sociologist.** She studies people and how they live. She looks at information, including people's education or background, to answer tough questions. Tienda charts this **data** to try to learn such things as why some people are rich and others are poor.

"I hope my work can help reduce **poverty** throughout the world," Tienda told TFK. "Kids deserve a better future."

Marta Tienda studies how groups of people behave and interact.

Kids must get moving and eat less to be healthy.

Shape Up, World

In the last few years, scientists have said that too many kids in the United States are **overweight.** A new study shows that this is not just an American problem. Kids in other countries are also eating too much junk food and have become less physically active.

The number of children in other countries who are overweight is expected to rise **dramatically** by 2010. For example, researchers say that if nothing is done, about 26 million kids in the European Union will be overweight or **obese.** The numbers are expected to increase in countries in the Middle East and Asia too.

Being obese is dangerous. It can lead to other serious health problems, including heart disease. Tim Lobstein is a doctor who worked on the study. Lobstein says that he hopes the study will make world leaders spring into action "to protect our children."

Top 5 Albums

Source: Billboard

Kids' music rules! Last week, the top three albums on *Billboard* magazine's "Billboard 200" list were CDs for kids. On one, *Kidz Bop 9,* average kids sing other artists' hits. CDs for adults, like the last two on this list, didn't sell as well. Here are the CDs rocking the charts.

① **High School Musical soundtrack**

② **Kidz Bop 9,** Kidz Bop Kids

③ **Curious George soundtrack,** Jack Johnson

④ **The Breakthrough,** Mary J. Blige

⑤ **Back to Bedlam,** James Blunt

LUCKY JUMBLE

March 17 is Saint Patrick's Day. It will take more than just luck to solve the riddle below. Unscramble the words. Use the letters underlined in red to spell out the answer.

SHIRI

_ _ _ _ _

EERNG

_ _ _ _ _

CKLU

_ _ _ _

SNIAT PKACTIR

_ _ _ _ _   _ _ _ _ _ _ _

What is in the middle of March?

The _ _ _ _ _ _ _ _ _ "_ _" _ _ _ _ _ _ _

TFK Challenge?

Use the numbers from the red blanks to learn a few facts.

1. Kennewick Man's skeleton was found in _ _ _ _ _.

2. Three of the top _ albums on the *Billboard* charts were CDs for kids. The soundtrack for the *Curious George* movie was number _.

3. Alyssa started saving in _ _ _ _.

FACTS: In _ _ _ _ _, Congress made March Irish-American Heritage Month. More than _ _ million Americans say they have an Irish background.

WHO'S NEWS

People call her the Penny Princess. She is also a dog's best friend. **ALYSSA MAYORGA**, 10, raises money to buy bullet-proof vests for police dogs. Alyssa started collecting pennies in 2004 after hearing about one doggy detective that died on the job. She has given more than 20 vests to police stations in California, her home state. Each vest costs about $400. Alyssa wants to protect pooches across the country. "I'm going to keep on saving so that I can keep these dogs safe," she told TFK.

MAYORGA FAMILY

Managing Editor: Martha Pickerill
Deputy Managing Editor: Nelida Gonzalez Cutler
Senior Editor: Kathryn R. Satterfield
Associate Editor: Andrea Delbanco
Writer/Reporter: Claudia Atticot
Letters Correspondent: Vickie An

Art Director: Jennifer Kraemer-Smith
Associate Art Director: Drew Willis
Picture Editor: Angelique LeDoux
Assistant Picture Editor: Don Heiny
Copy Editors: Michael DeCapite, Steve Levine

TIME Managing Editor: James Kelly
Contributors: Dan Cray/Los Angeles; Andrea Dorfman, Michael Lemonick and Jon Protas/New York
Cover: Raul Colon for TIME
Cover flap: Emily Thompson for TIME for Kids

TIME For Kids Publisher: Jodi Kahn
Business Manager: Regina Buckley
Customer Service Manager: Donna R. Gulledge
Public Affairs: Jennifer Zawadzinski
Production Manager: Gary Kelliher

ILLUSTRATION FOR TIME FOR KIDS BY EMILY THOMPSON

The Party
งานเลี้ยงฉลอง

12. caterer ผู้จัดอาหาร	**15.** banner ป้าย	**18.** gifts ของขวัญ	**H.** laugh หัวเราะ
13. buffet การเลี้ยงอาหารโดยให้แขก ตักอาหารเอง	**16.** dance floor พื้นที่สำหรับเต้นรำ	**F.** kiss จูบ	**I.** make a toast ดื่มอวยพร
14. guests แขก	**17.** DJ (disc jockey) เจ้าหน้าที่เปิดเพลง/ดีเจ	**G.** hug กอด	**J.** dance เต้นรำ

Share your answers. แลกเปลี่ยนคำตอบ

1. Did you ever go to a graduation? Whose?

2. Did you ever give a speech? Where?

3. Did you ever hear a great speaker? Where?

4. Did you ever go to a graduation party?

5. What do you like to eat at parties?

6. Do you like to dance at parties?

1. the city/an urban area
เมือง/บริเวณตัวเมือง

2. the suburbs
ชานเมือง

3. a small town
เมืองเล็ก

4. the country/a rural area
ชนบท

5. apartment building
อาคารห้องชุด

6. house
บ้าน

7. townhouse
ทาวเฮ้าส์ / ห้องแถว

8. mobile home
บ้านเคลื่อนที่ได้

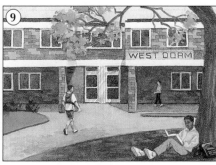

9. college dormitory
หอพักวิทยาลัย

10. shelter
ที่หลบภัย

11. nursing home
บ้านพักคนชรา

12. ranch
คอกปศุสัตว์

13. farm
ไร่นา

More vocabulary คำศัพท์เพิ่มเติม

duplex house: a house divided into two homes

condominium: an apartment building where each apartment is owned separately

co-op: an apartment building owned by the residents

Share your answers. แลกเปลี่ยนคำตอบ

1. Do you like where you live?

2. Where did you live in your country?

3. What types of housing are there near your school?

Renting an apartment การเช่าอพาร์ตเม้นท์/ห้องชุด

A. look for a new apartment
มองหาอพาร์ตเม้นท์ใหม่

B. talk to the manager
คุยกับผู้จัดการ

C. sign a rental agreement
เซ็นสัญญาเช่า

D. move in
ย้ายเข้า

E. unpack
แกะกล่อง

F. pay the rent
จ่ายค่าเช่า

Buying a house การซื้อบ้าน

G. talk to the Realtor
คุยกับนายหน้า

H. make an offer
ยื่นข้อเสนอ

I. get a loan
ได้เงินกู้

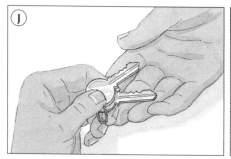

J. take ownership
รับกรรมสิทธิ์

K. arrange the furniture
จัดเฟอร์นิเจอร์

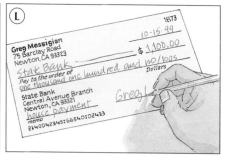

L. pay the mortgage
จ่ายค่าจำนอง

More vocabulary คำศัพท์เพิ่มเติม

lease: a rental agreement for a specific period of time

utilities: gas, water, and electricity for the home

Practice talking to an apartment manager.
พูดกับผู้จัดการอพาร์ตเม้นท์

How much is the rent?
Are utilities included?
When can I move in?

Entrance ทางเข้า

Apartment Avail
2 BD + 2 BA
Sec. Sys.
555-4263

Laundry Room ห้องซักรีด

Recreation Room ห้องนันทนาการ

Garage โรงจอดรถ

1. **first floor**
   ชั้นที่หนึ่ง

2. **second floor**
   ชั้นที่สอง

3. **third floor**
   ชั้นที่สาม

4. **fourth floor**
   ชั้นที่สี่

5. **roof garden**
   สวนบนหลังคา

6. **playground**
   สนามเด็กเล่น

7. **fire escape**
   ทางหนีไฟ

8. **intercom/speaker**
   การสื่อสารภายในสถานที่/ลำโพง

9. **security system**
   ระบบรักษาความปลอดภัย

10. **doorman**
    คนเปิดประตู

11. **vacancy sign**
    ป้ายบอกห้องว่าง

12. **manager/superintendent**
    ผู้จัดการ/ผู้ดูแล

13. **security gate**
    ประตูนิรภัย

14. **storage locker**
    ตู้เก็บของ

15. **parking space**
    ที่จอดรถ

More vocabulary คำศัพท์เพิ่มเติม

rec room: a short way of saying **recreation room**

basement: the area below the street level of an apartment
or a house

Talk about where you live. พูดเกี่ยวกับที่ที่คุณอาศัยอยู่

I live in <u>Apartment 3 near the entrance.</u>

I live in <u>Apartment 11 on the second floor near the fire
escape.</u>

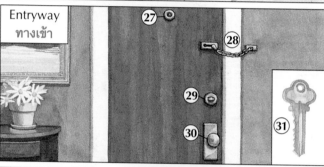

16. swimming pool สระว่ายน้ำ	**23.** fire exit ทางหนีไฟ	**30.** doorknob ลูกบิดประตู
17. balcony ระเบียง	**24.** trash chute ช่องสำหรับทิ้งขยะ	**31.** key กุญแจ
18. courtyard สนามหญ้า	**25.** smoke detector เครื่องจับควันไฟ	**32.** landlord เจ้าของบ้านเช่า
19. air conditioner เครื่องปรับอากาศ	**26.** stairway บันได	**33.** tenant ผู้เช่า
20. trash bin ถังขยะ	**27.** peephole รูที่เจาะไว้สำหรับดู	**34.** elevator ลิฟท์
21. alley ซอย	**28.** door chain โซ่ประตู	**35.** stairs บันได
22. neighbor เพื่อนบ้าน	**29.** dead-bolt lock กลอนด้านใน	**36.** mailboxes ตู้รับจดหมาย

Grammar point: *there is, there are* หลักไวยากรณ์

singular: *there is*   plural: *there are*

There is a fire exit in the hallway.

There are mailboxes in the lobby.

Talk about apartments. พูดเกี่ยวกับอพาตเม้นท์

My apartment has <u>an elevator</u>, <u>a lobby</u>, and <u>a rec room</u>.

My apartment doesn't have <u>a pool</u> or <u>a garage</u>.

My apartment needs <u>air conditioning</u>.

1. floor plan
แปลนบ้าน

2. backyard
สนามหญ้าหลังบ้าน

3. fence
รั้ว

4. mailbox
ตู้รับจดหมาย

5. driveway
ถนนส่วนตัว

6. garage
โรงเก็บรถ

7. garage door
ประตูโรงรถ

8. screen door
ประตูมุ้งลวด

9. porch light
ไฟหน้าบ้าน

10. doorbell
กริ่งเรียก

11. front door
ประตูหน้า

12. storm door
ประตูชั้นนอก

13. steps
ขั้นบันได

14. front walk
ทางเดินด้านหน้า

15. front yard
สนามหญ้าหน้าบ้าน

16. deck
ระเบียงนอกบ้าน

17. window
หน้าต่าง

18. shutter
บานเกล็ดหน้าต่าง

19. gutter
รางน้ำฝน

20. roof
หลังคา

21. chimney
ปล่องไฟ

22. TV antenna
เสาอากาศ

More vocabulary คำศัพท์เพิ่มเติม

two-story house: a house with two floors

downstairs: the bottom floor

upstairs: the part of a house above the bottom floor

Share your answers. แลกเปลี่ยนคำตอบ

1. What do you like about this house?

2. What's something you don't like about the house?

3. Describe the perfect house.

1. hedge รั้วต้นไม้	8. sprinkler เครื่องพ่นน้ำ	15. pruning shears กรรไกรตัดกิ่งไม้	22. lawn mower เครื่องตัดหญ้า
2. hammock เปลญวน	9. hose สายยาง	16. wheelbarrow รถเข็นล้อเดียว	A. **weed** the flower bed ถอนวัชพืชออกจากแปลงดอกไม้
3. garbage can ถังขยะ	10. compost pile กองปุ๋ยหมัก	17. watering can บัวรดน้ำ	B. **water** the plants รดน้ำต้นไม้
4. leaf blower เครื่องเป่าใบไม้	11. rake คราด	18. flowerpot กระถางต้นไม้	C. **mow** the lawn ตัดหญ้า
5. patio furniture โต๊ะเก้าอี้สนาม	12. hedge clippers กรรไกรตัดแต่งกิ่งไม้	19. flower ดอกไม้	D. **plant** a tree ปลูกต้นไม้
6. patio ลานบ้าน	13. shovel พลั่ว	20. bush พุ่มไม้	E. **trim** the hedge ตัดแต่งรั้ว
7. barbecue grill เตาย่างบาร์บีคิว	14. trowel พลั่วมือ	21. lawn สนามหญ้า	F. **rake** the leaves คราดใบไม้

Talk about your yard and gardening. พูดเกี่ยวกับสนามหญ้า
และสวนของคุณ

I like to plant trees.

I don't like to weed.

I like/don't like to work in the yard/garden.

Share your answers. แลกเปลี่ยนคำตอบ

1. What flowers, trees, or plants do you see in the picture? (Look at **Trees, Plants, and Flowers,** pages **128–129** for help.)

2. Do you ever use a barbecue grill to cook?

1. cabinet ตู้ติดผนัง	**8.** shelf ชั้นวางของ	**15.** toaster oven เตาอบขนมปัง	**22.** counter เคาเตอร์
2. paper towels กระดาษเช็ดมือ	**9.** refrigerator ตู้เย็น	**16.** pot หม้อ	**23.** drawer ลิ้นชัก
3. dish drainer ที่คว่ำจาน	**10.** freezer ช่องแช่แข็ง	**17.** teakettle กาต้มน้ำ	**24.** pan กะทะ
4. dishwasher เครื่องล้างจาน	**11.** coffeemaker เครื่องชงกาแฟ	**18.** stove เตาหุงต้ม	**25.** electric mixer เครื่องผสมอาหารไฟฟ้า
5. garbage disposal เครื่องกำจัดขยะ	**12.** blender เครื่องปั่น	**19.** burner หัวเตา	**26.** food processor เครื่องหั่นอาหารไฟฟ้า
6. sink อ่างล้างจาน	**13.** microwave oven เตาอบไมโครเวฟ	**20.** oven เตาอบ	**27.** cutting board เขียง
7. toaster เครื่องปิ้งขนมปัง	**14.** electric can opener ที่เปิดกระป๋องไฟฟ้า	**21.** broiler เตาย่าง	

Talk about the location of kitchen items. พูดเกี่ยวกับที่ตั้ง
ของอุปกรณ์ต่าง ๆ ในห้องครัว

The toaster oven is on the counter near the stove.

The microwave is above the stove.

Share your answers. แลกเปลี่ยนคำตอบ

1. Do you have a garbage disposal? a dishwasher?
a microwave?

2. Do you eat in the kitchen?

1. **china cabinet**
   ตู้เก็บจานกระเบื้อง

2. **set of dishes**
   จานชุด

3. **platter**
   จานอาหารขนาดใหญ่

4. **ceiling fan**
   พัดลมติดเพดาน

5. **light fixture**
   ไฟช่อติดเพดาน

6. **serving dish**
   จานเสริฟอาหาร

7. **candle**
   เทียน

8. **candlestick**
   เชิงเทียน

9. **vase**
   แจกัน

10. **tray**
    ถาดรอง

11. **teapot**
    กาน้ำชา

12. **sugar bowl**
    โถใส่น้ำตาล

13. **creamer**
    โถใส่ครีม

14. **saltshaker**
    ขวดเกลือป่น

15. **pepper shaker**
    ขวดพริกไทยป่น

16. **dining room chair**
    เก้าอี้ห้องอาหาร

17. **dining room table**
    โต๊ะอาหาร

18. **tablecloth**
    ผ้าปูโต๊ะ

19. **napkin**
    ผ้าเช็ดปาก

20. **place mat**
    ที่รองจานอาหาร

21. **fork**
    ส้อม

22. **knife**
    มีด

23. **spoon**
    ช้อน

24. **plate**
    จานแบน

25. **bowl**
    ชาม

26. **glass**
    แก้ว

27. **coffee cup**
    ถ้วยกาแฟ

28. **mug**
    เหยือกน้ำ

Practice asking for things in the dining room.
ฝึกการขอสิ่งของที่อยู่ในห้องรับประทานอาหาร

Please pass the platter.
May I have the creamer?
Could I have a fork, please?

Share your answers. แลกเปลี่ยนคำตอบ

1. What are the women in the picture saying?

2. In your home, where do you eat?

3. Do you like to make dinner for your friends?

1. bookcase ชั้นวางหนังสือ	**8.** mantel หิ้งเหนือเตาผิง	**15.** floor lamp โคมไฟตั้งพื้น	**22.** magazine holder ที่เก็บนิตยสาร
2. basket ตะกร้า	**9.** fireplace เตาผิง	**16.** drapes ม่านประดับ	**23.** coffee table โต๊ะเสริฟกาแฟ
3. track lighting รางสำหรับติดโคมไฟ	**10.** fire ไฟ	**17.** window หน้าต่าง	**24.** armchair/easy chair เก้าอี้มีที่วางแขน/เก้าอี้นวม
4. lightbulb หลอดไฟฟ้า	**11.** fire screen ตะแกรงหน้าเตาผิง	**18.** plant ไม้ประดับ	**25.** love seat โซฟาสองที่นั่ง
5. ceiling เพดาน	**12.** logs ฟืน	**19.** sofa/couch โซฟา/เก้าอี้นวมยาว	**26.** TV (television) โทรทัศน์
6. wall ฝาผนัง	**13.** wall unit ชั้นวางของ	**20.** throw pillow หมอนอิง	**27.** carpet พรม
7. painting ภาพเขียน	**14.** stereo system เครื่องเสียง	**21.** end table โต๊ะข้างโซฟา	

Use the new language. ใช้ภาษาใหม่

Look at **Colors**, page **12**, and describe this room.

There is a gray sofa and a gray armchair.

Talk about your living room. พูดเกี่ยวกับห้องนั่งเล่นของคุณ

In my living room I have a sofa, two chairs, and a coffee table.

I don't have a fireplace or a wall unit.

1. hamper ตะกร้ามีฝาปิด	**8.** towel rack ราวแขวนผ้าเช็ดตัว	**15.** toilet paper กระดาษชำระ	**22.** sink อ่างล้างมือ
2. bathtub อ่างอาบน้ำ	**9.** tile กระเบื้อง	**16.** toilet brush แปรงขัดโถส้วม	**23.** soap สบู่
3. rubber mat แผ่นยางกันลื่น	**10.** showerhead ฝักบัว	**17.** toilet โถส้วม	**24.** soap dish จานวางสบู่
4. drain ท่อระบายน้ำ	**11.** (mini)blinds ม่านบังตา	**18.** mirror กระจก	**25.** wastebasket ตะกร้าทิ้งขยะ
5. hot water น้ำร้อน	**12.** bath towel ผ้าเช็ดตัว	**19.** medicine cabinet ตู้ยา	**26.** scale เครื่องชั่งน้ำหนัก
6. faucet ก๊อกน้ำ	**13.** hand towel ผ้าเช็ดมือ	**20.** toothbrush แปรงสีฟัน	**27.** bath mat พรมเช็ดเท้า
7. cold water น้ำเย็น	**14.** washcloth ผ้าสำหรับเช็ดหน้า	**21.** toothbrush holder ที่เก็บแปรงสีฟัน	

More vocabulary คำศัพท์เพิ่มเติม

half bath: a bathroom without a shower or bathtub

linen closet: a closet or cabinet for towels and sheets

stall shower: a shower without a bathtub

Share your answers. แลกเปลี่ยนคำตอบ

1. Do you turn off the water when you brush your teeth? wash your hair? shave?

2. Does your bathroom have a bathtub or a stall shower?

1. mirror กระจก	**8.** bed เตียงนอน	**15.** headboard หัวเตียง	**22.** dust ruffle ครุยกันฝุ่น
2. dresser / bureau โต๊ะเครื่องแป้ง	**9.** pillow หมอน	**16.** clock radio วิทยุนาฬิกา	**23.** rug พรม
3. drawer ลิ้นชัก	**10.** pillowcase ปลอกหมอน	**17.** lamp โคมไฟ	**24.** floor พื้นห้อง
4. closet ตู้เสื้อผ้า	**11.** bedspread ผ้าคลุมเตียง	**18.** lampshade โป๊ะโคมไฟ	**25.** mattress ฟูกที่นอน
5. curtains ม่าน	**12.** blanket ผ้าห่ม	**19.** light switch สวิตช์ไฟ	**26.** box spring ฟูกรองที่ติดสปริง
6. window shade ม่านกันแสง	**13.** flat sheet ผ้าปูเตียง	**20.** outlet เต้ารับ/ปลั๊กไฟ	**27.** bed frame ขอบ/โครงเตียง
7. photograph รูปถ่าย	**14.** fitted sheet ผ้าปูเตียงแบบรัดมุม	**21.** night table โต๊ะข้างเตียงนอน	

Use the new language. ใช้ภาษาใหม่

Describe this room. (See **Describing Things**, page **11**, for help.)

I see a soft pillow and a beautiful bedspread.

Share your answers. แลกเปลี่ยนคำตอบ

1. What is your favorite thing in your bedroom?

2. Do you have a clock in your bedroom? Where is it?

3. Do you have a mirror in your bedroom? Where is it?

1. bunk bed เตียงนอนสองชั้น	**7.** bumper pad เบาะกันกระแทก	**13.** diaper pail ถังใส่ผ้าอ้อม	**19.** cradle เปล
2. comforter ผ้าห่มคลุมเตียง	**8.** chest of drawers ตู้ลิ้นชักเก็บเสื้อผ้า	**14.** dollhouse บ้านตุ๊กตา	**20.** coloring book สมุดภาพระบายสี
3. night-light ไฟหรี่ในห้องนอนเด็ก	**9.** baby monitor เครื่องฟังเสียงร้องเด็ก	**15.** blocks แท่งไม้	**21.** crayons สีเทียน
4. mobile โมบาย	**10.** teddy bear ตุ๊กตาหมี	**16.** ball ลูกบอล	**22.** puzzle เกมปริศนา
5. wallpaper กระดาษปิดฝาผนัง	**11.** smoke detector เครื่องจับสัญญาณควัน	**17.** picture book สมุดภาพ	**23.** stuffed animals ตุ๊กตาสัตว์ยัดนุ่น
6. crib เตียงนอนเด็กเล็ก	**12.** changing table โต๊ะแต่งตัวเด็กเล็ก	**18.** doll ตุ๊กตา	**24.** toy chest หีบของเล่น

Talk about where items are in the room.
พูดเกี่ยวกับสิ่งของในห้องนี้ว่าอยู่ที่ไหน
The dollhouse is near the coloring book.
The teddy bear is on the chest of drawers.

Share your answers. แลกเปลี่ยนคำตอบ
1. Do you think this is a good room for children? Why?
2. What toys did you play with when you were a child?
3. What children's stories do you know?

A. dust the furniture
ปัดฝุ่นเครื่องเรือน

B. recycle the newspapers
นำหนังสือพิมพ์มาใช้อีก

C. clean the oven
ทำความสะอาดเตาอบ

D. wash the windows
เช็ดกระจก

E. sweep the floor
กวาดพื้น

F. empty the wastebasket
เอาขยะไปทิ้ง

G. make the bed
เก็บที่นอน

H. put away the toys
เก็บของเล่นเข้าที่

I. vacuum the carpet
ดูดฝุ่นพรม

J. mop the floor
ถูพื้น

K. polish the furniture
ขัดถูเครื่องเรือน

L. scrub the floor
ขัดพื้น

M. wash the dishes
ล้างจาน

N. dry the dishes
เช็ดจาน

O. wipe the counter
เช็ดเคาน์เตอร์

P. change the sheets
เปลี่ยนผ้าปูที่นอน

Q. take out the garbage
เอาขยะออกไปทิ้ง

Talk about yourself. พูดเกี่ยวกับตัวของคุณ

I wash <u>the dishes</u> every day.
I change <u>the sheets</u> every week.
I never <u>dry the dishes</u>.

Share your answers. แลกเปลี่ยนคำตอบ

1. Who does the housework in your family?
2. What is your favorite cleaning job?
3. What is your least favorite cleaning job?

1. feather duster
   ไม้ขนนกปัดฝุ่น

2. recycling bin
   ถังขยะชนิดใส่ขยะนำมาใช้ได้อีก

3. oven cleaner
   น้ำยาทำความสะอาดเตาอบ

4. rubber gloves
   ถุงมือยาง

5. steel-wool soap pads
   ฝอยขัดหม้อ

6. rags
   ผ้าขี้ริ้ว

7. stepladder
   บันไดแบบพับได้

8. glass cleaner
   น้ำยาทำความสะอาดกระจก

9. squeegee
   ไม้ถูทำความสะอาดกระจก

10. broom
    ไม้กวาด

11. dustpan
    ที่ตักผง

12. trash bags
    ถุงขยะ

13. vacuum cleaner
    เครื่องดูดฝุ่น

14. vacuum cleaner attachments
    อุปกรณ์ที่ใช้กับเครื่องดูดฝุ่น

15. vacuum cleaner bag
    ถุงเก็บฝุ่น

16. wet mop
    ไม้ถูพื้น

17. dust mop
    ไม้เช็ดฝุ่น

18. furniture polish
    น้ำยาขัดเครื่องเรือน

19. scrub brush
    แปรงขัดพื้น

20. bucket / pail
    ถังน้ำ/ถัง

21. dishwashing liquid
    น้ำยาล้างจาน

22. dish towel
    ผ้าเช็ดจาน

23. cleanser
    น้ำยาทำความสะอาด

24. sponge
    ฟองน้ำ

Practice asking for the items. ฝึกการขอสิ่งของ

I want to <u>wash the windows</u>.

Please hand me <u>the squeegee</u>.

I have to <u>sweep the floor</u>.

Can you get me <u>the broom</u>, please?

1. The water heater is **not working**.
   เครื่องทำน้ำร้อน**เสีย**

2. The power is **out**.
   ไฟฟ้าดับ

3. The roof is **leaking**.
   หลังคา**รั่ว**

4. The wall is **cracked**.
   ฝาผนัง**ร้าว**

5. The window is **broken**.
   กระจกหน้าต่าง**แตก**

6. The lock is **broken**.
   กุญแจ**เสีย**

7. The steps are **broken**.
   บันได**หัก**

8. roofer
   ช่างซ่อมหลังคา

9. electrician
   ช่างไฟ

10. repair person
    ช่างซ่อม

11. locksmith
    ช่างทำกุญแจ

12. carpenter
    ช่างไม้

13. fuse box
    กล่องฟิวส์

14. gas meter
    มาตรวัดแก๊ส

Use the new language. ใช้ภาษาใหม่

Look at **Tools and Building Supplies**, pages **150–151**.

Name the tools you use for household repairs.

I use <u>a hammer and nails</u> to fix <u>a broken step</u>.

I use <u>a wrench</u> to repair <u>a dripping faucet</u>.

15. The furnace is **broken**.
เครื่องทำความร้อน**เสีย**

16. The faucet is **dripping**.
ก๊อกน้ำ**หยด**

17. The sink is **overflowing**.
น้ำล้น/อ่างล้างจาน**ตัน**

18. The toilet is **stopped up**.
ท่อส้วม**ตัน**

19. The pipes are **frozen**.
ท่อน้ำเย็นจนเป็นน้ำแข็ง

20. plumber
ช่างประปา

21. exterminator
พนักงานกำจัดปลวกและแมลงต่างๆ

Household pests
สัตว์ที่สร้างความรำคาญภายในบ้าน

22. termite(s)
ปลวก

23. flea(s)
หมัด

24. ant(s)
มด

25. cockroach(es)
แมลงสาบ

26. mice*
หนู

27. rat(s)
หนู

*Note: *one mouse, two mice*

More vocabulary คำศัพท์เพิ่มเติม

fix: to repair something that is broken

exterminate: to kill household pests

pesticide: a chemical that is used to kill household pests

Share your answers. แลกเปลี่ยนคำตอบ

1. Who does household repairs in your home?

2. What is the worst problem a home can have?

3. What is the most expensive problem a home can have?

49

1. grapes องุ่น	**9.** grapefruit ส้มสรวง	**17.** strawberries สตรอเบอร์รี่	**25.** dates อินทผาลัม
2. pineapples สับปะรด	**10.** oranges ส้ม	**18.** raspberries ราสเบอร์รี่	**26.** prunes ลูกพรุน
3. bananas กล้วย	**11.** lemons มะนาวเปลือกสีเหลือง	**19.** blueberries บลูเบอร์รี่	**27.** raisins ลูกเกด
4. apples แอปเปิ้ล	**12.** limes มะนาว	**20.** papayas มะละกอ	**28.** not ripe ดิบ
5. peaches ลูกพีช	**13.** tangerines ส้มจีน	**21.** mangoes มะม่วง	**29.** ripe สุก
6. pears ลูกแพร์	**14.** avocadoes อะโวคาโด้	**22.** coconuts มะพร้าว	**30.** rotten เน่า
7. apricots ผลแอพริคอท	**15.** cantaloupes แคนตาลูพ	**23.** nuts ลูกนัท	
8. plums ลูกพลัม	**16.** cherries เชอร์รี่	**24.** watermelons แตงโม	

Language note: *a bunch of* ข้อสังเกตทางภาษา

We say *a bunch of grapes* and *a bunch of bananas*.

Share your answers. แลกเปลี่ยนคำตอบ

1. Which fruits do you put in a fruit salad?

2. Which fruits are sold in your area in the summer?

3. What fruits did you have in your country?

1. lettuce ผักกาดหอม	**9.** celery ผักคื่นฉ่าย	**17.** scallions ต้นหอม	**25.** string beans ถั่วแขก
2. cabbage กะหล่ำปลี	**10.** parsley ผักชีฝรั่ง	**18.** eggplants มะเขือม่วง	**26.** mushrooms เห็ด
3. carrots แครอท	**11.** spinach ผักขม	**19.** peas ถั่วลันเตา	**27.** corn ข้าวโพด
4. zucchini แตงชนิดหนึ่งสีเขียวเข้ม	**12.** cucumbers แตงกวา	**20.** artichokes อาทิโชค	**28.** onions หัวหอม
5. radishes หัวผักกาดแดง	**13.** squash แตงน้ำเต้า	**21.** potatoes มันฝรั่ง	**29.** garlic กระเทียม
6. beets บีท/ผักชนิดลงหัว	**14.** turnips หัวผักกาดชนิดหนึ่ง	**22.** yams มันเทศ	
7. sweet peppers พริกหยวก	**15.** broccoli ดอกบรอคโคลี่	**23.** tomatoes มะเขือเทศ	
8. chili peppers พริกชี้ฟ้า	**16.** cauliflower กะหล่ำดอก	**24.** asparagus หน่อไม้ฝรั่ง	

Language note: *a bunch of, a head of* ข้อสังเกตทางภาษา

We say *a bunch of carrots, a bunch of celery*, and *a bunch of spinach*.

We say *a head of lettuce, a head of cabbage*, and *a head of cauliflower*.

Share your answers. แลกเปลี่ยนคำตอบ

1. Which vegetables do you eat raw? cooked?

2. Which vegetables need to be in the refrigerator?

3. Which vegetables don't need to be in the refrigerator?

Beef เนื้อวัว

1. roast beef
เนื้อวัวสำหรับย่าง

2. steak
เนื้อสเต็ค

3. stewing beef
เนื้อสำหรับทำสตู

4. ground beef
เนื้อบด

5. beef ribs
ซี่โครงวัว

6. veal cutlets
เนื้อลูกวัว

7. liver
ตับ

8. tripe
ผ้าขี้ริ้ว (เครื่องใน)

Pork เนื้อหมู

9. ham
เนื้อต้นขาหลังของหมู

10. pork chops
เนื้อแดงติดมัน

11. bacon
หมูเบคอน/หมูเค็ม

12. sausage
ไส้กรอก

Lamb เนื้อแกะ

13. lamb shanks
เนื้อขาส่วนล่าง

14. leg of lamb
เนื้อขาส่วนบน

15. lamb chops
เนื้อแดงติดมัน

16. chicken
เนื้อไก่

17. turkey
เนื้อไก่งวง

18. duck
เนื้อเป็ด

19. breasts
เนื้อหน้าอก

20. wings
ปีก

21. thighs
โคนขา

22. drumsticks
น่อง

23. gizzards
กึ๋นไก่

24. **raw** chicken
ไก่ดิบ

25. **cooked** chicken
ไก่สุก

More vocabulary คำศัพท์เพิ่มเติม

vegetarian: a person who doesn't eat meat

Meat and poultry without bones are called **boneless**.

Poultry without skin is called **skinless**.

Share your answers. แลกเปลี่ยนคำตอบ

1. What kind of meat do you eat most often?

2. What kind of meat do you use in soup?

3. What part of the chicken do you like the most?

1. **white bread**
ขนมปังสีขาว

2. **wheat bread**
ขนมปังแป้งสาลี

3. **rye bread**
ขนมปังข้าวไร

4. **smoked turkey**
เนื้อไก่งวงรมควัน

5. **salami**
ไส้กรอกใส่กระเทียม

6. **pastrami**
เนื้อวัวอบใส่เครื่องเทศ

7. **roast beef**
เนื้อย่าง

8. **corned beef**
เนื้อเค็ม

9. **American cheese**
เนยแข็งอเมริกัน

10. **cheddar cheese**
เนยแข็งชนิดหนึ่ง

11. **Swiss cheese**
เนยแข็งสวิส

12. **jack cheese**
เนยแข็งชนิดหนึ่ง

13. **potato salad**
สลัดมันฝรั่ง

14. **coleslaw**
โคลสลอ/สลัดกระหล่ำปลี

15. **pasta salad**
สลัดพาสต้า

Fish เนื้อปลา

16. **trout**
ปลาเทร้า

17. **catfish**
ปลาดุก

18. **whole salmon**
ปลาแซลมอน

19. **salmon steak**
เนื้อปลาแซลมอน

20. **halibut**
ปลาทะเลชนิดหนึ่ง

21. **filet of sole**
เนื้อปลาโซล

Shellfish สัตว์น้ำที่มีเปลือกแข็ง

22. **crab**
ปู

23. **lobster**
กุ้งก้ามกราม

24. **shrimp**
กุ้ง

25. **scallops**
หอยแครง

26. **mussels**
หอยแมลงภู่

27. **oysters**
หอยนางรม

28. **clams**
หอยกาบ

29. **fresh** fish
ปลาสด

30. **frozen** fish
ปลาแช่แข็ง

Practice ordering a sandwich. ฝึกการสั่งแซนวิช

I'd like roast beef and American cheese on rye bread.

Tell what you want on it.

Please put tomato, lettuce, onions, and mustard on it.

Share your answers. แลกเปลี่ยนคำตอบ

1. Do you like to eat fish?

2. Do you buy fresh or frozen fish?

1. bottle return ที่คืนขวด	**3.** shopping cart รถเข็นใส่ของ	**6.** baked goods อาหารประเภทอบ	**9.** dairy section แผนกผลิตภัณฑ์นม
2. meat and poultry section แผนกเนื้อและสัตว์ปีก	**4.** canned goods อาหารกระป๋อง	**7.** shopping basket ตะกร้าใส่ของ	**10.** pet food อาหารสัตว์
	5. aisle ทางเดินระหว่างชั้นวางของ	**8.** manager ผู้จัดการ	**11.** produce section แผนกผักสด

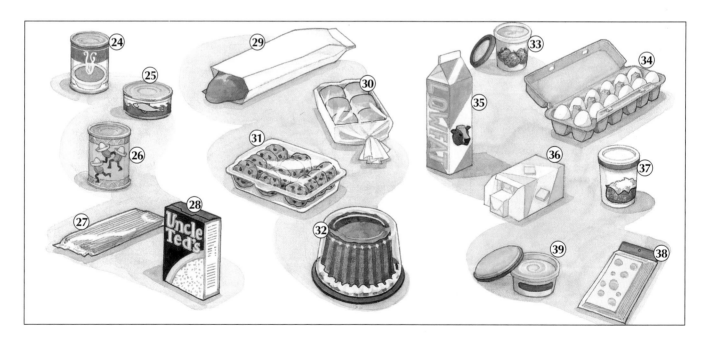

24. soup ซุปกระป๋อง	**28.** rice ข้าว	**32.** cake ขนมเค้ก	**36.** butter เนย
25. tuna ปลาทูน่ากระป๋อง	**29.** bread ขนมปัง	**33.** yogurt โยเกิร์ต	**37.** sour cream ครีมเปรี้ยว
26. beans ถั่วกระป๋อง	**30.** rolls ขนมปังม้วนกลม	**34.** eggs ไข่	**38.** cheese เนยแข็ง
27. spaghetti เส้นสปาเก็ตตี้	**31.** cookies ขนมคุ้กกี้	**35.** milk นม	**39.** margarine เนยเทียม

12. frozen foods อาหารแช่แข็ง	**15.** beverages เครื่องดื่ม	**18.** cash register เครื่องบันทึกจำนวนเงิน	**21.** bagger พนักงานใส่ของลงถุง
13. baking products สินค้าประเภททำขนมปัง	**16.** snack foods อาหารว่าง	**19.** checker พนักงานเก็บเงิน	**22.** paper bag ถุงกระดาษ
14. paper products สินค้าประเภทกระดาษชำระ	**17.** checkstand ที่วางของรอคิดเงิน	**20.** line คิว/แถว	**23.** plastic bag ถุงพลาสติก

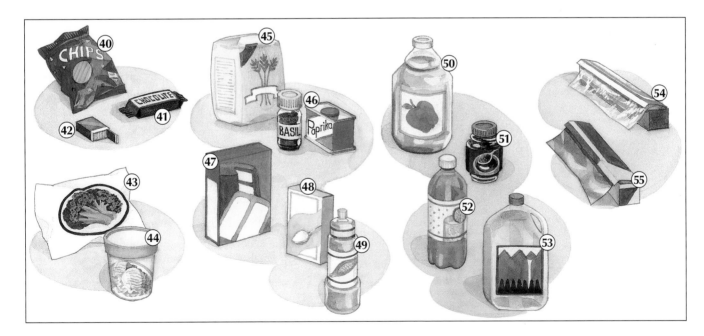

40. potato chips มันฝรั่งกรอบ	**44.** ice cream ไอศครีม	**48.** sugar น้ำตาล	**52.** soda โซดา
41. candy bar ขนมหวานชนิดแท่ง	**45.** flour แป้ง	**49.** oil น้ำมันพืช	**53.** bottled water น้ำดื่มบรรจุขวด
42. gum หมากฝรั่ง	**46.** spices เครื่องเทศ	**50.** apple juice น้ำแอปเปิ้ล	**54.** plastic wrap พลาสติกใช้ห่ออาหาร
43. frozen vegetables ผักแช่แข็ง	**47.** cake mix แป้งเค้กสำเร็จรูป	**51.** instant coffee กาแฟสำเร็จรูป	**55.** aluminum foil แผ่นอลูมิเนียมฟอยล์

Containers and Packaged Foods ภาชนะและอาหารบรรจุหีบห่อ

 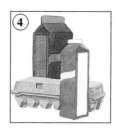    

1. bottle
ขวด

2. jar
ขวดทรงเตี้ย
ปากกว้าง

3. can
กระป๋อง

4. carton
กล่องกระดาษ

5. container
ภาชนะที่มีฝาปิด

6. box
กล่อง

7. bag
ถุงกระดาษ

8. package
ซอง/ห่อ

9. six-pack
ชุดครึ่งโหล

10. loaf
ก้อนขนมปัง

11. roll
ม้วน

12. tube
หลอด

 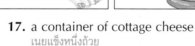  

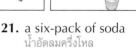

13. a bottle of soda
น้ำอัดลมหนึ่งขวด

14. a jar of jam
แยมหนึ่งกระปุก

15. a can of soup
ซุปหนึ่งกระป๋อง

16. a carton of eggs
ไข่หนึ่งกล่อง

17. a container of cottage cheese
เนยแข็งหนึ่งถ้วย

18. a box of cereal
ธัญพืชหนึ่งกล่อง

19. a bag of flour
แป้งหนึ่งถุง

20. a package of cookies
คุ้กกี้หนึ่งห่อ

21. a six-pack of soda
น้ำอัดลมครึ่งโหล

22. a loaf of bread
ขนมปังหนึ่งแถว

23. a roll of paper towels
กระดาษเช็ดมือหนึ่งม้วน

24. a tube of toothpaste
ยาสีฟันหนึ่งหลอด

Grammar point: *How much? How many?*

การใช้ How much? How many?
Some foods can be counted: *one apple, two apples.*
How many apples do you need? I need ***two*** apples.

Some foods cannot be counted, like liquids, grains, spices, or dairy foods. For these, count containers: *one box of rice, two boxes of rice.*

How much rice do you need? I need ***two boxes.***

56

A. Measure the ingredients.
ตวงส่วนผสม

B. Weigh the food.
ชั่งอาหาร

C. Convert the measurements.
เปลี่ยนหน่วยการชั่ง ตวง วัด

Liquid measures การตวงของเหลว

1 fl. oz.　　　　1 c.　　　　1 pt.　　　　1 qt.　　　　1 gal.

Dry measures การตวงของแห้ง

1 tsp.　　　　1 TBS.　　　　1/4 c.　　　　1/2 c.　　　　1 c.

Weight น้ำหนัก

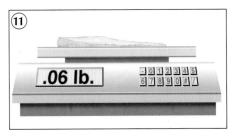
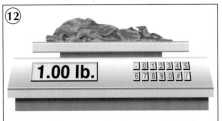

1. a fluid ounce of water
น้ำหนึ่งออนซ์

2. a cup of oil
น้ำมันหนึ่งถ้วย

3. a pint of yogurt
โยเกิร์ตหนึ่งไพนต์

4. a quart of milk
นมหนึ่งควอท

5. a gallon of apple juice
น้ำแอปเปิ้ลหนึ่งแกลลอน

6. a teaspoon of salt
เกลือหนึ่งช้อนชา

7. a tablespoon of sugar
น้ำตาลหนึ่งช้อนโต๊ะ

8. a 1/4 cup of brown sugar
น้ำตาลทรายเศษหนึ่งส่วนสี่ถ้วย

9. a 1/2 cup of raisins
ลูกเกตครึ่งถ้วย

10. a cup of flour
แป้งหนึ่งถ้วย

11. an ounce of cheese
เนยแข็งหนึ่งออนซ์

12. a pound of roast beef
เนื้อวัวย่างหนึ่งปอนด์

VOLUME ปริมาตร
1 fl. oz. = 30 milliliters (ml.)
1 c. = 237 ml.
1 pt. = .47 liters (l.)
1 qt. = .95 l.
1 gal. = 3.79 l.

EQUIVALENCIES
เปรียบเทียบความเท่ากัน

3 tsp. = 1 TBS.	2 c. = 1 pt.
2 TBS. = 1 fl. oz.	2 pt. = 1 qt.
8 fl. oz. = 1 c.	4 qt. = 1 gal.

WEIGHT น้ำหนัก
1 oz. = 28.35 grams (g.)
1 lb. = 453.6 g.
2.205 lbs. = 1 kilogram
1 lb. = 16 oz.

Scrambled eggs ไข่เจียวชนิดคนให้เละ

A. Break 3 eggs.
ตอกไข่ไก่ 3 ฟอง

B. Beat well.
ตีให้เข้ากัน

C. Grease the pan.
ใส่เนยหรือน้ำมัน
ในกะทะ

D. Pour the eggs into the pan.
เทไข่ลงในกะทะ

E. Stir.
คนไปมา

F. Cook until done.
ปรุงจนไข่สุก

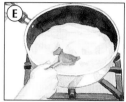

Vegetable casserole การอบผัก

G. Chop the onions.
หั่นหัวหอม

H. Sauté the onions.
ผัดหัวหอมในน้ำมัน

I. Steam the broccoli.
นึ่งดอกบรอคโคลี่

J. Grate the cheese.
ขูดเนยแข็ง

K. Mix the ingredients.
ผสมส่วนประกอบทั้งหมด

L. Bake at 350° for 45 minutes.
อบที่อุณหภูมิ 350 องศา
ประมาณ 45 นาที

Chicken soup ซุปไก่

M. Cut up the chicken.
หั่นเนื้อไก่

N. Peel the carrots.
ปอกเปลือกหัวแครอท

O. Slice the carrots.
ฝานแครอท

P. Boil the chicken.
ต้มเนื้อไก่

Q. Add the vegetables.
เติมผัก

R. Simmer for 1 hour.
เคี่ยวไฟอ่อนประมาณ
1 ชม.

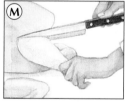

Five ways to cook chicken ห้าวิธีในการปรุงเนื้อไก่

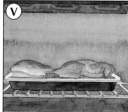

S. fry
ทอด

T. barbecue / grill
บาร์บีคิว/ย่างบน
ตะแกรง

U. roast
อบในเตาอบ

V. broil
ย่างในเตาอบ

W. stir-fry
ผัด

Talk about the way you prepare these foods.
พูดเกี่ยวกับวิธีที่คุณเตรียมอาหารเหล่านี้

I _fry_ eggs.

I _bake_ potatoes.

Share your answers. แลกเปลี่ยนคำตอบ

1. What are popular ways in your country to make rice? vegetables? meat?

2. What is your favorite way to cook chicken?

1. can opener
   ที่เปิดกระป๋อง

2. grater
   ที่ขูด/ไส

3. plastic storage
   container
   ภาชนะพลาสติกสำหรับใส่ของ

4. steamer
   ภาชนะใช้นึ่งอาหาร

5. frying pan
   กะทะก้นแบน

6. pot
   หม้อ

7. ladle
   ทัพพี

8. double boiler
   หม้อต้มสองชั้น

9. wooden spoon
   ช้อนไม้

10. garlic press
    เครื่องบีบกระเทียม

11. casserole dish
    ชามมีฝาใช้อบอาหาร

12. carving knife
    มีดหั่นเนื้อก้อน

13. roasting pan
    ถาดสำหรับอบหรือย่าง

14. roasting rack
    ตะแกรงสำหรับอบหรือย่าง

15. vegetable peeler
    ที่ปอกเปลือกผัก

16. paring knife
    มีดปอกเปลือก

17. colander
    ตะแกรงล้างผัก

18. kitchen timer
    นาฬิกาตั้งเวลา

19. spatula
    ไม้พายผสมอาหาร

20. eggbeater
    เครื่องตีไข่

21. whisk
    ที่ตีไข่

22. strainer
    กระชอน

23. tongs
    คีมหนีบ

24. lid
    ฝาปิด

25. saucepan
    หม้อที่มีฝาปิดและด้ามถือ

26. cake pan
    ถาดใช้อบเค้ก

27. cookie sheet
    ถาดใช้อบคุ้กกี้

28. pie pan
    ถาดใช้อบพาย

29. pot holders
    ผ้าสำหรับใช้จับหม้อที่ร้อน

30. rolling pin
    ไม้นวดแป้ง

31. mixing bowl
    ชามสำหรับผสมแป้ง

Talk about how to use the utensils.
พูดเกี่ยวกับการใช้เครื่องครัว

You use a peeler to peel potatoes.

You use a pot to cook soup.

Use the new language.
ใช้ภาษาใหม่

Look at **Food Preparation,** page **58.**

Name the different utensils you see.

1. hamburger
แฮมเบอร์เกอร์

2. french fries
มันทอด

3. cheeseburger
ชีสเบอร์เกอร์

4. soda
น้ำอัดลม

5. iced tea
ชาดำเย็น

6. hot dog
ฮ้อทดอก

7. pizza
พิซซ่า

8. green salad
สลัดผัก

9. taco
ทาโก้

10. nachos
นาโชส

11. frozen yogurt
โยเกิร์ตแช่แข็ง

12. milk shake
นมปั่น

13. counter
เคาเตอร์

14. muffin
มัฟฟิน

15. doughnut
โดนัท

16. salad bar
โต๊ะสลัด

17. lettuce
ผักกาดหอม

18. salad dressing
น้ำสลัด

19. booth
โต๊ะแยกเฉพาะส่วน

20. straw
หลอดดูด

21. sugar
น้ำตาล

22. sugar substitute
น้ำตาลเทียม

23. ketchup
ชอสมะเขือเทศ

24. mustard
มัสตาร์ด

25. mayonnaise
น้ำสลัดข้น/มายองเนส

26. relish
เครื่องปรุงรส

A. eat
รับประทานอาหาร

B. drink
ดื่ม

More vocabulary คำศัพท์เพิ่มเติม

donut: doughnut (spelling variation)

condiments: relish, mustard, ketchup, mayonnaise, etc.

Share your answers. แลกเปลี่ยนคำตอบ

1. What would you order at this restaurant?

2. Which fast foods are popular in your country?

3. How often do you eat fast food? Why?

Breakfast อาหารเช้า

Lunch อาหารกลางวัน

Dinner อาหารเย็น

ของหวาน
Desserts

Beverages เครื่องดื่ม

1. scrambled eggs
ไข่เจียวชนิดคนเละ

2. sausage
ไส้กรอก

3. toast
ขนมปังปิ้ง

4. waffles
ขนมรังผึ้ง

5. syrup
น้ำเชื่อม

6. pancakes
ขนมแพนเค้ก

7. bacon
เบคอน/หมูเค็ม

8. grilled cheese sandwich
แซนวิชกรอบไส้เนยแข็ง

9. chef's salad
สลัดชนิดหนึ่ง

10. soup of the day
ซุปประจำวัน

11. mashed potatoes
มันฝรั่งบด

12. roast chicken
ไก่ย่าง

13. steak
สเต็ก/เนื้อย่าง

14. baked potato
มันฝรั่งอบ

15. pasta
พาสต้า

16. garlic bread
ขนมปังกระเทียม

17. fried fish
ปลาทอด

18. rice pilaf
ข้าวผัด

19. cake
ขนมเค้ก

20. pudding
ขนมพุดดิ้ง

21. pie
ขนมพาย

22. coffee
กาแฟ

23. decaf coffee
กาแฟที่ไม่มีคาเฟอีน

24. tea
ชา

Practice ordering from the menu. ฝึกการสั่งจากเมนู
I'd like a grilled cheese sandwich and some soup.
I'll have the chef's salad and a cup of decaf coffee.

Use the new language. ใช้ภาษาใหม่
Look at **Fruit,** page **50.**
Order a slice of pie using the different fruit flavors.
Please give me a slice of apple pie.

A Restaurant ภัตตาคาร

1. hostess
พนักงานต้อนรับหญิง

2. dining room
ห้องรับประทานอาหาร

3. menu
รายการอาหาร

4. server/waiter
บริกรชาย

5. patron/diner
ลูกค้า/แขกที่มารับประทานอาหาร

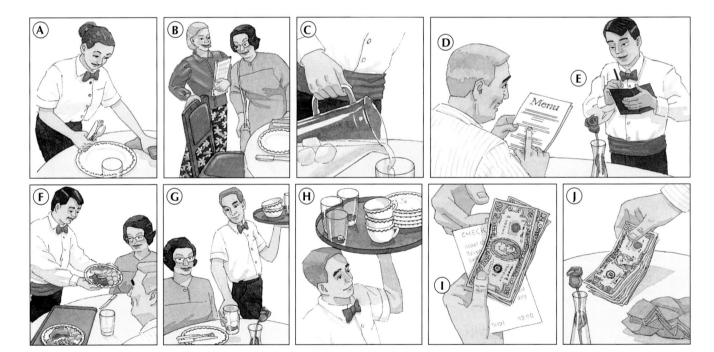

A. set the table
จัดโต๊ะอาหาร

B. seat the customer
พาลูกค้านั่งโต๊ะ

C. pour the water
รินน้ำใส่แก้ว

D. order from the menu
สั่งอาหารตามรายการ

E. take the order
จดรายการอาหารที่สั่ง

F. serve the meal
เสิร์ฟอาหาร

G. clear the table
เก็บโต๊ะอาหาร

H. carry the tray
ถือถาด

I. pay the check
จ่ายเงิน

J. leave a tip
ให้ทิปเป็นค่าบริการ

More vocabulary คำศัพท์เพิ่มเติม

eat out: to go to a restaurant to eat

take out: to buy food at a restaurant and take it home to eat

Practice giving commands. ฝึกการใช้คำสั่ง

Please <u>set the table</u>.

I'd like you to <u>clear the table</u>.

It's time to <u>serve the meal</u>.

6. server / waitress
บริกรหญิง

7. dessert tray
ถาดขนมหวาน

8. bread basket
ตะกร้าขนมปัง

9. busperson
พนักงานขนถ้วยชาม

10. kitchen
ห้องครัว

11. chef
พ่อครัว

12. dishroom
ห้องเก็บจาน

13. dishwasher
คนล้างจาน

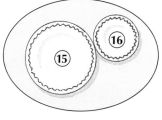
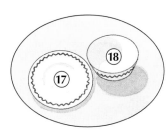
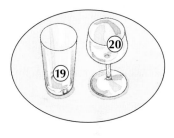

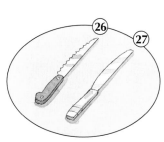
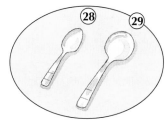

14. place setting
ตำแหน่งอุปกรณ์การ
รับประทาน

15. dinner plate
จานอาหาร

16. bread-and-butter plate
จานขนมปังและเนย

17. salad plate
จานสลัด

18. soup bowl
ถ้วยซุป

19. water glass
แก้วน้ำ

20. wine glass
แก้วไวน์

21. cup
ถ้วยกาแฟ

22. saucer
จานรอง

23. napkin
ผ้าเช็ดปาก

24. salad fork
ส้อมสลัด

25. dinner fork
ส้อมใช้รับประทานอาหาร

26. steak knife
มีดหั่นสเต็ก

27. knife
มีด

28. teaspoon
ช้อนชา

29. soupspoon
ช้อนตักซุป

Talk about how you set the table in your home.
พูดเกี่ยวกับวิธีการจัดโต๊ะอาหารในบ้านของคุณ

The glass is on the right.
The fork goes on the left.
The napkin is next to the plate.

Share your answers. แลกเปลี่ยนคำตอบ

1. Do you know anyone who works in a restaurant? What does he or she do?

2. In your opinion, which restaurant jobs are hard? Why?

1. three-piece suit
ชุดสูทสามชิ้น/สูทนักธุรกิจ

2. suit
ชุดสูท

3. dress
ชุดเสื้อกระโปรงติดกัน

4. shirt
เสื้อเชิ้ต

5. jeans
กางเกงยีนส์

6. sports coat
เสื้อสูทลำลอง

7. turtleneck
เสื้อยืดรัดคอ

8. slacks/pants
กางเกงขายาว

9. blouse
เสื้อสุภาพสตรี

10. skirt
กระโปรง

11. pullover sweater
เสื้อกันหนาวที่สวมทางศีรษะ

12. T-shirt
เสื้อยืดคอกลม

13. shorts
กางเกงขาสั้น

14. sweatshirt
เสื้อใส่ออกกำลังกาย

15. sweatpants
กางเกงใส่ออกกำลังกาย

More vocabulary: คำศัพท์เพิ่มเติม

outfit: clothes that look nice together

When clothes are popular, they are **in fashion.**

Talk about what you're wearing today and what you wore yesterday. พูดเกี่ยวกับเสื้อผ้าที่คุณใส่วันนี้ และเสื้อผ้าที่คุณใส่เมื่อวานนี้

I'm wearing a gray sweater, a red T-shirt, and blue jeans.

Yesterday I wore a green pullover sweater, a white shirt, and black slacks.

16. jumpsuit
ชุดทำงานที่เป็นเสื้อกางเกงติดกัน

17. uniform
เครื่องแบบ

18. jumper
ชุดกระโปรงเด็กสวมทับเสื้อ

19. maternity dress
ชุดคลุมท้อง

20. knit shirt
เสื้อเชิ้ตผ้ายืด

21. overalls
ชุดเอี๊ยม

22. tunic
เสื้อตัวยาวมีแขน

23. leggings
กางเกงขายาวแนบเนื้อ

24. vest
เสื้อกั๊กคอแหลม

25. split skirt
กระโปรงกางเกง

26. sports shirt
เสื้อยืดคอปก

27. cardigan sweater
เสื้อกันหนาวไหมพรม

28. tuxedo
ชุดเต้นรำ/ทักซี่โดยาว

29. evening gown
ชุดราตรี

Use the new language. ใช้ภาษาใหม่

Look at **A Graduation**, pages **32–33.**

Name the clothes you see.

The man at the podium is wearing <u>*a suit*</u>.

Share your answers. แลกเปลี่ยนคำตอบ

1. Which clothes in this picture are in fashion now?

2. Who is the best-dressed person in this line? Why?

3. What do you wear when you go to the movies?

1. **hat**
หมวก

2. **overcoat**
เสื้อคลุมกันหนาวยาวเกินหัวเข่า

3. **leather jacket**
เสื้อแจ๊คเก็ตหนัง

4. **wool scarf/muffler**
ผ้าพันคอขนสัตว์/ผ้าพันคอ

5. **gloves**
ถุงมือ

6. **cap**
หมวกแก๊ป

7. **jacket**
เสื้อแจ็คเก็ต

8. **parka**
เสื้อคลุมมีหมวก

9. **mittens**
ถุงมือชนิดไม่มีนิ้ว

10. **ski cap**
หมวกไหมพรม

11. **tights**
กางเกงยืดแนบเนื้อ

12. **earmuffs**
ที่ครอบหูกันหนาว

13. **down vest**
เสื้อกั๊กบุฟองน้ำ

14. **ski mask**
หน้ากากกันหิมะ

15. **down jacket**
เสื้อแจ็คเก็ตบุฟองน้ำ

16. **umbrella**
ร่ม

17. **raincoat**
เสื้อกันฝน

18. **poncho**
เสื้อคลุมกันฝน

19. **rain boots**
รองเท้าบู๊ทกันน้ำ

20. **trench coat**
เสื้อโค้ทกันฝน

21. **sunglasses**
แว่นกันแดด

22. **swimming trunks**
กางเกงว่ายน้ำ

23. **straw hat**
หมวกปีกกว้าง

24. **windbreaker**
เสื้อผ้าร่มกันลม

25. **cover-up**
เสื้อคลุมว่ายน้ำ

26. **swimsuit/bathing suit**
ชุดว่ายน้ำ

27. **baseball cap**
หมวกเบสบอล

Use the new language. ใช้ภาษาใหม่

Look at **Weather**, page **10**.

Name the clothing for each weather condition.

Wear a jacket when it's windy.

Share your answers. แลกเปลี่ยนคำตอบ

1. Which is better in the rain, an umbrella or a poncho?

2. Which is better in the cold, a parka or a down jacket?

3. Do you have more summer clothes or winter clothes?

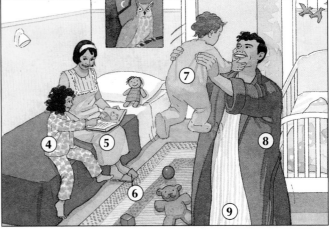

1. leotard
กางเกงแนบเนื้อใส่ออกกำลังกาย

2. tank top
เสื้อกล้าม

3. bike shorts
กางเกงขาสั้นใส่ขี่จักรยาน

4. pajamas
ชุดนอน

5. nightgown
ชุดนอนติดกัน

6. slippers
รองเท้าแตะ

7. blanket sleeper
ชุดนอนหมี

8. bathrobe
เสื้อคลุมอาบน้ำ

9. nightshirt
เสื้อนอนตัวยาว

10. undershirt
เสื้อชั้นในของผู้ชาย

11. long underwear
เสื้อกางเกงชั้นในยาว

12. boxer shorts
กางเกงนักมวย

13. briefs
กางเกงในผู้ชาย

14. athletic supporter / jockstrap
กระจับ

15. socks
ถุงเท้า

16. (bikini) panties
กางเกงในสตรี

17. briefs / underpants
กางเกงชั้นในยืดเต็มตัว

18. girdle
กางเกงชั้นในสตรีรัดเอวและตะโพก

19. garter belt
สายรัดถุงน่อง

20. bra
เสื้อชั้นใน

21. camisole
เสื้อใส่ทับเสื้อชั้นใน

22. full slip
ชุดใส่ทับชั้นในแบบเต็มตัว

23. half slip
กระโปรงใส่ทับชั้นในแบบครึ่งตัว

24. knee-highs
ถุงน่องยาวแค่เข่า

25. kneesocks
ถุงเท้ายาวถึงเข่า

26. stockings
ถุงน่อง

27. pantyhose
ถุงน่องยาวครึ่งตัว

More vocabulary คำศัพท์เพิ่มเติม

lingerie: underwear or sleepwear for women

loungewear: clothing (sometimes sleepwear) people wear around the home

Share your answers. แลกเปลี่ยนคำตอบ

1. What do you wear when you exercise?

2. What kind of clothing do you wear for sleeping?

Shoes and Accessories รองเท้าและอุปกรณ์

1. salesclerk
พนักงานขาย

2. suspenders
สายดึงกางเกง

3. shoe department
แผนกรองเท้า

4. silk scarves*
ผ้าพันคอไหม

5. hats
หมวก

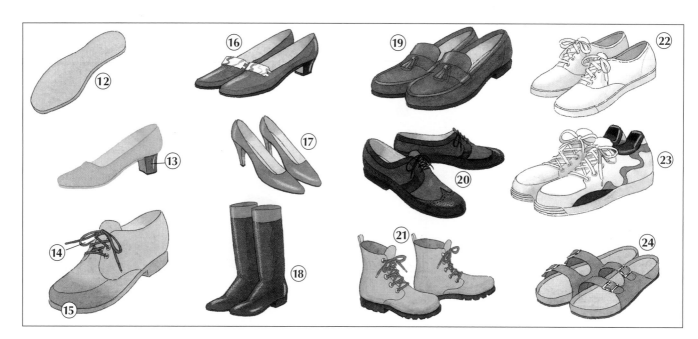

12. sole
พื้นรองเท้า

13. heel
ส้นรองเท้า

14. shoelace
เชือกผูกรองเท้า

15. toe
นิ้วเท้า

16. pumps
รองเท้าส้นเตี้ย

17. high heels
รองเท้าส้นสูง

18. boots
รองเท้าบู๊ท

19. loafers
รองเท้าพื้นราบไม่มีเชือกผูก

20. oxfords
รองเท้าพื้นราบมีเชือกผูก

21. hiking boots
รองเท้าบู๊ทสำหรับปีนเขา

22. tennis shoes
รองเท้าเทนนิส

23. athletic shoes
รองเท้ากีฬา

24. sandals
รองเท้าแตะ

*Note: one scarf, two scarves

Talk about the shoes you're wearing today.
พูดเกี่ยวกับรองเท้าที่คุณกำลังใส่วันนี้
I'm wearing a pair of white sandals.

Practice asking a salesperson for help.
ฝึกการถามพนักงานขายเพื่อขอความช่วยเหลือ
Could I try on these sandals in size 10?
Do you have any silk scarves?
Where are the hats?

6. purses/handbags
กระเป๋าถือสตรี

7. display case
ตู้โชว์

8. jewelry
เครื่องประดับ/เพชรพลอย

9. necklaces
สร้อยคอ

10. ties
เนคไท

11. belts
เข็มขัด

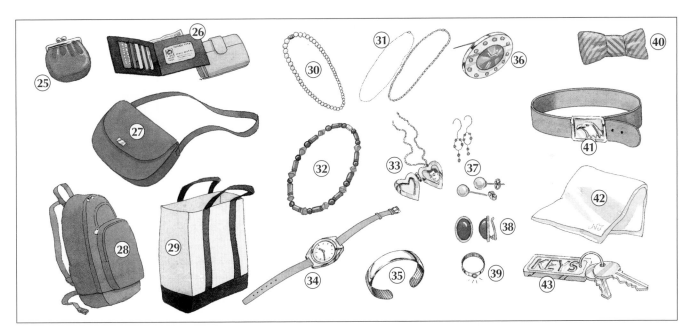

25. change purse
กระเป๋าใส่เศษสตางค์

26. wallet
กระเป๋าเงิน

27. shoulder bag
กระเป๋าสะพายไหล่

28. backpack/bookbag
กระเป๋าสะพายหลัง/กระเป๋า
หนังสือ

29. tote bag
ย่ามหรือถุง

30. string of pearls
สร้อยไข่มุก

31. chain
สายสร้อย

32. beads
สร้อยลูกปัด

33. locket
ตลับจี้ห้อยคอ

34. (wrist) watch
นาฬิกาข้อมือ

35. bracelet
กำไลข้อมือ

36. pin
เข็มหมุด

37. pierced earrings
ต่างหูแบบเจาะ

38. clip-on earrings
ต่างหูแบบหนีบ

39. ring
แหวน

40. bow tie
หูกระต่าย

41. belt buckle
หัวเข็มขัด

42. handkerchief
ผ้าเช็ดหน้า

43. key chain
พวงกุญแจ

Share your answers. แลกเปลี่ยนคำตอบ

1. Which of these accessories are usually worn by
women? by men?

2. Which of these do you wear every day?

3. Which of these would you wear to a job interview?
Why?

4. Which accessory would you like to receive as a
present? Why?

Describing Clothes การบรรยายเสื้อผ้า

Sizes ขนาด

1. extra small
ขนาดเล็กพิเศษ

2. small
ขนาดเล็ก

3. medium
ขนาดกลาง

4. large
ขนาดใหญ่

5. extra large
ขนาดใหญ่พิเศษ

Patterns ลวดลาย

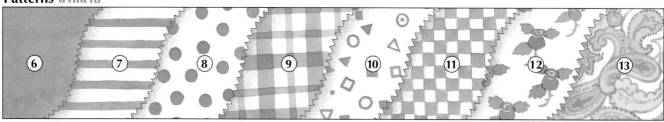

6. solid green
ผ้าสีเขียวล้วน

7. striped
ผ้าลายทาง

8. polka-dotted
ผ้าลายจุด

9. plaid
ผ้าลายสก็อต

10. print
ผ้าพิมพ์

11. checked
ผ้าลายตาหมากรุก

12. floral
ผ้าลายดอกไม้

13. paisley
ผ้าลายโค้ง

Types of material ชนิดของวัสดุ

   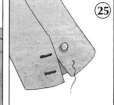

14. wool sweater
เสื้อกันหนาว**ขนแกะ**

15. silk scarf
ผ้าพันคอ**ไหม**

16. cotton T-shirt
เสื้อคอกลม**ผ้าฝ้าย**

17. linen jacket
เสื้อแจ็คเก็ต**ผ้าลินิน**

18. leather boots
รองเท้าบู๊ท**หนัง**

19. nylon stockings*
ถุงน่อง**ไนล่อน**

Problems ปัญหา

   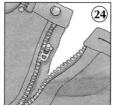 

20. too small
เล็กเกินไป

21. too big
ใหญ่เกินไป

22. stain
รอยคราบสกปรก

23. rip/tear
ขาด/ฉีกขาด

24. broken zipper
ซิปแตก

25. missing button
กระดุม**หลุด**

***Note:** Nylon, polyester, rayon, and plastic are synthetic materials.

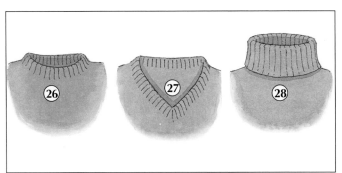

26. crewneck sweater
เสื้อกันหนาว**คอกลม**

27. V-neck sweater
เสื้อกันหนาว**คอวี**

28. turtleneck sweater
เสื้อกันหนาว**คอตั้ง**

29. sleeveless shirt
เสื้อเชิ้ตแขนกุด

30. short-sleeved shirt
เสื้อเชิ้ต**แขนสั้น**

31. long-sleeved shirt
เสื้อเชิ้ต**แขนยาว**

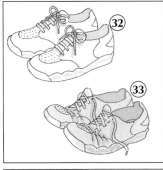
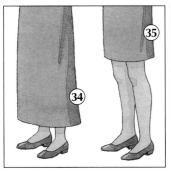

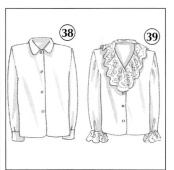

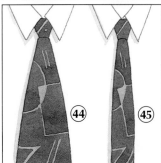

32. new shoes
รองเท้า**ใหม่**

33. old shoes
รองเท้า**เก่า**

34. long skirt
กระโปรง**ยาว**

35. short skirt
กระโปรง**สั้น**

36. formal dress
ชุด**พิธีการ**

37. casual dress
ชุด**ลำลอง**

38. plain blouse
เสื้อแบบ**เรียบ**

39. fancy blouse
เสื้อตกแต่ง**แบบหรูหรา**

40. light jacket
เสื้อแจ็คเก็ต**บาง**

41. heavy jacket
เสื้อแจ็คเก็ต**หนา**

42. loose pants / **baggy** pants
กางเกง**ทรงหลวม**

43. tight pants
กางเกง**ทรงรัดรูป**

44. wide tie
เนคไทชนิด**กว้าง**

45. narrow tie
เนคไทชนิด**แคบ**

46. low heels
รองเท้า**ส้นเตี้ย**

47. high heels
รองเท้า**ส้นสูง**

Talk about yourself. พูดเกี่ยวกับตัวของคุณเอง
I like <u>long-sleeved</u> shirts and <u>baggy</u> pants.
I like <u>short skirts</u> and <u>high heels</u>.
I usually wear <u>plain</u> clothes.

Share your answers. แลกเปลี่ยนคำตอบ
1. What type of material do you usually wear in the summer? in the winter?
2. What patterns do you see around you?
3. Are you wearing casual or formal clothes?

71

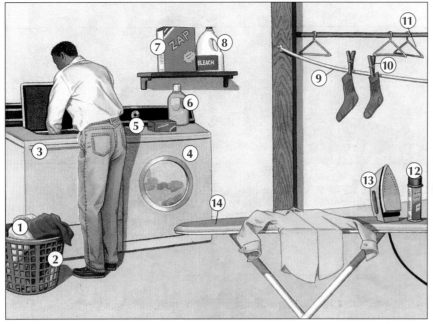
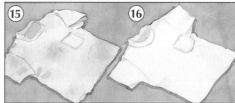
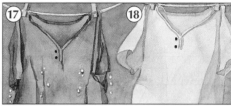
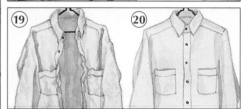

1. laundry
เสื้อผ้าที่ส่งซักรีด

2. laundry basket
ตะกร้าใส่ผ้า

3. washer
เครื่องซักผ้า

4. dryer
เครื่องอบผ้า

5. dryer sheets
แผ่นใส่ในเครื่องอบป้องกันผ้า
ติดกัน

6. fabric softener
น้ำยาปรับผ้านุ่ม

7. laundry detergent
ผงซักฟอก

8. bleach
น้ำยาฟอกขาว

9. clothesline
ราวตากผ้า

10. clothespin
ไม้หนีบผ้า

11. hanger
ไม้แขวนเสื้อ

12. spray starch
สเปรย์รีดผ้าเรียบ

13. iron
เตารีด

14. ironing board
โต๊ะรีดผ้า

15. dirty T-shirt
เสื้อยืด**สกปรก**

16. clean T-shirt
เสื้อยืด**สะอาด**

17. wet T-shirt
เสื้อยืด**เปียก**

18. dry T-shirt
เสื้อยืด**แห้ง**

19. wrinkled shirt
เสื้อเชิ้ต**ยับยู่ยี่**

20. ironed shirt
เสื้อเชิ้ต**รีดแล้ว**

A. Sort the laundry.
แยกผ้าที่จะซัก

B. Add the detergent.
เติมผงซักฟอก

C. Load the washer.
ใส่ผ้าลงในเครื่องซักผ้า

D. Clean the lint trap.
ทำความสะอาดช่องเศษผ้า

E. Unload the dryer.
เอาผ้าออกจากเครื่องอบ

F. Fold the laundry.
พับผ้าที่ซักแล้ว

G. Iron the clothes.
รีดเสื้อผ้า

H. Hang up the clothes.
แขวนเสื้อผ้า

More vocabulary คำศัพท์เพิ่มเติม

dry cleaners: a business that cleans clothes using chemicals, not water and detergent

wash in cold water only

no bleach

line dry

dry-clean only, do not wash

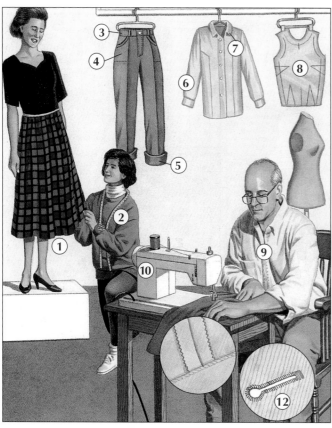

A. sew by hand
เย็บด้วยมือ

B. sew by machine
เย็บด้วยจักร

C. lengthen
ทำให้ยาว

D. shorten
ทำให้สั้น

E. take in
เย็บเข้า

F. let out
ขยายออก

1. hemline
ชายกระโปรง

2. dressmaker
ช่างตัดเสื้อสตรี

3. waistband
ขอบเอวกางเกง

4. pocket
กระเป๋ากางเกง

5. cuff
ขอบชายกางเกง

6. sleeve
แขนเสื้อ

7. collar
ปกเสื้อ

8. pattern
แบบกระดาษสำหรับตัดเสื้อ

9. tailor
ช่างตัดเสื้อบุรุษ

10. sewing machine
จักรเย็บผ้า

11. seam
ตะเข็บผ้า

12. buttonhole
รังดุม

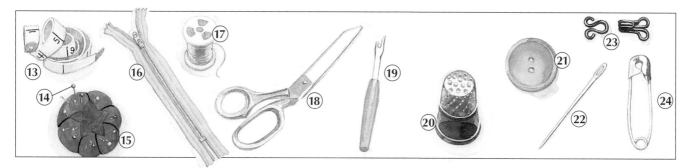

13. tape measure
สายวัดตัว

14. pin
เข็มหมุด

15. pin cushion
หมอนปักเข็มหมุด

16. zipper
ซิป

17. spool of thread
หลอดด้าย

18. (pair of) scissors
กรรไกร

19. seam ripper
ที่เลาะตะเข็บผ้า

20. thimble
ปลอกสวมนิ้วสำหรับเย็บผ้า

21. button
กระดุม

22. needle
เข็ม

23. hook and eye
ตะขอและที่เกาะ

24. safety pin
เข็มกลัด

More vocabulary คำศัพท์เพิ่มเติม

pattern maker: a person who makes patterns

garment worker: a person who works in a clothing factory

fashion designer: a person who makes original clothes

Share your answers. แลกเปลี่ยนคำตอบ

1. Do you know how to use a sewing machine?

2. Can you sew by hand?

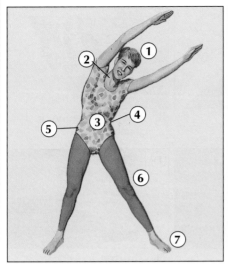
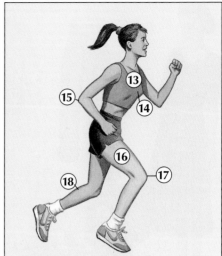

1. head
ศีรษะ

2. neck
คอ

3. abdomen
ท้อง

4. waist
เอว

5. hip
สะโพก

6. leg
ขา

7. foot
เท้า

8. hand
มือ

9. arm
แขน

10. shoulder
ไหล่

11. back
หลัง

12. buttocks
ก้น

13. chest
หน้าอก

14. breast
เต้านม

15. elbow
ข้อศอก

16. thigh
ขาอ่อน

17. knee
เข่า

18. calf
น่อง

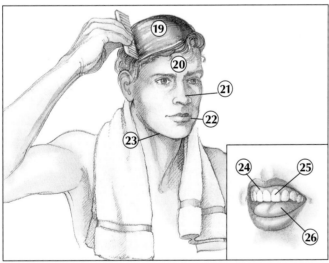
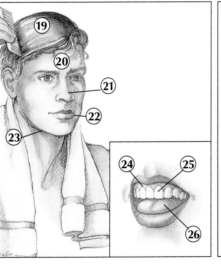
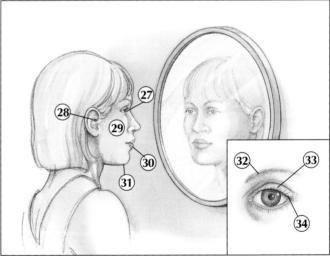

The face ใบหน้า

19. hair
ผม

20. forehead
หน้าผาก

21. nose
จมูก

22. mouth
ปาก

23. jaw
ขากรรไกร

24. gums
เหงือก

25. teeth
ฟัน

26. tongue
ลิ้น

27. eye
ตา

28. ear
หู

29. cheek
แก้ม

30. lip
ริมฝีปาก

31. chin
คาง

32. eyebrow
คิ้ว

33. eyelid
เปลือกตา

34. eyelashes
ขนตา

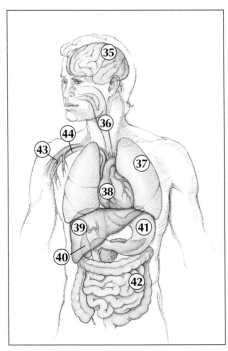

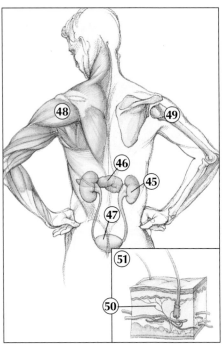

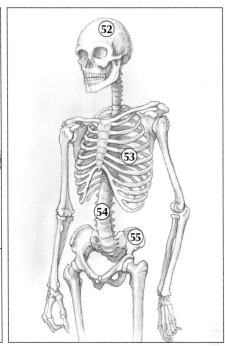

Inside the body
ภายในร่างกาย

35. brain
สมอง

36. throat
ลำคอ

37. lung
ปอด

38. heart
หัวใจ

39. liver
ตับ

40. gallbladder
ถุงน้ำดี

41. stomach
กระเพาะ

42. intestines
ลำไส้ใหญ่

43. artery
เส้นโลหิตแดง

44. vein
เส้นโลหิตดำ

45. kidney
ไต

46. pancreas
ตับอ่อน

47. bladder
กระเพาะปัสสาวะ

48. muscle
กล้ามเนื้อ

49. bone
กระดูก

50. nerve
เส้นประสาท

51. skin
ผิวหนัง

The skeleton
โครงกระดูก

52. skull
หัวกะโหลก

53. rib cage
กระดูกซี่โครง

54. spinal column
กระดูกสันหลัง

55. pelvis
กระดูกเชิงกราน

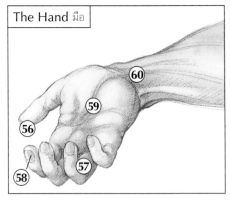

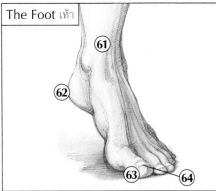

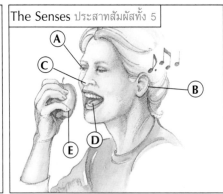

56. thumb
นิ้วหัวแม่มือ

57. fingers
นิ้วมือ

58. fingernail
เล็บมือ

59. palm
ฝ่ามือ

60. wrist
ข้อมือ

61. ankle
ข้อเท้า

62. heel
ส้นเท้า

63. toe
นิ้วเท้า

64. toenail
เล็บเท้า

A. see
เห็น

B. hear
ได้ยิน

C. smell
ดม

D. taste
ชิม

E. touch
จับ/สัมผัส

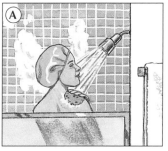

A. take a shower
อาบน้ำฝักบัว

B. bathe/take a bath
อาบน้ำในอ่าง

C. use deodorant
ใช้น้ำหอมดับกลิ่นตัว

D. put on sunscreen
ทาครีมกันแดด

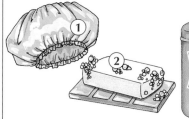

1. shower cap
   หมวกอาบน้ำ

2. soap
   สบู่

3. bath powder/talcum powder
   แป้งทาตัว

4. deodorant
   น้ำหอมดับกลิ่นตัว

5. perfume/cologne
   น้ำหอม/โคโลญจ์

6. sunscreen
   ครีมกันแดด

7. body lotion
   โลชั่นบำรุงผิว

8. moisturizer
   ครีมบำรุงผิวหน้า

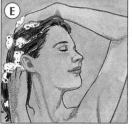
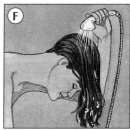
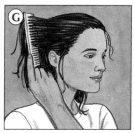
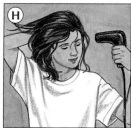

E. wash...hair
สระผม

F. rinse...hair
ล้างผม

G. comb...hair
หวีผม

H. dry...hair
เป่าผม

I. brush...hair
แปรงผม

9. shampoo
   ยาสระผม

10. conditioner
    ครีมนวดผม

11. hair gel
    เจลใส่ผม

12. hair spray
    สเปรย์ฉีดผม

13. comb
    หวี

14. brush
    แปรง

15. curling iron
    คีมทำลอนผม

16. blow dryer
    เครื่องเป่าผม

17. hair clip
    กิ๊บปากเป็ด

18. barrette
    กิ๊บติดผม

19. bobby pins
    กิ๊บหนีบผม

J. brush…teeth
แปรงฟัน

K. floss…teeth
ใช้ไหมขัดฟัน

L. gargle
กลั้วคอ

M. shave
โกนหนวด

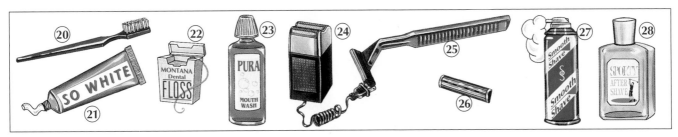

20. toothbrush
แปรงสีฟัน

21. toothpaste
ยาสีฟัน

22. dental floss
ไหมขัดฟัน

23. mouthwash
น้ำยาบ้วนปาก

24. electric shaver
ที่โกนหนวดไฟฟ้า

25. razor
มีดโกนหนวด

26. razor blade
ใบมีดโกน

27. shaving cream
ครีมโกนหนวด

28. aftershave
น้ำยาทาหลังโกนหนวด

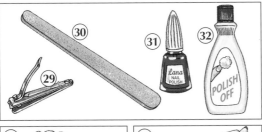

N. cut…nails
ตัดเล็บ

O. polish…nails
ทาเล็บ

P. put on…makeup
แต่งหน้า

29. nail clipper
กรรไกรตัดเล็บ

30. emery board
ตะไบถูเล็บ

31. nail polish
น้ำยาทาเล็บ

32. nail polish remover
น้ำยาล้างเล็บ

33. eyebrow pencil
ดินสอเขียนคิ้ว

34. eye shadow
อายแชโดว์/สีทาเปลือกตา

35. eyeliner
ดินสอเขียนขอบตา

36. blush / rouge
ที่ปัดแก้ม

37. lipstick
ลิปสติค

38. mascara
ที่ปัดขนตา

39. face powder
แป้งทาหน้า

40. foundation
ครีมรองพื้น

More vocabulary คำศัพท์เพิ่มเติม

A product without perfume or scent is **unscented.**

A product that is better for people with allergies is **hypoallergenic.**

Share your answers. แลกเปลี่ยนคำตอบ

1. What is your morning routine if you stay home? if you go out?

2. Do women in your culture wear makeup? How old are they when they begin to use it?

1. headache
   ปวดหัว

2. toothache
   ปวดฟัน

3. earache
   ปวดหู

4. stomachache
   ปวดท้อง

5. backache
   ปวดหลัง

6. sore throat
   เจ็บคอ

7. nasal congestion
   คัดจมูก

8. fever/temperature
   เป็นไข้

9. chills
   หนาวสั่น

10. rash
    ผื่นแดง

A. **cough**
   ไอ

B. **sneeze**
   จาม

C. **feel** dizzy
   รู้สึกวิงเวียนศีรษะ

D. **feel** nauseous
   รู้สึกคลื่นเหียน

E. **throw up/vomit**
   อาเจียน

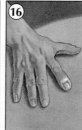

11. insect bite
    แมลงกัดต่อย

12. bruise
    แผลฟกช้ำ

13. cut
    บาดแผล

14. sunburn
    ผิวเกรียมเพราะถูกแดด

15. blister
    แผลพุพอง

16. **swollen** finger
    นิ้วมือบวม

17. **bloody** nose
    เลือดกำเดาไหล

18. **sprained** ankle
    ข้อเท้าแพลง

Use the new language. ใช้ภาษาใหม่

Look at **Health Care,** pages **80–81.**

Tell what medication or treatment you would use for each health problem.

Share your answers. แลกเปลี่ยนคำตอบ

1. For which problems would you go to a doctor? use medication? do nothing?

2. What do you do for a sunburn? for a headache?

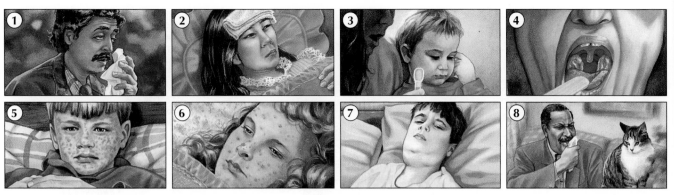

Common illnesses and childhood diseases โรคทั่วไปและโรคเด็ก

1. cold
หวัด

2. flu
ไข้หวัดใหญ่

3. ear infection
หูน้ำหนวก

4. strep throat
คออักเสบ

5. measles
โรคหัด

6. chicken pox
อีสุกอีใส

7. mumps
คางทูม

8. allergies
ภูมิแพ้

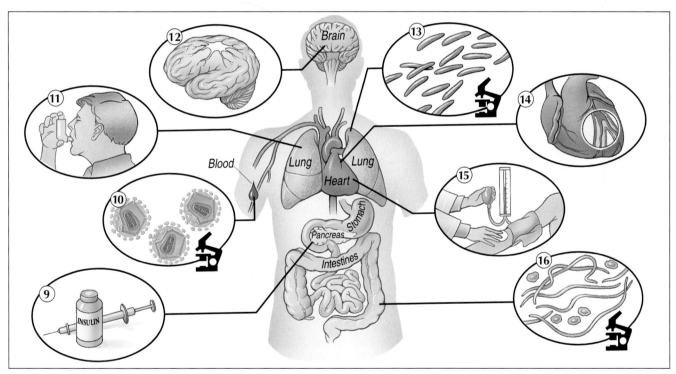

Medical conditions and serious diseases โรคร้ายแรงบางชนิด

9. diabetes
โรคเบาหวาน

10. HIV (human immunodeficiency virus)
เอชไอวี โรคภูมิคุ้มกันบกพร่อง

11. asthma
โรคหอบหืด

12. brain cancer
มะเร็งในสมอง

13. TB (tuberculosis)
วัณโรค

14. heart disease
โรคหัวใจ

15. high blood pressure
ความดันโลหิตสูง

16. intestinal parasites
โรคพยาธิ

More vocabulary คำศัพท์เพิ่มเติม

AIDS (acquired immunodeficiency syndrome): a medical condition that results from contracting the HIV virus

influenza: flu

hypertension: high blood pressure

infectious disease: a disease that is spread through air or water

Share your answers. แลกเปลี่ยนคำตอบ

Which diseases on this page are infectious?

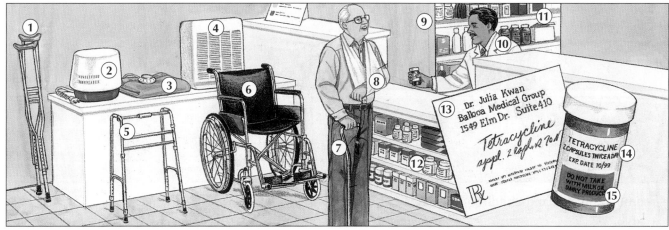

 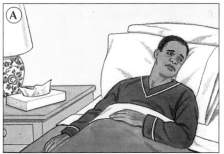

  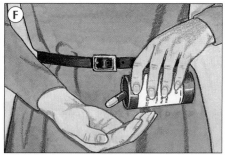

1. crutches
ไม้ยันรักแร้

2. humidifier
เครื่องควบคุมปริมาณความชื้น

3. heating pad
ถุงน้ำร้อน

4. air purifier
เครื่องกรองอากาศ

5. walker
อุปกรณ์ช่วยเดิน

6. wheelchair
รถเข็น

7. cane
ไม้เท้า

8. sling
ผ้าพยุงแขน

9. pharmacy
ร้านขายยา

10. pharmacist
เภสัชกร

11. prescription medication
ยาที่ต้องมีใบสั่งยาจากแพทย์

12. over-the-counter medication
ยาที่ซื้อโดยไม่ต้องมีใบสั่งยา

13. prescription
ใบสั่งยา

14. prescription label
ฉลากยา

15. warning label
ฉลากคำเตือน

A. Get bed rest.
นอนพักฟื้น

B . Drink fluids.
ดื่มน้ำ

C. Change your diet.
เปลี่ยนอุปนิสัยการกินอาหาร

D. Exercise.
ออกกำลังกาย

E. Get an injection.
ฉีดยา

F. Take medicine.
กินยา

More vocabulary คำศัพท์เพิ่มเติม

dosage: how much medicine you take and how many times a day you take it

expiration date: the last day the medicine can be used

treatment: something you do to get better

Staying in bed, drinking fluids, and getting physical therapy are treatments.

An injection that stops a person from getting a serious disease is called **an immunization** or **a vaccination.**

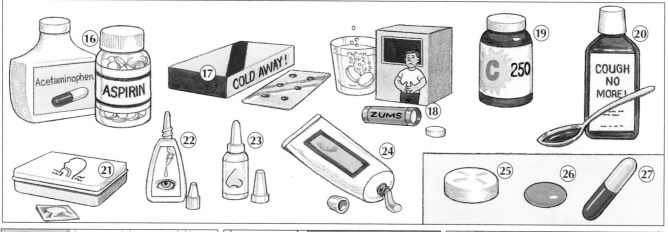

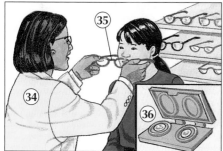
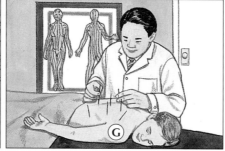

16. pain reliever
ยาบรรเทาปวด

17. cold tablets
ยาเม็ดแก้ไข้หวัด

18. antacid
ยาลดกรด

19. vitamins
วิตามิน

20. cough syrup
ยาแก้ไอน้ำเชื่อม

21. throat lozenges
ยาอมแก้เจ็บคอ

22. eyedrops
ยาหยอดตา

23. nasal spray
ยาพ่นจมูก

24. ointment
ยาขี้ผึ้ง

25. tablet
ยาเม็ดกลมแบน

26. pill
ยาเม็ด

27. capsule
ยาบรรจุแคปซูล

28. orthopedist
หมอกระดูก

29. cast
เฝือก

30. physical therapist
นักกายภาพบำบัด

31. brace
เฝือกโลหะชนิดถอดได้

32. audiologist
ผู้ชำนาญด้านการได้ยิน

33. hearing aid
เครื่องช่วยฟัง

34. optometrist
ผู้ชำนาญด้านสายตา/ช่างประกอบแว่นตา

35. (eye) glasses
แว่นสายตา

36. contact lenses
คอนแทคเลนส์

G. **Get** acupuncture.
ฝังเข็ม

H. **Go** to a chiropractor.
ไปพบผู้ชำนาญการจัดหรือดัดกระดูก

Share your answers. แลกเปลี่ยนคำตอบ

1. What's the best treatment for a headache? a sore throat? a stomachache? a fever?

2. Do you think vitamins are important? Why or why not?

3. What treatments are popular in your culture?

A. be injured / be hurt ได้รับบาดเจ็บ	**G. get** frostbite มีอาการชาจนเจ็บเนื่องจากเย็นจัด	**L. choke** อาหารติดคอ/สำลัก
B. be unconscious หมดสติ	**H. burn** (your)self ถูกน้ำร้อนลวก	**M. bleed** เลือดออก
C. be in shock อยู่ในอาการช็อค	**I. drown** จมน้ำ	**N. can't breathe** หายใจไม่ออก
D. have a heart attack มีอาการหัวใจวาย	**J. swallow** poison กลืนกินยาพิษ	**O. fall** หกล้ม
E. have an allergic reaction มีอาการแพ้	**K. overdose** on drugs กินยาเกินขนาด	**P. break** a bone กระดูกหัก
F. get an electric shock ถูกไฟฟ้าช็อต		

Grammar point: past tense หลักไวยากรณ์

burn	— burned	choke	— choked	bleed	— bled
drown	— drowned	be	— was, were	can't	— couldn't
swallow	— swallowed	have	— had	fall	— fell
overdose	— overdosed	get	— got	break	— broke

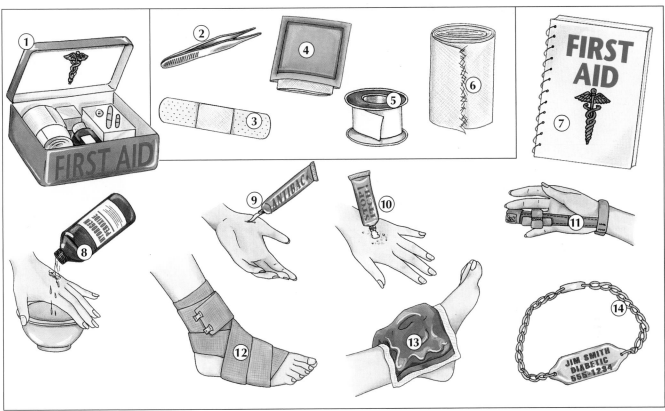

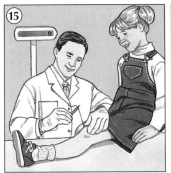 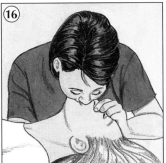 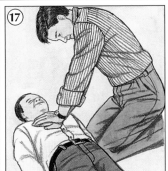 

1. first aid kit
อุปกรณ์ที่ใช้ในการปฐมพยาบาล

2. tweezers
คีมคีบ

3. adhesive bandage
พลาสเตอร์ยาปิดแผล

4. sterile pad
แผ่นปิดแผลฆ่าเชื้อ

5. tape
แถบกาว

6. gauze
ผ้าโปร่งใช้ปิดแผล/ผ้าก๊อส

7. first aid manual
คู่มือปฐมพยาบาล

8. hydrogen peroxide
น้ำยาล้างแผล

9. antibacterial ointment
ยาขี้ผึ้งฆ่าเชื้อแบคทีเรีย

10. antihistamine cream
ครีมรักษาอาการแพ้

11. splint
เฝือกค้ำหรือพยุงกระดูก

12. elastic bandage
ผ้ายืดพันแผล

13. ice pack
ถุงน้ำแข็ง

14. medical emergency bracelet
กำไลข้อมือบอกชื่อใช้กรณีฉุกเฉิน

15. stitches
เย็บแผล

16. rescue breathing
ผายปอด

17. CPR (cardiopulmonary resuscitation)
ปั๊มหัวใจเพื่อกู้ภาวะล้มเหลวทางหัวใจ

18. Heimlich maneuver
เฮมลิช แมนนูเวอร์ แก้อาการติดคอ

Important Note: Only people who are properly trained should give stitches or do CPR.

Share your answers. แลกเปลี่ยนคำตอบ

1. Do you have a First Aid kit in your home? Where can you buy one?

2. When do you use hydrogen peroxide? an elastic support bandage? antihistamine cream?

3. Do you know first aid? Where did you learn it?

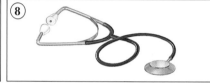

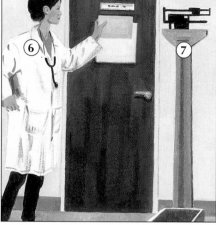

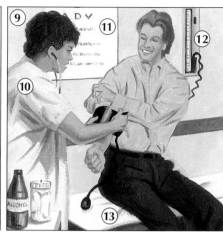

Medical clinic คลีนิคแพทย์

1. waiting room
   ห้องนั่งรอ

2. receptionist
   พนักงานต้อนรับ

3. patient
   คนไข้

4. insurance card
   บัตรประกันสุขภาพ

5. insurance form
   แบบฟอร์มประกันสุขภาพ

6. doctor
   แพทย์

7. scale
   เครื่องชั่งน้ำหนัก

8. stethoscope
   เครื่องมือสำหรับตรวจ/หูฟัง

9. examining room
   ห้องตรวจโรค

10. nurse
    พยาบาล

11. eye chart
    แผนภูมิวัดสายตา

12. blood pressure gauge
    เครื่องวัดความดันโลหิต

13. examination table
    เตียงตรวจโรค

14. syringe
    เข็มฉีดยา

15. thermometer
    ปรอทวัดไข้

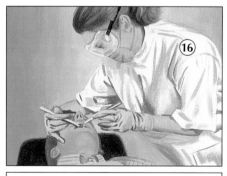

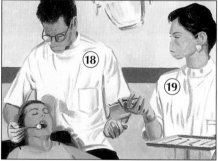

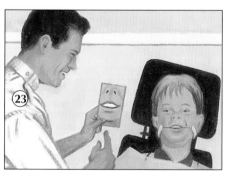

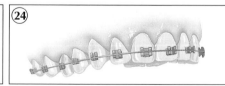

Dental clinic คลีนิคหมอฟัน

16. dental hygienist
    ทันตนามัย

17. tartar
    หินปูน

18. dentist
    ทันตแพทย์

19. dental assistant
    ผู้ช่วยทันตแพทย์

20. cavity
    ช่องฟันผุ

21. drill
    เครื่องกรอฟัน

22. filling
    การอุดฟัน

23. orthodontist
    ทันตแพทย์ที่เชี่ยวชาญด้านการจัดฟัน

24. braces
    ลวดดัดฟัน

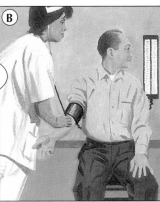

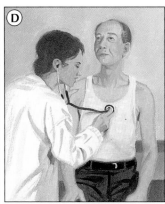

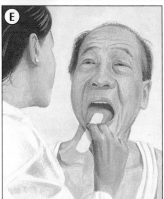
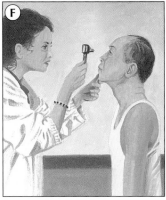
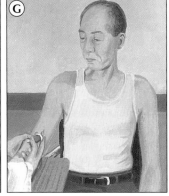
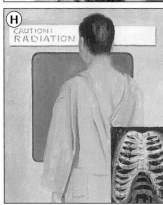

A. make an appointment
ทำการนัดหมาย

B. check…blood pressure
วัดความดันโลหิต

C. take…temperature
วัดอุณหภูมิ

D. listen to…heart
ฟังการเต้นของหัวใจ

E. look in…throat
ตรวจลำคอ

F. examine…eyes
ตรวจตา

G. draw…blood
เจาะเลือด

H. get an X ray
ฉายเอกซเรย์

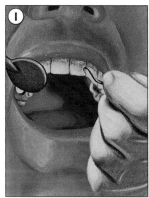
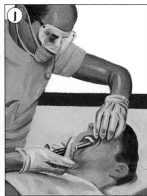
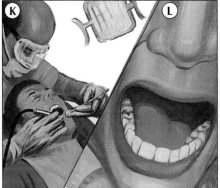
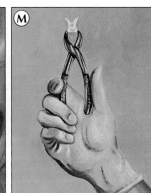

I. clean…teeth
ขูดหินปูน

J. give…a shot of anesthetic
ฉีดยาชา

K. drill a tooth
กรอฟัน

L. fill a cavity
อุดฟัน

M. pull a tooth
ถอนฟัน

More vocabulary คำศัพท์เพิ่มเติม

get a checkup: to go for a medical exam

extract a tooth: to pull out a tooth

Share your answers. แลกเปลี่ยนคำตอบ

1. What is the average cost of a medical exam in your area?

2. Some people are nervous at the dentist's office. What can they do to relax?

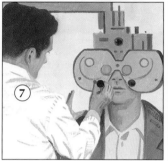
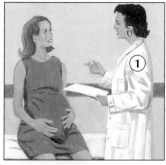

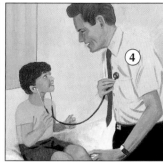

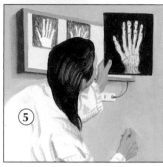

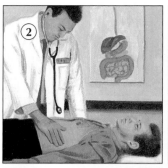
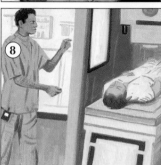

Hospital staff เจ้าหน้าที่โรงพยาบาล

1. obstetrician
   สูติแพทย์
2. internist
   อายุรแพทย์
3. cardiologist
   แพทย์หัวใจ

4. pediatrician
   กุมารแพทย์
5. radiologist
   นักรังสีวิทยา
6. psychiatrist
   จิตแพทย์

7. ophthalmologist
   จักษุแพทย์
8. X-ray technician
   เจ้าหน้าที่เอกซเรย์

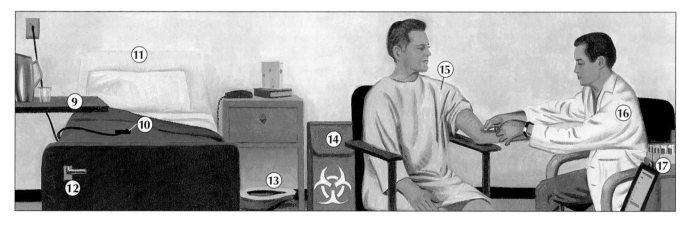

Patient's room ห้องคนไข้

9. bed table
   โต๊ะอาหารสำหรับคนไข้บนเตียง
10. call button
    ปุ่มเรียกพยาบาล
11. hospital bed
    เตียงคนไข้

12. bed control
    ที่ปรับระดับเตียง
13. bedpan
    โถอุจจาระ - ปัสสาวะ
14. medical waste disposal
    ถังขยะติดเชื้อโรค

15. hospital gown
    ชุดคนไข้
16. lab technician
    เจ้าหน้าที่ห้องปฏิบัติการ
17. blood work / blood test
    ตรวจเลือด

More vocabulary คำศัพท์เพิ่มเติม

nurse practitioner: a nurse licensed to give medical exams

specialist: a doctor who only treats specific medical problems

gynecologist: a specialist who examines and treats women

nurse midwife: a nurse practitioner who examines pregnant women and delivers babies

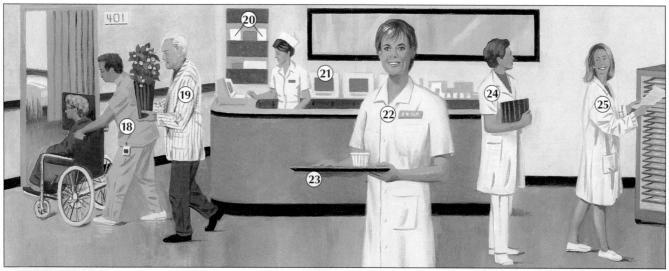

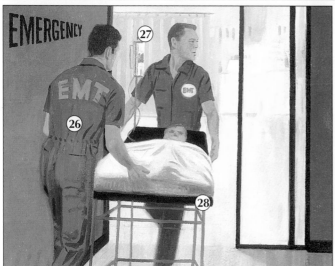

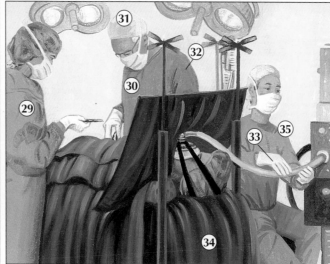

Nurse's station หน่วยพยาบาล

18. orderly
เจ้าหน้าที่เข็นรถผู้ป่วย

19. volunteer
อาสาสมัคร

20. medical charts
แผ่นข้อมูลผู้ป่วย

21. vital signs monitor
เครื่องตรวจวัดสัญญาณชีพ

22. RN (registered nurse)
พยาบาลที่จดทะเบียนแล้ว

23. medication tray
ถาดใส่ยา

24. LPN (licensed practical nurse)/
LVN (licensed vocational nurse)
พยาบาลที่มีใบประกอบวิชาชีพ

25. dietician
โภชนากร

Emergency room ห้องฉุกเฉิน

26. emergency medical technician
(EMT)
เจ้าหน้าที่ห้องฉุกเฉิน

27. IV (intravenous drip)
ให้น้ำเกลือ

28. stretcher/gurney
เตียงเข็นคนไข้

Operating room ห้องผ่าตัด

29. surgical nurse
พยาบาลผ่าตัด

30. surgeon
ศัลยแพทย์

31. surgical cap
หมวกสำหรับศัลยแพทย์ใส่คลุมผม

32. surgical gown
ชุดผ่าตัด

33. latex gloves
ถุงมือยาง

34. operating table
เตียงผ่าตัด

35. anesthesiologist
วิสัญญีแพทย์

Practice asking for the hospital staff.
ฝึกการถามหาเจ้าหน้าที่โรงพยาบาล

Please get <u>the nurse</u>. I have a question for <u>her</u>.
Where's <u>the anesthesiologist</u>? I need to talk to <u>her</u>.
I'm looking for <u>the lab technician</u>. Have you seen <u>him</u>?

Share your answers. แลกเปลี่ยนคำตอบ

1. Have you ever been to an emergency room? Who helped you?

2. Have you ever been in the hospital? How long did you stay?

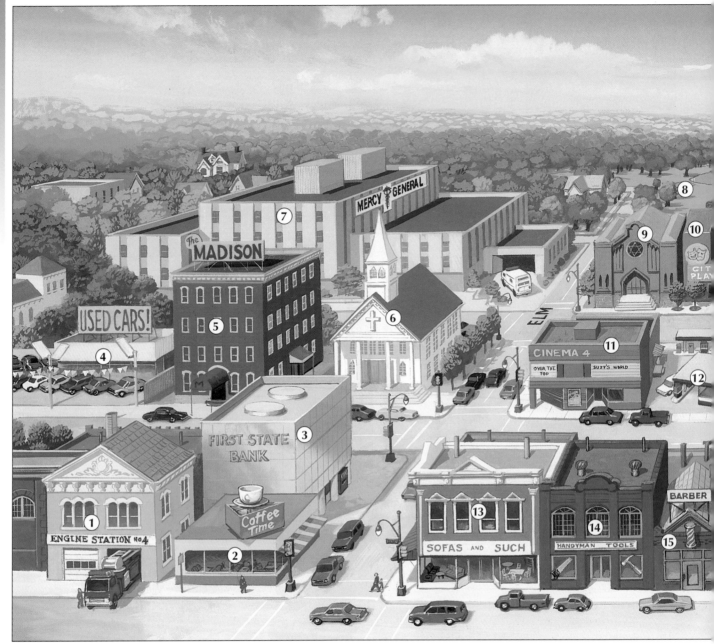

1. fire station
สถานีดับเพลิง

2. coffee shop
ร้านกาแฟ

3. bank
ธนาคาร

4. car dealership
ตัวแทนจำหน่ายรถยนต์

5. hotel
โรงแรม

6. church
โบสถ์

7. hospital
โรงพยาบาล

8. park
สวนสาธารณะ

9. synagogue
สุเหร่ายิว

10. theater
โรงละคร

11. movie theater
โรงภาพยนตร์

12. gas station
สถานีบริการน้ำมัน

13. furniture store
ร้านเฟอร์นิเจอร์

14. hardware store
ร้านฮาร์ดแวร์ / ร้านเครื่องมือ

15. barber shop
ร้านตัดผมชาย

More vocabulary คำศัพท์เพิ่มเติม

skyscraper: a very tall office building

downtown/city center: the area in a city with the
city hall, courts, and businesses

Practice giving your destination. ฝึกพูดบอกจุดหมายปลายทาง

I'm going to go <u>downtown</u>.

I have to go to <u>the post office</u>.

16. bakery ร้านขนมปัง	**21.** health club สโมสรเพื่อสุขภาพ	**26.** parking garage อาคารจอดรถ
17. city hall ศาลากลาง	**22.** motel ที่พักสำหรับผู้เดินทางที่มีห้องนอน ติดกับที่จอดรถ	**27.** school โรงเรียน
18. courthouse ศาล	**23.** mosque สุเหร่า	**28.** library ห้องสมุด
19. police station สถานีตำรวจ	**24.** office building อาคารสำนักงาน	**29.** post office ที่ทำการไปรษณีย์
20. market ตลาด	**25.** high-rise building อาคารสูง	

Practice asking for and giving the locations of buildings.
ฝึกถามและตอบเกี่ยวกับสถานที่ตั้งของอาคาร

Where's <u>thepost office</u>?

It's on <u>Oak Street</u>.

Share your answers. แลกเปลี่ยนคำตอบ

1. Which of the places in this picture do you go to every week?

2. Is it good to live in a city? Why or why not?

3. What famous cities do you know?

1. **Laundromat**
   ร้านซักรีด

2. **drugstore / pharmacy**
   ร้านขายยา

3. **convenience store**
   ร้านสะดวกซื้อ

4. **photo shop**
   ร้านถ่ายรูป

5. **parking space**
   ที่สำหรับจอดรถ

6. **traffic light**
   ไฟจราจร

7. **pedestrian**
   คนเดินเท้า

8. **crosswalk**
   ทางข้ามถนน

9. **street**
   ถนน

10. **curb**
    ขอบถนน

11. **newsstand**
    แผงหนังสือพิมพ์

12. **mailbox**
    ตู้รับจดหมาย

13. **drive-thru window**
    ร้านขายอาหารริมทางสำหรับรถยนต์

14. **fast food restaurant**
    ภัตตาคารอาหารจานด่วน

15. **bus**
    รถประจำทาง

A. **cross** the street
   ข้ามถนน

B. **wait** for the light
   รอสัญญาณไฟ

C. **drive** a car
   ขับรถยนต์

More vocabulary คำศัพท์เพิ่มเติม

neighborhood: the area close to your home

do errands: to make a short trip from your home to buy or pick up something.

Talk about where to buy things. พูดเกี่ยวกับสถานที่ที่จะซื้อของ

You can buy <u>newspapers</u> at <u>a newsstand</u>.

You can buy <u>donuts</u> at <u>a donut shop</u>.

You can buy <u>food</u> at <u>a convenience store</u>.

16. bus stop
ที่จอดรถประจำทาง

17. corner
มุม

18. parking meter
มิเตอร์วัดเวลาการจอดรถ

19. motorcycle
รถจักรยานยนต์

20. donut shop
ร้านขนมโดนัท

21. public telephone
โทรศัพท์สาธารณะ

22. copy center/print shop
ร้านถ่ายเอกสาร

23. streetlight
ไฟถนน

24. dry cleaners
ร้านซักแห้ง

25. nail salon
ร้านแต่งเล็บสุภาพสตรี

26. sidewalk
ทางเดินเท้า

27. garbage truck
รถเก็บขยะ

28. fire hydrant
หัวท่อน้ำดับเพลิง

29. sign
สัญลักษณ์

30. street vendor
คนขายของหาบเร่

31. cart
รถเข็น

D. **park** the car
จอดรถยนต์

E. **ride** a bicycle
ขี่จักรยาน

Share your answers. แลกเปลี่ยนคำตอบ

1. Do you like to do errands?

2. Do you always like to go to the same stores?

3. Which businesses in the picture are also in your neighborhood?

4. Do you know someone who has a small business? What kind?

5. What things can you buy from a street vendor?

1. music store
ร้านขายเทปเพลง

2. jewelry store
ร้านอัญมณี

3. candy store
ร้านขายลูกกวาด

4. bookstore
ร้านขายหนังสือ

5. toy store
ร้านขายของเล่น

6. pet store
ร้านขายสัตว์เลี้ยง

7. card store
ร้านขายบัตรอวยพร

8. optician
ร้านขายแว่น

9. travel agency
ตัวแทนบริษัทท่องเที่ยว

10. shoe store
ร้านขายรองเท้า

11. fountain
น้ำพุ

12. florist
ร้ายขายดอกไม้

More vocabulary คำศัพท์เพิ่มเติม

beauty shop: hair salon

men's store: a store that sells men's clothing

dress shop: a store that sells women's clothing

Talk about where you want to shop in this mall.
พูดคุยถึงสถานที่ที่คุณจะจับจ่ายในศูนย์การค้านี้
Let's go to the card store.
I need to buy a card for Maggie's birthday.

13. department store ห้างสรรพสินค้า	17. maternity shop ร้านขายของสำหรับคุณแม่	21. escalator บันไดเลื่อน
14. food court ศูนย์อาหาร	18. electronics store ร้านอุปกรณ์ไฟฟ้า	22. information booth แผนกประชาสัมพันธ์
15. video store ร้านขายวีดีโอ	19. directory แผ่นป้ายแสดงสถานที่ต่างๆ	
16. hair salon ร้านแต่งผมสุภาพสตรี	20. ice cream stand ร้านไอศครีม	

Practice asking for and giving the location of different shops.

ฝึกถามและตอบเกี่ยวกับที่ตั้งของร้านต่าง ๆ

Where's the maternity shop?

It's on the first floor, next to the hair salon.

Share your answers. แลกเปลี่ยนคำตอบ

1. Do you like shopping malls? Why or why not?

2. Some people don't go to the mall to shop.
   Name some other things you can do in a mall.

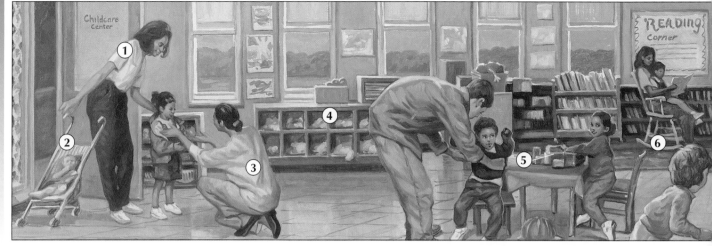

1. parent
พ่อ - แม่

2. stroller
รถเข็นเด็ก 4 ล้อ

3. childcare worker
เจ้าหน้าที่เลี้ยงเด็ก

4. cubby
ช่องเก็บของ

5. toys
ของเล่น

6. rocking chair
เก้าอี้โยก

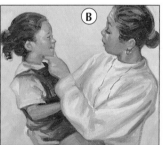

A. **drop off**
มาฝากไว้

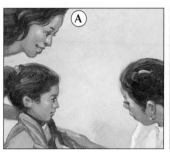

B. **hold**
อุ้ม

C. **nurse**
เลี้ยงลูก

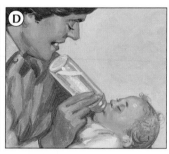

D. **feed**
ป้อน

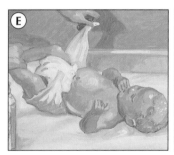

E. **change** diapers
เปลี่ยนผ้าอ้อม

F. **read** a story
อ่านเรื่องให้ฟัง

G. **pick up**
ยกขึ้น / อุ้มขึ้น

H. **rock**
โยก

I. **tie** shoes
ผูกเชือกรองเท้า

J. **dress**
แต่งตัว

K. **play**
เล่น

L. **take** a nap
นอนกลางวัน

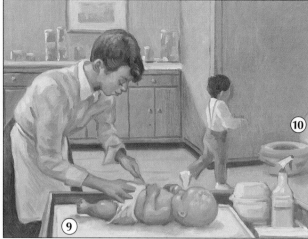

7. high chair
เก้าอี้สูงสำหรับเด็ก

8. bib
ผ้ากันเปื้อน

9. changing table
โต๊ะเปลี่ยนผ้าอ้อม

10. potty seat
โถปัสสาวะ

11. playpen
คอกสำหรับปล่อยเด็กเล่น

12. walker
รถสำหรับเด็กหัดเดิน

13. car safety seat
ที่นั่งนิรภัยสำหรับเด็กในรถ

14. baby carrier
ตะกร้าใส่เด็ก

15. baby backpack
ถุงใส่เด็กสะพายหลัง

16. carriage
รถเข็นเด็ก

17. wipes
ผ้าสำหรับเช็ด

18. baby powder
แป้งเด็ก

19. disinfectant
ยาฆ่าเชื้อโรค

20. disposable diapers
ผ้าอ้อมชนิดใช้แล้วทิ้ง

21. cloth diapers
ผ้าอ้อม

22. diaper pins
เข็มกลัดผ้าอ้อม

23. diaper pail
ถังเก็บผ้าอ้อม

24. training pants
การเกงฝึกขับถ่าย

25. formula
นมผงสำเร็จรูป

26. bottle
ขวด

27. nipple
หัวนมสำหรับขวด

28. baby food
อาหารเด็ก

29. pacifier
หัวนมปลอม

30. teething ring
ยางฝึกกัดสำหรับเด็ก

31. rattle
ของเล่นเด็กใช้เขย่าให้ดัง

1. envelope
ซองจดหมาย

2. letter
จดหมาย

3. postcard
ไปรษณียบัตร

4. greeting card
บัตรอวยพร / ทักทาย

5. package
หีบห่อ

6. letter carrier
บุรุษไปรษณีย์

7. return address
ที่อยู่ผู้ส่ง

8. mailing address
ที่อยู่ผู้รับ

9. postmark
ตราประทับไปรษณีย์

10. stamp / postage
ดวงตราไปรษณียากร

11. certified mail
ไปรษณีย์รับรอง

12. priority mail
ไปรษณีย์ด่วนพิเศษ

13. air letter / aerogramme
ไปรษณีย์อากาศ

14. ground post /
parcel post
พัสดุไปรษณีย์

15. Express Mail /
overnight mail
ไปรษณีย์ด่วน

A. **address** a postcard
จ่าหน้าซองไปรษณียบัตร

B. **send** it / **mail** it
ส่งจดหมาย

C. **deliver** it
ส่งตามบ้าน

D. **receive** it
รับจดหมาย

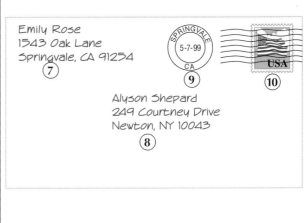

Emily Rose
1543 Oak Lane
Springvale, CA 91254

SPRINGVALE
5-7-99
CA

USA

Alyson Shepard
249 Courtney Drive
Newton, NY 10043

CERTIFIED MAIL

PRIORITY MAIL

AEROGRAMME - VIA AIRMAIL PAR AVION

FRAGILE

EXPRESS MAIL
UNITED STATES POSTAL SERVICE

1. teller
พนักงานธนาคาร

2. vault
ตู้เซฟ

3. ATM (automated teller machine)
ตู้ถอนเงินอัตโนมัติ / เอทีเอ็ม

4. security guard
เจ้าหน้าที่รักษาความปลอดภัย

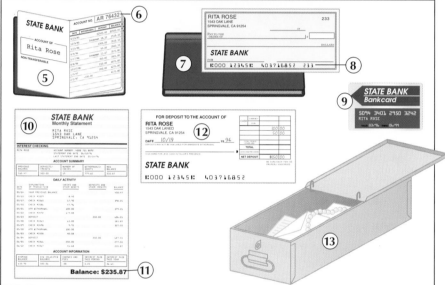

5. passbook
สมุดฝาก - ถอน

6. savings account number
เลขบัญชีสะสมทรัพย์

7. checkbook
สมุดเช็ค

8. checking account number
หมายเลขบัญชีเช็ค

9. ATM card
บัตรเอทีเอ็ม

10. monthly statement
รายการประจำเดือน

11. balance
ยอดเงินคงเหลือ

12. deposit slip
ใบฝากเงิน

13. safe-deposit box
ตู้ฝากนิรภัย

Using the ATM machine การใช้เครื่องเอทีเอ็ม

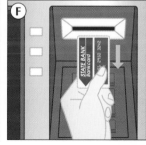

A. **Insert** your ATM card.
สอดบัตรเอทีเอ็ม

B. **Enter** your PIN number.*
กดรหัสของท่าน

C. **Make** a deposit.
ฝากเงิน

D. **Withdraw** cash.
ถอนเงินสด

E. **Transfer** funds.
โอนเงิน

F. **Remove** your ATM card.
รับบัตรเอทีเอ็มคืน

*PIN: personal identification number

More vocabulary คำศัพท์เพิ่มเติม

overdrawn account: When there is not enough money in an account to pay a check, we say the account is overdrawn.

Share your answers. แลกเปลี่ยนคำตอบ

1. Do you use a bank?

2. Do you use an ATM card?

3. Name some things you can put in a safe-deposit box.

1. reference librarian บรรณารักษ์อ้างอิง	**7.** magazine นิตยสาร	**13.** videocassette ม้วนวีดีโอเทป	**19.** library card บัตรห้องสมุด
2. reference desk แผนกอ้างอิง	**8.** newspaper หนังสือพิมพ์	**14.** CD (compact disc) แผ่นซีดี	**20.** library book หนังสือห้องสมุด
3. atlas แผนที่	**9.** online catalog บัตรรายการออนไลน์	**15.** record แผ่นเสียง	**21.** title ชื่อเรื่อง
4. microfilm reader เครื่องอ่านไมโครฟิล์ม	**10.** card catalog บัตรรายการ	**16.** checkout desk แผนกบริการให้ยืม	**22.** author ผู้แต่ง
5. microfilm ฟิล์มขนาดเล็กสำหรับ ย่อเอกสาร	**11.** media section แผนกสื่ออุปกรณ์ต่างๆ	**17.** library clerk เจ้าหน้าที่ห้องสมุด	
6. periodical section แผนกวารสาร	**12.** audiocassette เทปคาสเซ็ท	**18.** encyclopedia สารานุกรม	

More vocabulary คำศัพท์เพิ่มเติม

check a book out: to borrow a book from the library

nonfiction: real information, history or true stories

fiction: stories from the author's imagination

Share your answers. แลกเปลี่ยนคำตอบ

1. Do you have a library card?

2. Do you prefer to buy books or borrow them from the library?

A. arrest a suspect
จับผู้ต้องสงสัย

1. police officer
เจ้าหน้าที่ตำรวจ

2. handcuffs
กุญแจมือ

B. hire a lawyer/**hire** an attorney
จ้างทนายความ

3. guard
เจ้าหน้าที่รักษาความปลอดภัย

4. defense attorney
ทนายจำเลย

C. appear in court
ขึ้นศาล

5. defendant
จำเลย

6. judge
ผู้พิพากษา

D. stand trial
พิจารณาคดี

7. courtroom
ห้องพิจารณาคดี

8. jury
คณะลูกขุน

9. evidence
หลักฐาน

10. prosecuting attorney
อัยการ

11. witness
พยาน

12. court reporter
ผู้พิมพ์รายงานศาล

13. bailiff
เจ้าหน้าที่ออกหมายจับ / ยึด
ทรัพย์

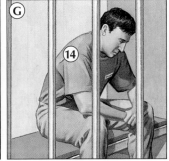

E. give the verdict*
ตัดสิน

F. sentence the
defendant
พิพากษาวางโทษ จำเลย

14. convict
นักโทษ

G. go to jail/**go** to prison
ติดคุก / เข้าเรือนจำ

H. be released
พ้นโทษ

*__Note:__ There are two possible verdicts, "guilty" and "not guilty."

Share your answers. แลกเปลี่ยนคำตอบ

1. What are some differences between the legal system
in the United States and the one in your country?

2. Do you want to be on a jury? Why or why not?

99

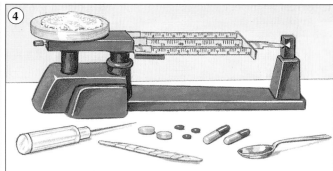

1. vandalism
ความป่าเถื่อน / ชอบทำลาย

2. gang violence
กลุ่มอันธพาล / รุนแรง

3. drunk driving
เมาในขณะขับ

4. illegal drugs
ยาเสพติดที่ผิดกฎหมาย

5. mugging
วิ่งราว

6. burglary
การลักขโมย

7. assault
ทำร้ายร่างกาย

8. murder
ฆาตกรรม

9. gun
ปืน

More vocabulary คำศัพท์เพิ่มเติม

commit a crime: to do something illegal

criminal: someone who commits a crime

victim: someone who is hurt or killed by someone else

Share your answers. แลกเปลี่ยนคำตอบ

1. Is there too much crime on TV? in the movies?

2. Do you think people become criminals from watching crime on TV?

A. **Walk** with a friend.
เดินกับเพื่อน

B. **Stay** on well-lit streets.
อยู่บนถนนที่สว่าง

C. **Hold** your purse close to your body.
ถือกระเป๋าให้ชิดตัวอยู่เสมอ

D. **Protect** your wallet.
ปกป้องกระเป๋าเงิน

E. **Lock** your doors.
ล็อคประตูบ้าน

F. **Don't open** your door to strangers.
อย่าเปิดประตูให้คนแปลกหน้า

G. **Don't drink** and **drive**.
อย่าดื่มสุราเมื่อขับขี่

H. **Report** crimes to the police.
แจ้งเรื่องอาชญากรรมต่อตำรวจ

More vocabulary คำศัพท์เพิ่มเติม

Neighborhood Watch: a group of neighbors who watch for criminals in their neighborhood

designated drivers: people who don't drink alcoholic beverages so that they can drive drinkers home

Share your answers. แลกเปลี่ยนคำตอบ

1. Do you feel safe in your neighborhood?

2. Look at the pictures. Which of these things do you do?

3. What other things do you do to stay safe?

1. lost child
เด็กหาย

2. car accident
อุบัติเหตุทางรถยนต์

3. airplane crash
เครื่องบินตก

4. explosion
การระเบิด

5. earthquake
แผ่นดินไหว

6. mudslide
โคลนถล่ม

7. fire
ไฟไหม้

8. firefighter
พนักงานดับเพลิง

9. fire truck
รถดับเพลิง

Practice reporting a fire. ฝึกการบอกเหตุไฟไหม้

This is <u>Lisa Broad</u>. There is a fire.

The address is <u>323 Oak Street.</u>

Please send someone quickly.

Share your answers. แลกเปลี่ยนคำตอบ

1. Can you give directions to your home if there is a fire?

2. What information do you give to the other driver if you are in a car accident?

10. drought
ความแห้งแล้ง

11. blizzard
พายุหิมะ

12. hurricane
พายุเฮอริเคน

13. tornado
พายุทอร์นาโด

14. volcanic eruption
ภูเขาไฟระเบิด

15. tidal wave
คลื่นยักษ์

16. flood
น้ำท่วม

17. search and rescue team
ชุดค้นหาและช่วยชีวิต

Share your answers. แลกเปลี่ยนคำตอบ

1. Which disasters are common in your area? Which never happen?

2. What can you do to prepare for emergencies?

3. Do you have emergency numbers near your telephone?

4. What organizations will help you in an emergency?

103

1. **bus stop**
   ที่จอดรถประจำทาง

2. **route**
   เส้นทาง

3. **schedule**
   ตารางเวลา

4. **bus**
   รถประจำทาง

5. **fare**
   ค่าโดยสาร

6. **transfer**
   การถ่ายโอน/เปลี่ยนรถ

7. **passenger**
   ผู้โดยสาร

8. **bus driver**
   พนักงานขับรถประจำทาง

9. **subway**
   รถไฟใต้ดิน

10. **track**
    ทางรถไฟ

11. **token**
    เหรียญ

12. **fare card**
    บัตรโดยสาร

13. **train station**
    สถานีรถไฟ

14. **ticket**
    ตั๋ว

15. **platform**
    ชานชาลา

16. **conductor**
    พนักงานเดินตั๋ว

17. **train**
    รถไฟ

18. **taxi / cab**
    แท็กซี่/รถรับจ้าง

19. **taxi stand**
    ที่จอดรถแท็กซี่

20. **taxi driver**
    คนขับแท็กซี่

21. **meter**
    มิเตอร์/มาตรวัด

22. **taxi license**
    บัตรประจำตัวผู้ขับแท็กซี่

23. **ferry**
    เรือข้ามฟาก

More vocabulary คำศัพท์เพิ่มเติม

hail a taxi: to get a taxi driver's attention by raising your hand

miss the bus: to arrive at the bus stop late

Talk about how you and your friends come to school.
พูดเกี่ยวกับวิธีมาโรงเรียน

I take <u>the bus</u> to school.
You take <u>the train</u>.
We take <u>the subway</u>.

He <u>drives</u> to school.
She <u>walks</u> to school.
They <u>ride</u> bikes.

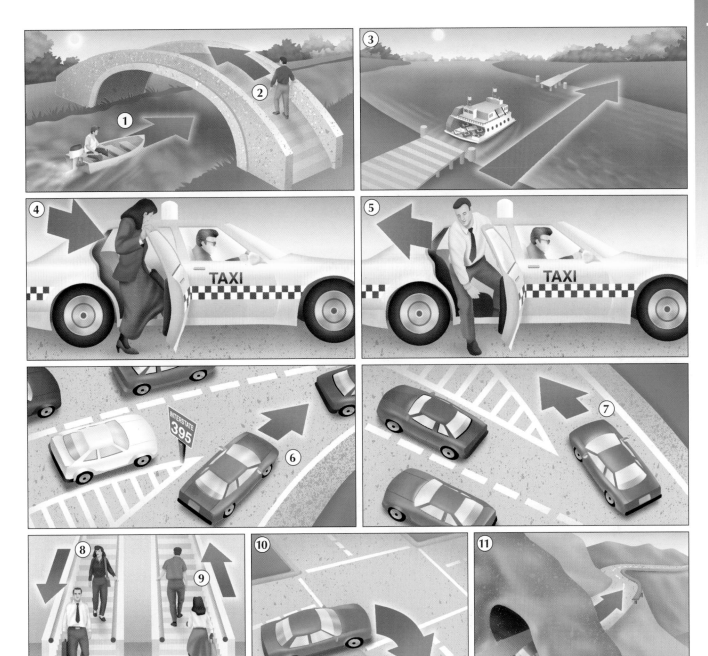

1. **under** the bridge
   ใต้สะพาน

2. **over** the bridge
   เหนือสะพาน

3. **across** the water
   ข้ามแม่น้ำ

4. **into** the taxi
   ขึ้นแท็กซี่

5. **out of** the taxi
   ลงจากแท็กซี่

6. **onto** the highway
   ขึ้นทางหลวง

7. **off** the highway
   ออกจากทางหลวง

8. **down** the stairs
   ลงชั้นล่าง

9. **up** the stairs
   ขึ้นชั้นบน

10. **around** the corner
    เลี้ยวหัวมุม

11. **through** the tunnel
    ลอดอุโมงค์

Grammar point: *into, out of, on, off* หลักไวยากรณ์

We say, *get **into** a taxi or a car.*

But we say, *get **on** a bus, a train, or a plane.*

We say, *get **out of** a taxi or a car.*

But we say, *get **off** a bus, a train, or a plane.*

1. subcompact
   รถยนต์ขนาดเล็ก

2. compact
   รถยนต์ขนาดย่อม

3. midsize car
   รถยนต์ขนาดกลาง

4. full-size car
   รถยนต์ขนาดใหญ่

5. convertible
   รถเปิดประทุน

6. sports car
   รถสปอร์ต

7. pickup truck
   รถกระบะ

8. station wagon
   รถยนต์ส่วนตัวท้ายยาว

9. SUV (sports utility vehicle)
   รถแวนเอนกประสงค์

10. minivan
    รถแวนเล็ก

11. camper
    รถออกแค้มป์

12. dump truck
    รถบรรทุกชนิดเทได้/รถดั้มพ์

13. tow truck
    รถลาก/รถยก

14. moving van
    รถขนของย้ายบ้าน

15. tractor trailer / semi
    เทรลเลอร์

16. cab
    ห้องผู้โดยสาร

17. trailer
    รถพ่วง

More vocabulary คำศัพท์เพิ่มเติม

make: the name of the company that makes the car

model: the style of car

Share your answers. แลกเปลี่ยนคำตอบ

1. What is your favorite kind of car?

2. What kind of car is good for a big family? for a single person?

Directions ทิศทาง

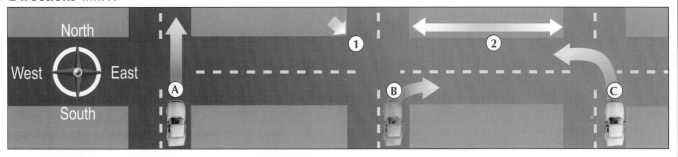

A. go straight
ตรงไป

B. turn right
เลี้ยวขวา

C. turn left
เลี้ยวซ้าย

1. corner
มุม

2. block
บล็อคถนน/ช่วงถนน

Signs สัญลักษณ์/เครื่องหมาย

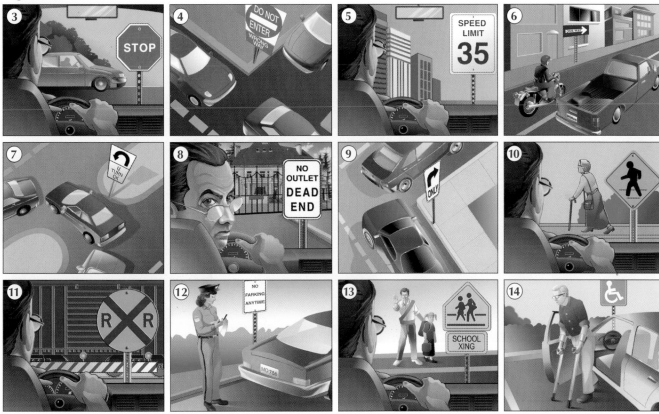

3. stop
หยุด

4. do not enter / wrong way
ห้ามเข้า

5. speed limit
จำกัดความเร็ว

6. one way
เดินรถทางเดียว

7. U-turn OK
กลับรถได้

8. no outlet / dead end
ทางตัน

9. right turn only
เลี้ยวขวาเท่านั้น

10. pedestrian crossing
ทางคนข้าม

11. railroad crossing
ทางรถไฟตัดผ่าน

12. no parking
ห้ามจอด

13. school crossing
ทางข้ามหน้าโรงเรียน

14. handicapped parking
ที่จอดรถคนพิการ

More vocabulary คำศัพท์เพิ่มเติม

right-of-way: the right to go first

yield: to give another person or car the right-of-way

Share your answers. แลกเปลี่ยนคำตอบ

1. Which traffic signs are the same in your country?

2. Do pedestrians have the right-of-way in your city?

3. What is the speed limit in front of your school? your home?

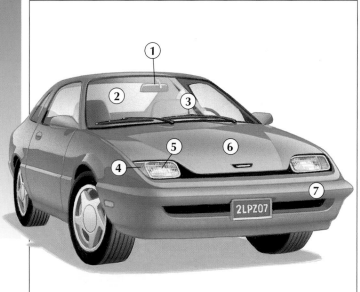

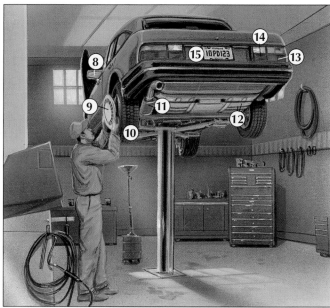

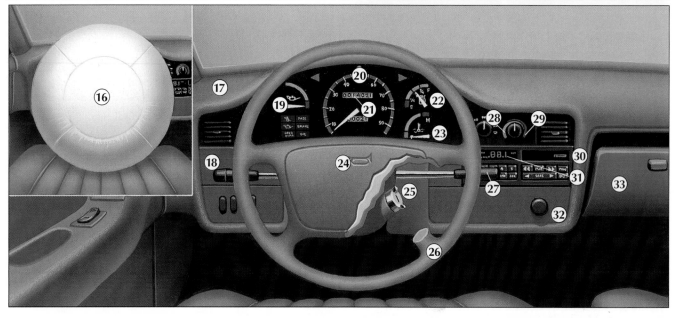

1. rearview mirror กระจกมองหลัง	**10.** tire ยาง	**19.** oil gauge ที่วัดน้ำมันเครื่อง	**28.** air conditioning ปุ่มปรับอากาศ
2. windshield กระจกหน้า	**11.** muffler ท่อไอเสีย	**20.** speedometer เครื่องวัดความเร็ว	**29.** heater ปุ่มทำความร้อน
3. windshield wipers ที่ปัดกระจกหน้า	**12.** gas tank ถังน้ำมัน	**21.** odometer เครื่องวัดระยะทาง	**30.** tape deck เทปรถยนต์
4. turn signal ไฟเลี้ยว	**13.** brake light ไฟเบรค	**22.** gas gauge เครื่องวัดน้ำมัน	**31.** radio วิทยุ
5. headlight ไฟหน้า	**14.** taillight ไฟท้าย	**23.** temperature gauge เครื่องวัดอุณหภูมิ	**32.** cigarette lighter ที่จุดบุหรี่
6. hood กระโปรงหน้า	**15.** license plate ป้ายทะเบียน	**24.** horn แตร	**33.** glove compartment ช่องเก็บของ
7. bumper กันชน	**16.** air bag ถุงลม	**25.** ignition ที่เสียบกุญแจสำหรับติดเครื่อง	
8. sideview mirror กระจกมองข้าง	**17.** dashboard แผ่นคลุมหน้าปัดต่างๆ	**26.** steering wheel พวงมาลัย	
9. hubcap ฝาครอบล้อ	**18.** turn signal สัญญาณเลี้ยว	**27.** gearshift คันเกียร์	

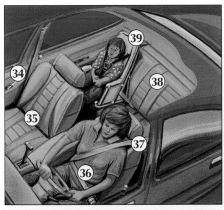
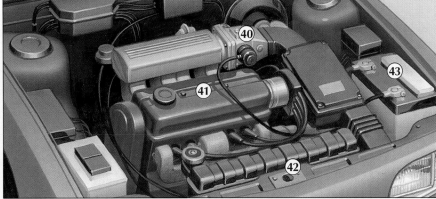

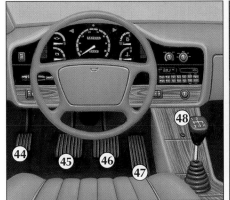

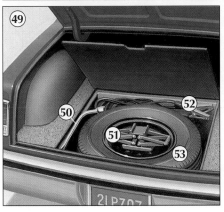

34. lock
ที่ล็อคประตู

35. front seat
ที่นั่งด้านหน้า

36. seat belt
เข็มขัดนิรภัย

37. shoulder harness
ที่ยึดเข็มขัดนิรภัย

38. backseat
ที่นั่งด้านหลัง

39. child safety seat
ที่นั่งเด็กเล็ก

40. fuel injection system
ระบบสูบฉีดเชื้อเพลิง

41. engine
เครื่องยนต์

42. radiator
หม้อน้ำรถยนต์

43. battery
แบตเตอรี่

44. emergency brake
เบรคฉุกเฉิน

45. clutch*
คลัทช์

46. brake pedal
คันเบรค

47. accelerator/gas pedal
คันเร่งน้ำมันเครื่องยนต์

48. stick shift
คันเกียร์

49. trunk
กระโปรงหลัง

50. lug wrench
กุญแจด้ามมากากบาท

51. jack
แม่แรง

52. jumper cables
สายจั้มไฟ

53. spare tire
ยางอะไหล่

54. The car needs **gas**.
น้ำมันจะหมด

55. The car needs **oil**.
เติมน้ำมันเครื่อง

56. The radiator needs **coolant**.
เติมสารให้ความเย็นในหม้อน้ำ

57. The car needs **a smog check**.
การตรวจสอบเขม่าควัน

58. The battery needs **recharging**.
การเติมไฟแบตเตอรี่

59. The tires need **air**.
เติมลมยาง

***Note:** Standard transmission cars have a clutch; automatic transmission cars do not.

1. airline terminal
อาคารสายการบิน

2. airline representative
ตัวแทนสายการบิน

3. check-in counter
เคาเตอร์เช็คตั๋ว

4. arrival and departure monitors
จอแสดงตารางขาเข้าและขาออก

5. gate
ประตูขึ้นเครื่อง

6. boarding area
บริเวณที่จะขึ้นเครื่อง

7. control tower
หอควบคุม

8. helicopter
เฮลิคอปเตอร์

9. airplane
เครื่องบินโดยสาร

10. overhead compartment
ชั้นวางของเหนือศีรษะ

11. cockpit
ห้องนักบิน

12. pilot
นักบิน

13. flight attendant
เจ้าหน้าที่เที่ยวบิน

14. oxygen mask
หน้ากากอ๊อกซิเจน

15. airsickness bag
ถุงสำหรับใส่อาเจียน

16. tray table
โต๊ะถาดสำหรับวางของ

17. baggage claim area
ที่รับกระเป๋า

18. carousel
สายพานหมุนไปรอบๆ

19. luggage carrier
รถเข็นกระเป๋า

20. customs
ด่านศุลกากร

21. customs officer
เจ้าหน้าที่ศุลกากร

22. declaration form
แบบฟอร์มแสดงรายการที่ต้องเสียภาษี

23. passenger
ผู้โดยสาร

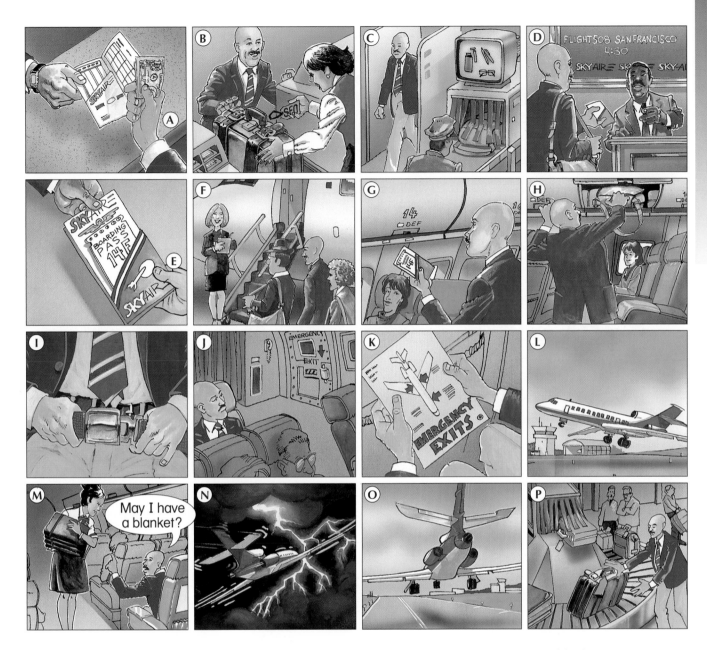

A. **buy** your ticket
ซื้อตั๋ว

B. **check** your bags
ตรวจกระเป๋า

C. **go through** security
ผ่านเครื่องตรวจความปลอดภัย

D. **check in** at the gate
เข้าสู่ประตู

E. **get** your boarding pass
รับบัตรขึ้นเครื่องบิน

F. **board** the plane
ขึ้นเครื่องบิน

G. **find** your seat
หาที่นั่ง

H. **stow** your carry-on bag
เก็บสัมภาระที่หิ้วขึ้นเครื่องมาด้วยให้เข้าที่

I. **fasten** your seat belt
รัดเข็มขัด

J. **look for** the emergency exit
มองหาทางออกฉุกเฉิน

K. **look at** the emergency card
ศึกษาบัตรแสดงทางออกฉุกเฉิน

L. **take off / leave**
เครื่องบิน**กำลังขึ้น**

M. **request** a blanket
ขอผ้าห่ม

N. **experience** turbulence
ประสบอากาศแปรปรวน

O. **land / arrive**
ลงจอด / มาถึง

P. **claim** your baggage
รับกระเป๋า

More vocabulary คำศัพท์เพิ่มเติม

destination: the place the passenger is going

departure time: the time the plane takes off

arrival time: the time the plane lands

direct flight: a plane trip between two cities with no stops

stopover: a stop before reaching the destination, sometimes to change planes

1. public school
โรงเรียนรัฐบาล

2. private school
โรงเรียนเอกชน

3. parochial school
โรงเรียนสอนศาสนา

4. preschool
โรงเรียนก่อนวัยเรียน

5. elementary school
โรงเรียนประถม

6. middle school/
junior high school
โรงเรียนมัธยมต้น

7. high school
โรงเรียนมัธยมปลาย

8. adult school
โรงเรียนผู้ใหญ่

9. vocational school/trade school
โรงเรียนอาชีวศึกษา

10. college/university
วิทยาลัย/มหาวิทยาลัย

Note: In the U.S. most children begin school at age 5 (in kindergarten) and graduate from high school at 17 or 18.

More vocabulary คำศัพท์เพิ่มเติม

When students graduate from a college or university they receive a **degree:**

Bachelor's degree—usually 4 years of study

Master's degree—an additional 1–3 years of study

Doctorate—an additional 3–5 years of study

community college: a two-year college where students can get an Associate of Arts degree.

graduate school: a school in a university where students study for their master's and doctorates.

1. writing assignment
ให้งานเกี่ยวกับการเขียน

A. Write a first draft.
เขียนฉบับร่าง

B. Edit your paper.
แก้ไขงาน

C. Get feedback.
รับฟังข้อติ-ชม

D. Rewrite your paper.
เขียนงานใหม่

E. Turn in your paper.
ส่งงาน

2. paper / composition
งานเขียน/เรียงความ

My life in the U.S.

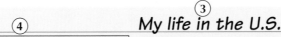

I arrived in this country in 1996. My family did not come with me. I was homesick, nervous, and a little excited. I had no job and no friends here. I lived with my aunt and my daily routine was always the same: get up, look for a job, go to bed. At night I remembered my mother's words to me, "Son, you can always come home!" I was homesick and scared, but I did not go home.

I started to study English at night. English is a difficult language and many times I was too tired to study. One teacher, Mrs. Armstrong, was very kind to me. She showed me many

3. title
ชื่อเรื่อง

4. sentence
ประโยค

5. paragraph
หนึ่งย่อหน้า

Punctuation เครื่องหมายวรรคตอน

6. period
เครื่องหมายมหัพภาค

7. question mark
เครื่องหมายคำถาม

8. exclamation mark
เครื่องหมายอัศเจรีย์

9. quotation marks
เครื่องหมายคำพูด

10. comma
เครื่องหมายจุลภาค

11. apostrophe
จุดลูกน้ำใช้แสดงว่าเป็นเจ้าของหรือ
แสดงการย่อคำ

12. colon
เครื่องหมายจุดคู่

13. semicolon
เครื่องหมายอัฒภาค

113

Exploration การสำรวจ

War สงคราม

Immigration การอพยพ

Historical and Political Events เหตุการณ์ทางประวัติ-ศาสตร์และการเมือง	**1492 →** French, Spanish, English explorers นักสำรวจชาวฝรั่งเศส, สเปน, อังกฤษ	**1607–1750** Colonies along Atlantic coast founded by Northern Europeans การสร้างอาณานิคมตามแนวฝั่งแอตแลนติคโดยชาวยุโรปตอนเหนือ	**1619** 1st African slave sold in Virginia ทาสชาวอัฟริกาคนแรกถูกขายในรัฐเวอร์จิเนีย **1653** 1st Indian reservation in Virginia มีเขตสงวนสำหรับชาวอินเดียแดง เป็นครั้งแรกในรัฐเวอร์จิเนีย

Before 1700   1700

Immigration* การอพยพ	**1607** 1st English in Virginia ชาวอังกฤษคนแรกในรัฐเวอร์จิเนีย	**1610** Spanish at Santa Fe ชาวสเปนมาอยู่ที่ซานตาเฟ่
Population** ประชากร	Before 1700: Native American: 1,000,000+ ก่อนปี 1700 ชาวพื้นเมืองอเมริกันมี 1,000,000 ขึ้นไป	1700: colonists: 250,000 ผู้คนที่อพยพเข้ามาเป็น 250,000 คน

1803 Louisiana Purchase ซื้อรัฐหลุยเซียน่า	**1812** War of 1812 สงคราม 1812	**1820** Missouri Compromise ข้อตกลงมิชซูรี่	**1830** Indian Removal Act กฎหมายเกี่ยวกับอินเดียแดง	**1835–1838** Cherokee Trail of Tears สงครามกับเผ่าเชอโรกี	**1846–1848** U.S. war with Mexico สงครามระหว่างสหรัฐกับแม็กซิโก

1800   1810   1820   1830   1840

1815 → Irish
ชาวไอริสเริ่มเข้ามา

1800: citizens and free blacks: 5,300,000   slaves: 450,000
ประชากรรวมทั้งชาวผิวดำ   ทาส

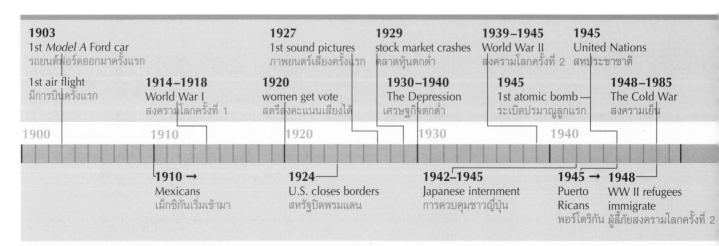

1903 1st *Model A* Ford car รถยนต์ฟอร์ดออกมาครั้งแรก		**1927** 1st sound pictures ภาพยนตร์เสียงครั้งแรก	**1929** stock market crashes ตลาดหุ้นตกต่ำ	**1939–1945** World War II สงครามโลกครั้งที่ 2	**1945** United Nations สหประชาชาติ
1st air flight มีการบินครั้งแรก	**1914–1918** World War I สงครามโลกครั้งที่ 1	**1920** women get vote สตรีลงคะแนนเสียงได้	**1930–1940** The Depression เศรษฐกิจตกต่ำ	**1945** 1st atomic bomb ระเบิดปรมาณูลูกแรก	**1948–1985** The Cold War สงครามเย็น

1900   1910   1920   1930   1940

1910 → Mexicans เม็กซิกันเริ่มเข้ามา	**1924** U.S. closes borders สหรัฐปิดพรมแดน	**1942–1945** Japanese internment การควบคุมชาวญี่ปุ่น	**1945 →** Puerto Ricans พอร์โตริกัน	**1948** WW II refugees immigrate ผู้ลี้ภัยสงครามโลกครั้งที่ 2

1900: 75,994,000

*Immigration dates indicate a time when large numbers of that group first began to immigrate to the U.S.
**All population figures before 1790 are estimates. Figures after 1790 are based on the official U.S. census.

Movement การเดินขบวนเคลื่อนไหว

Election การเลือกตั้ง

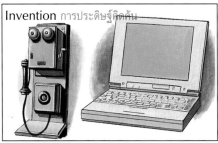

Invention การประดิษฐ์คิดค้น

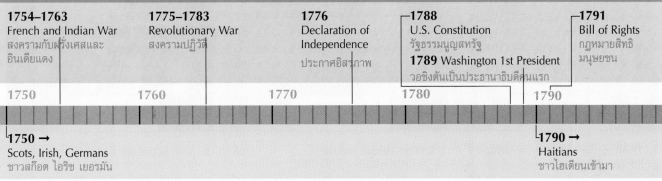

1754–1763
French and Indian War
สงครามกับฝรั่งเศสและ
อินเดียแดง

1775–1783
Revolutionary War
สงครามปฏิวัติ

1776
Declaration of
Independence
ประกาศอิสรภาพ

1788
U.S. Constitution
รัฐธรรมนูญสหรัฐ

1789 Washington 1st President
วอชิงตันเป็นประธานาธิบดีคนแรก

1791
Bill of Rights
กฎหมายสิทธิ
มนุษยชน

1750   1760   1770   1780   1790

1750 →
Scots, Irish, Germans
ชาวสก๊อต ไอริช เยอรมัน

1790 →
Haitians
ชาวไฮเตียนเข้ามา

1750: Native American: 1,000,000 +
ชาวอเมริกันพื้นเมือง

colonists and free blacks: 1,171,000
ชาวอาณานิคมและคนผิวดำ

slaves: 200,000
ทาส

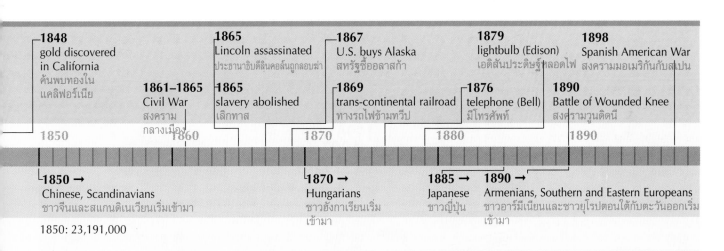

1848
gold discovered
in California
ค้นพบทองใน
แคลิฟอร์เนีย

1865
Lincoln assassinated
ประธานาธิบดีลินคอล์นถูกลอบฆ่า

1867
U.S. buys Alaska
สหรัฐซื้ออลาสก้า

1879
lightbulb (Edison)
เอดิสันประดิษฐ์หลอดไฟ

1898
Spanish American War
สงครามอเมริกันกับสเปน

1861–1865
Civil War
สงคราม
กลางเมือง

1865
slavery abolished
เลิกทาส

1869
trans-continental railroad
ทางรถไฟข้ามทวีป

1876
telephone (Bell)
มีโทรศัพท์

1890
Battle of Wounded Knee
สงครามวูนดิดนี

1850   1860   1870   1880   1890

1850 →
Chinese, Scandinavians
ชาวจีนและสแกนดิเนเวียนเริ่มเข้ามา

1870 →
Hungarians
ชาวฮังกาเรียนเริ่ม
เข้ามา

1885 →
Japanese
ชาวญี่ปุ่น

1890 →
Armenians, Southern and Eastern Europeans
ชาวอาร์มีเนียนและชาวยุโรปตอนใต้กับตะวันออกเริ่ม
เข้ามา

1850: 23,191,000

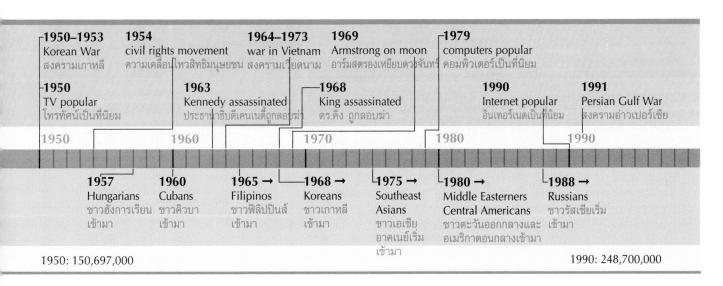

1950–1953
Korean War
สงครามเกาหลี

1954
civil rights movement
ความเคลื่อนไหวสิทธิมนุษยชน

1964–1973
war in Vietnam
สงครามเวียดนาม

1969
Armstrong on moon
อาร์มสตรองเหยียบดวงจันทร์

1979
computers popular
คอมพิวเตอร์เป็นที่นิยม

1950
TV popular
โทรทัศน์เป็นที่นิยม

1963
Kennedy assassinated
ประธานาธิบดีเคนเนดี้ถูกลอบฆ่า

1968
King assassinated
ดร.คิง ถูกลอบฆ่า

1990
Internet popular
อินเทอร์เนตเป็นที่นิยม

1991
Persian Gulf War
สงครามอ่าวเปอร์เซีย

1950   1960   1970   1980   1990

1957
Hungarians
ชาวฮังการีเรียน
เข้ามา

1960
Cubans
ชาวคิวบา
เข้ามา

1965 →
Filipinos
ชาวฟิลิปปินส์
เข้ามา

1968 →
Koreans
ชาวเกาหลี
เข้ามา

1975 →
Southeast
Asians
ชาวเอเชีย
อาคเนย์เริ่ม
เข้ามา

1980 →
Middle Easterners
Central Americans
ชาวตะวันออกกลางและ
อเมริกาตอนกลางเข้ามา

1988 →
Russians
ชาวรัสเซียเริ่ม
เข้ามา

1950: 150,697,000

1990: 248,700,000

BRANCHES OF GOVERNMENT
ฝ่ายต่างๆ ของการปกครอง

Legislative
ฝ่ายนิติบัญญัติ

Executive
ฝ่ายบริหาร

Judicial
ฝ่ายตุลาการ

1. The House of Representatives
สภาผู้แทนราษฎร

2. congresswoman / congressman
ผู้แทนราษฎร

3. The Senate
วุฒิสภา

4. senator
วุฒิสมาชิก

5. The White House
ทำเนียบขาว

6. president
ประธานาธิบดี

7. vice president
รองประธานาธิบดี

8. The Supreme Court
ศาลสูงสุด/ศาลฎีกา

9. chief justice
หัวหน้าผู้พิพากษา

10. justices
ผู้พิพากษา

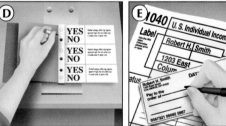

Citizenship application requirements
คุณสมบัติในการสมัครเป็นพลเมืองสหรัฐ

A. **be** 18 years old
อายุ 18 ปี

B. **live** in the U.S. for five years
อาศัยอยู่ในสหรัฐ 5 ปี

C. **take** a citizenship test
เข้าทดสอบเพื่อการเป็นพลเมืองสหรัฐ

Rights and responsibilities
สิทธิและหน้าที่ในการเป็นพลเมืองสหรัฐ

D. **vote**
ออกเสียงเลือกตั้ง

E. **pay** taxes
เสียภาษี

F. **register** with Selective Service*
ลงทะเบียนเพื่อคัดเลือกทหาร

G. **serve** on a jury
เป็นสมาชิกในคณะลูกขุน

H. **obey** the law
เคารพกฎหมาย

*Note: All males 18 to 26 who live in the U.S. are required to register with Selective Service.

1. **rain forest**
   ป่าดิบชื้น

2. **waterfall**
   น้ำตก

3. **river**
   แม่น้ำ

4. **desert**
   ทะเลทราย

5. **sand dune**
   เนินทราย

6. **ocean**
   มหาสมุทร

7. **peninsula**
   คาบสมุทร

8. **island**
   เกาะ

9. **bay**
   อ่าว

10. **beach**
    ชายหาด

11. **forest**
    ป่า

12. **shore**
    ชายฝั่ง

13. **lake**
    ทะเลสาป

14. **mountain peak**
    ยอดเขา

15. **mountain range**
    เทือกเขา

16. **hills**
    เนินเขา

17. **canyon**
    หุบเขาลึก

18. **valley**
    หุบเขา/บริเวณระหว่างภูเขา

19. **plains**
    ที่ราบ

20. **meadow**
    ทุ่งหญ้า

21. **pond**
    แอ่งน้ำ/บ่อน้ำ

More vocabulary คำศัพท์เพิ่มเติม

a body of water: a river, lake, or ocean

stream/creek: a very small river

Talk about where you live and where you like to go.

I live in a valley. There is a lake nearby.

I like to go to the beach.

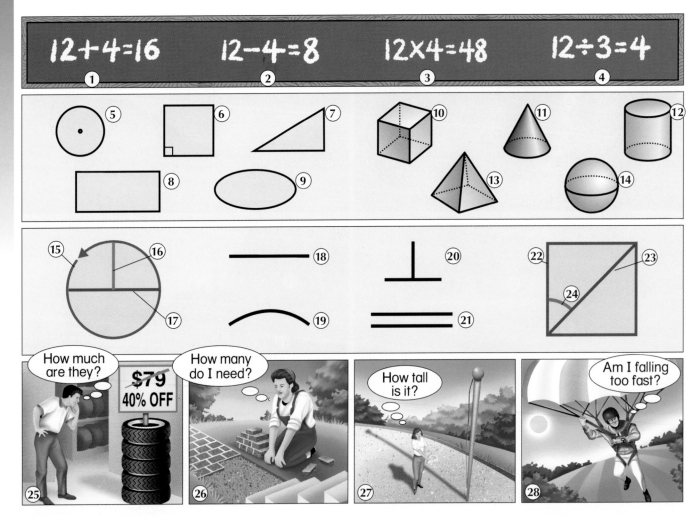

Operations การดำเนินการ

1. addition
การบวก

2. subtraction
การลบ

3. multiplication
การคูณ

4. division
การหาร

Shapes รูปทรง

5. circle
วงกลม

6. square
สี่เหลี่ยมจัตุรัส

7. triangle
สามเหลี่ยม

8. rectangle
สี่เหลี่ยมผืนผ้า

9. oval/ellipse
วงรี

Solids รูปทรงตัน

10. cube
สี่เหลี่ยมลูกบาศก์

11. cone
ทรงกรวย

12. cylinder
ทรงกระบอก

13. pyramid
ทรงพีระมิด

14. sphere
ทรงกลม

Parts of a circle
ส่วนต่าง ๆ ของวงกลม

15. circumference
เส้นรอบวง

16. radius
รัศมี

17. diameter
เส้นผ่าศูนย์กลาง

Lines เส้นต่าง ๆ

18. straight
เส้นตรง

19. curved
เส้นโค้ง

20. perpendicular
เส้นตั้งฉาก

21. parallel
เส้นขนาน

Parts of a square
ส่วนต่าง ๆ ของสี่เหลี่ยมจัตุรัส

22. side
ด้าน

23. diagonal
เส้นทแยงมุม

24. angle
มุม

Types of math
สาขา/แขนงในคณิตศาสตร์

25. algebra
พีชคณิต

26. geometry
เรขาคณิต

27. trigonometry
ตรีโกณมิติ

28. calculus
แคลคูลัส

More vocabulary คำศัพท์เพิ่มเติม

total: the answer to an addition problem

difference: the answer to a subtraction problem

product: the answer to a multiplication problem

quotient: the answer to a division problem

pi (π): the number when you divide the circumference of a circle by its diameter (approximately = 3.14)

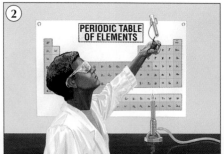

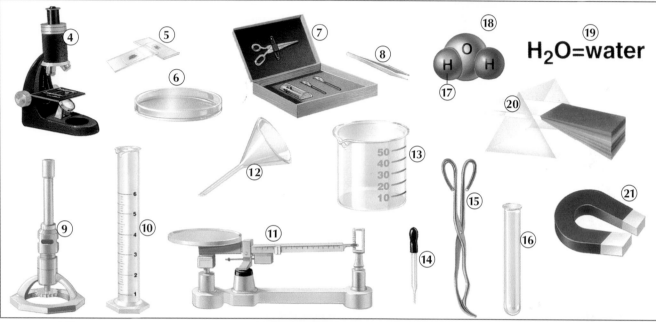

H₂O=water

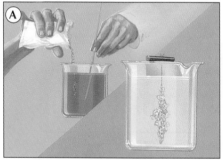

1. biology
ชีววิทยา

2. chemistry
วิชาเคมี

3. physics
วิชาฟิสิกส์

4. microscope
กล้องจุลทรรศน์

5. slide
แผ่นสไลด์

6. petri dish
จานเพาะเชื้อ

7. dissection kit
อุปกรณ์ผ่าตัด

8. forceps
คีมใช้ในการผ่าตัด

9. Bunsen burner
ตะเกียง

10. graduated cylinder
กระบอกวัดปริมาตร

11. balance
คันชั่ง

12. funnel
กรวย

13. beaker
บีกเกอร์

14. dropper
หลอดหยด

15. crucible tongs
คีมคีบ

16. test tube
หลอดทดลอง

17. atom
อะตอม/ปรมาณู

18. molecule
โมเลกุล

19. formula
สูตร

20. prism
แท่งปริซึม

21. magnet
แม่เหล็ก

A. **do** an experiment
ทำการทดลอง

B. **observe**
สังเกต

C. **record** results
บันทึกผล

A. play an instrument
เล่นเครื่องดนตรี

B. sing a song
ร้องเพลง

1. orchestra
วงดนตรีออเค็ชทระ

2. rock band
วงดนตรีร็อค

Woodwinds เครื่องเป่า

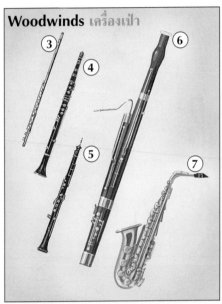

Strings เครื่องสาย

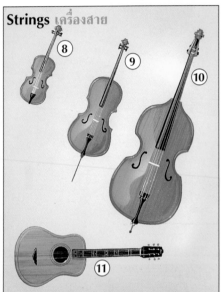

Brass แตรทองเหลือง

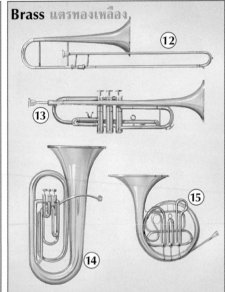

Percussion
เครื่องตี
หรือเคาะ

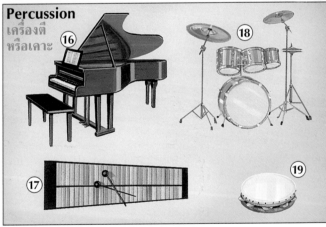

Other Instruments เครื่องดนตรีอื่นๆ

3. flute ขลุ่ย	**8.** violin ไวโอลิน	**13.** trumpet/horn ทรัมเป็ท/แตร	**18.** drums กลองชุด
4. clarinet คลาริเนท	**9.** cello เชลโล	**14.** tuba ทูบ้า	**19.** tambourine แทมบูรีน
5. oboe โอโบ	**10.** bass ดับเบิลเบส	**15.** French horn เฟรนซ ฮอร์น	**20.** electric keyboard คีย์บอร์ดไฟฟ้า
6. bassoon ปี่ทุ้ม/บาสซูน	**11.** guitar กีตาร์	**16.** piano เปียโน	**21.** accordion แอคคอเดียน/หีบเพลง
7. saxophone แซกโซโฟน	**12.** trombone ทรัมโบน	**17.** xylophone ระนาดฝรั่ง	**22.** organ ออแกน

1. art
ศิลปะ

2. business education
ธุรกิจศึกษา

3. chorus
การประสานเสียง

4. computer science
วิทยาการคอมพิวเตอร์

5. driver's education
การสอนขับรถยนต์

6. economics
เศรษฐศาสตร์

7. English as a second language
ภาษาอังกฤษในฐานะภาษาที่สอง

8. foreign language
ภาษาต่างประเทศ

9. home economics
คหกรรมศาสตร์

10. industrial arts / shop
อุตสาหกรรมศิลป์

11. PE (physical education)
พลศึกษา

12. theater arts
ศิลปะการแสดง

More vocabulary คำศัพท์เพิ่มเติม

core course: a subject students have to take

elective: a subject students choose to take

Share your answers. แลกเปลี่ยนคำตอบ

1. What are your favorite subjects?

2. In your opinion, what subjects are most important? Why?

3. What foreign languages are taught in your school?

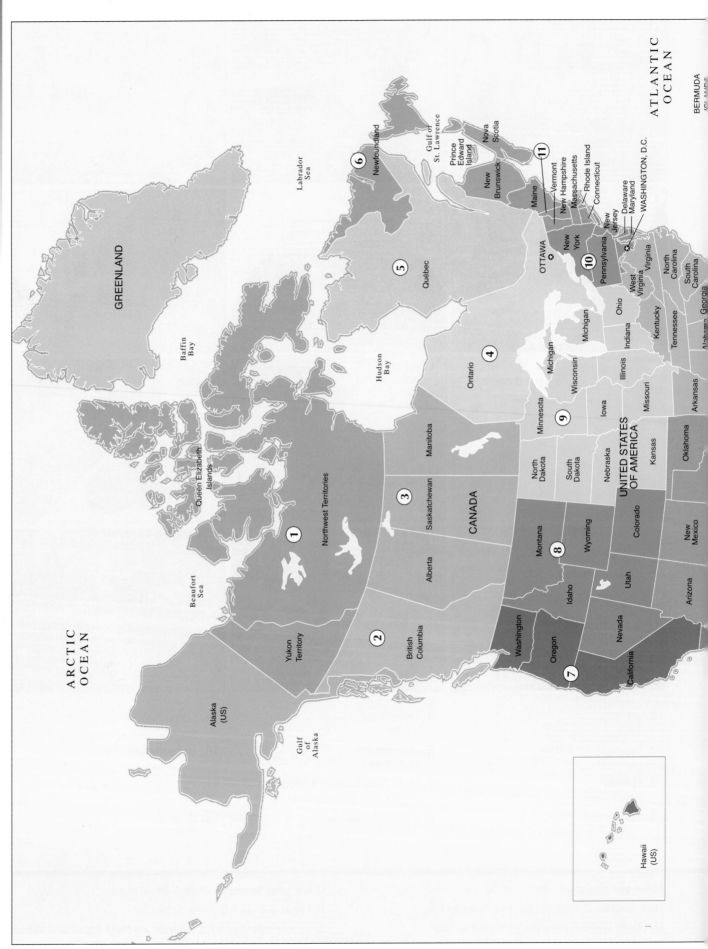

ARCTIC OCEAN

ATLANTIC OCEAN

BERMUDA

GREENLAND

Labrador Sea

Baffin Bay

Beaufort Sea

Queen Elizabeth Islands

Hudson Bay

Gulf of St. Lawrence

Newfoundland

⑥

Prince Edward Island

Nova Scotia

New Brunswick

Maine

Vermont

New Hampshire

Massachusetts

Rhode Island

Connecticut

Delaware

Maryland

WASHINGTON, D.C.

⑪

Québec

⑤

New York

⑩

OTTAWA

Pennsylvania

New Jersey

West Virginia

Virginia

North Carolina

South Carolina

Georgia

Ontario

④

Michigan

Michigan

Ohio

Kentucky

Tennessee

Alabama

Wisconsin

Indiana

Illinois

Missouri

Arkansas

Minnesota

⑨

Iowa

Manitoba

North Dakota

South Dakota

Nebraska

Kansas

Oklahoma

Northwest Territories

Saskatchewan

③

CANADA

UNITED STATES OF AMERICA

New Mexico

Alberta

British Columbia

②

Montana

Wyoming

Colorado

⑧

Idaho

Utah

Arizona

Yukon Territory

①

Nevada

Washington

Oregon

⑦

California

Alaska (US)

Gulf of Alaska

Hawaii (US)

122

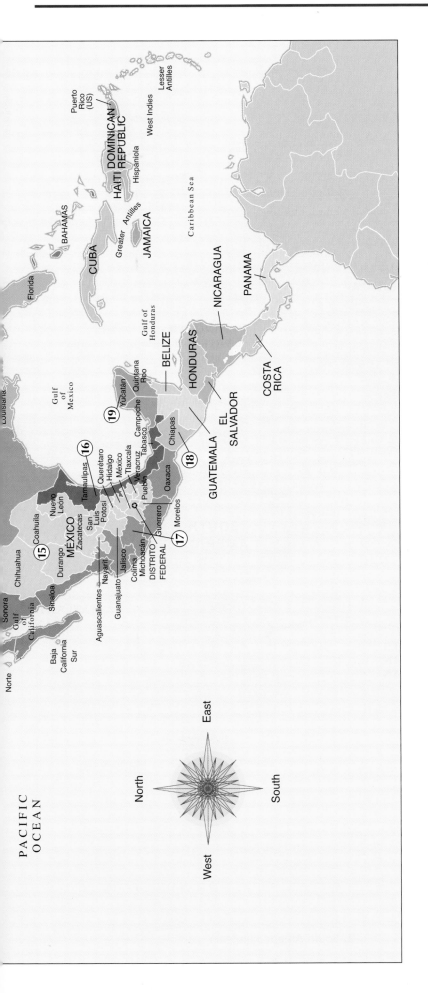

Regions of Canada
ภูมิภาคต่าง ๆ ของแคนาดา

1. Northern Canada
   แคนาดาเหนือ

2. British Columbia
   บริทิชโคลัมเบีย

3. The Prairie Provinces
   แถบทุ่งหญ้า

4. Ontario
   ออนแทรีโอ

5. Québec
   ควิเบก

6. The Atlantic Provinces
   แถบมหาสมุทรแอตแลนติก

Regions of the United States
ภูมิภาคต่าง ๆ ของสหรัฐ

7. The Pacific States/the West Coast
   รัฐแถบมหาสมุทรแปซิฟิก/ชายฝั่งทะเลวันตก

8. The Rocky Mountain States
   รัฐแถบเทือกเขาร็อกกี

9. The Midwest
   รัฐแถบมิดเวสต์

10. The Mid-Atlantic States
    รัฐทางตอนกลางมหาสมุทรแอตแลนติก

11. New England
    รัฐนิวอิงแลนด์

12. The Southwest
    รัฐตะวันตกเฉียงใต้

13. The Southeast/the South
    รัฐตะวันออกเฉียงใต้/ทิศใต้

Regions of Mexico
ภูมิภาคต่าง ๆ ของเม็กซิโก

14. The Pacific Northwest
    แถบตะวันตกเฉียงเหนือมหาสมุทรแปซิฟิก

15. The Plateau of Mexico
    ที่ราบสูงเม็กซิโก

16. The Gulf Coastal Plain
    ที่ราบชายฝั่ง

17. The Southern Uplands
    ที่ดอนทางตอนใต้

18. The Chiapas Highlands
    ที่ราบสูงชิเอพัส

19. The Yucatan Peninsula
    แหลมคาบสมุทรยูกะทาน

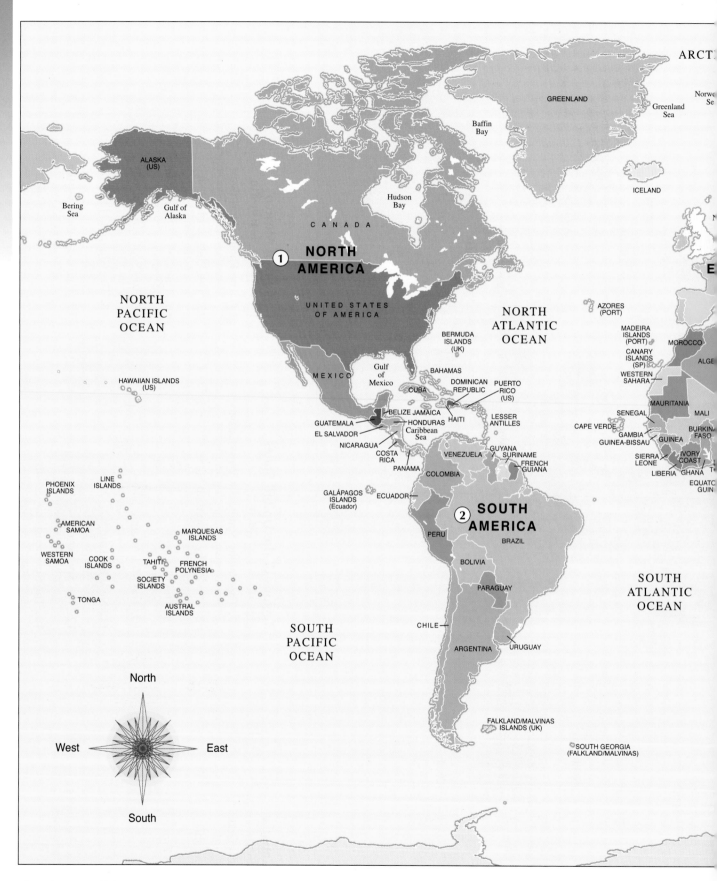

Map labels:

ARCTI

GREENLAND

Norwe Se

Baffin Bay

Greenland Sea

ICELAND

ALASKA (US)

Bering Sea

Gulf of Alaska

Hudson Bay

C A N A D A

① NORTH AMERICA

NORTH PACIFIC OCEAN

UNITED STATES OF AMERICA

NORTH ATLANTIC OCEAN

AZORES (PORT)

E

MADEIRA ISLANDS (PORT)

MOROCCO

CANARY ISLANDS (SP)

ALGE

BERMUDA ISLANDS (UK)

WESTERN SAHARA

MEXICO

Gulf of Mexico

BAHAMAS

CUBA

DOMINICAN REPUBLIC

PUERTO RICO (US)

MAURITANIA

MALI

HAWAIIAN ISLANDS (US)

BELIZE JAMAICA

HAITI

LESSER ANTILLES

SENEGAL

CAPE VERDE

GAMBIA

GUINEA-BISSAU

GUINEA

BURKIN FASO

GUATEMALA

HONDURAS

Caribbean Sea

EL SALVADOR

NICARAGUA

COSTA RICA

PANAMA

VENEZUELA

GUYANA

SURINAME

FRENCH GUIANA

SIERRA LEONE

IVORY COAST

LIBERIA

GHANA

COLOMBIA

EQUATC GUIN

PHOENIX ISLANDS

LINE ISLANDS

GALÁPAGOS ISLANDS (Ecuador)

ECUADOR

② SOUTH AMERICA

AMERICAN SAMOA

MARQUESAS ISLANDS

PERU

BRAZIL

WESTERN SAMOA

COOK ISLANDS

TAHITI

FRENCH POLYNESIA

BOLIVIA

SOUTH ATLANTIC OCEAN

SOCIETY ISLANDS

PARAGUAY

TONGA

AUSTRAL ISLANDS

CHILE

SOUTH PACIFIC OCEAN

ARGENTINA

URUGUAY

North

West — East

South

FALKLAND/MALVINAS ISLANDS (UK)

SOUTH GEORGIA (FALKLAND/MALVINAS)

Continents ทวีป

1. North America อเมริกาเหนือ

2. South America อเมริกาใต้

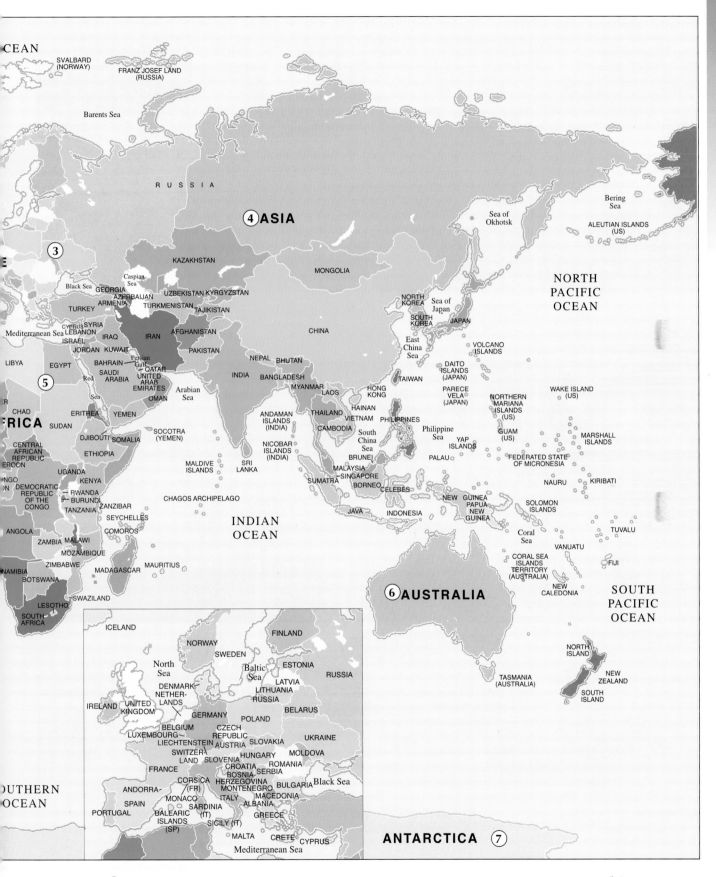

3. Europe ยุโรป

4. Asia เอเชีย

5. Africa อัฟริกา

6. Australia ออสเตรเลีย

7. Antarctica แอนตาร์กติกา

Energy resources แหล่งพลังงาน

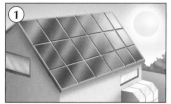

1. solar energy
พลังงานแสงอาทิตย์

2. wind
ลม

3. natural gas
ก๊าซธรรมชาติ

4. coal
ถ่านหิน

5. hydroelectric power
ไฟฟ้าพลังน้ำ

6. oil / petroleum
น้ำมัน

7. geothermal energy
พลังงานความร้อนใต้พิภพ

8. nuclear energy
พลังงานนิวเคลียร์

Pollution มลภาวะ

9. hazardous waste
ขยะที่เป็นอันตราย

10. air pollution / smog
มลภาวะทางอากาศ/เขม่าควัน

11. acid rain
ฝนกรด

12. water pollution
มลภาวะทางน้ำ

13. radiation
กัมมันตภาพรังสี

14. pesticide poisoning
สารพิษจากยาฆ่าแมลง

15. oil spill
น้ำมันรั่วไหล

Conservation การอนุรักษ์

A. **recycle**
นำกลับมาใช้ใหม่

B. **save** water / **conserve** water
ประหยัดน้ำ/อนุรักษ์น้ำ

C. **save** energy / **conserve** energy
ประหยัดพลังงาน/อนุรักษ์พลังงาน

Share your answers. แลกเปลี่ยนคำตอบ

1. How do you heat your home?

2. Do you have a gas stove or an electric stove?

3. What are some ways you can save energy when it's cold?

4. Do you recycle? What products do you recycle?

5. Does your market have recycling bins?

The Solar System
ระบบสุริยะจักรวาล

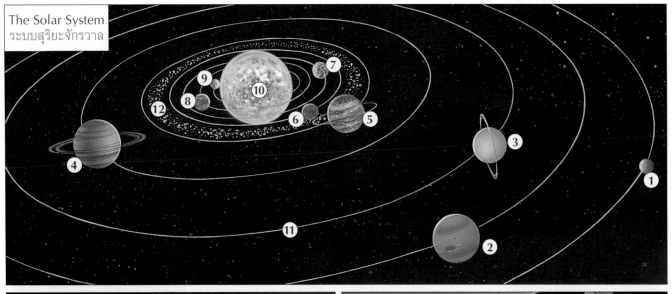

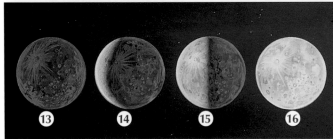

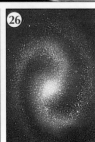

The planets
ดาวเคราะห์ต่าง ๆ

1. Pluto
ดาวพลูโต

2. Neptune
ดาวเนปจูน

3. Uranus
ดาวยูเรนัส

4. Saturn
ดาวเสาร์

5. Jupiter
ดาวพฤหัส

6. Mars
ดาวอังคาร

7. Earth
โลก

8. Venus
ดาวพระศุกร์

9. Mercury
ดาวพุธ

10. sun
ดวงอาทิตย์

11. orbit
วงโคจรรอบดวงอาทิตย์

12. asteroid belt
กลุ่มดาวเคราะห์น้อยที่หมุน
รอบดวงอาทิตย์

13. new moon
พระจันทร์ข้างขึ้น

14. crescent moon
พระจันทร์เสี้ยว

15. quarter moon
พระจันทร์ครึ่งซีก

16. full moon
พระจันทร์เต็มดวง

17. astronaut
นักบินอวกาศ

18. space station
สถานีอวกาศ

19. observatory
หอดูดาว

20. astronomer
นักดาราศาสตร์

21. telescope
กล้องส่องทางไกล

22. space
อวกาศ

23. star
ดวงดาว

24. constellation
หมู่ดาว

25. comet
ดาวหาง

26. galaxy
ทางช้างเผือก/แกแล็คซี่

More vocabulary คำศัพท์เพิ่มเติม

lunar eclipse: when the earth is between the sun and the moon

solar eclipse: when the moon is between the earth and the sun

Share your answers. แลกเปลี่ยนคำตอบ

1. Do you know the names of any constellations?

2. How do you feel when you look up at the night sky?

3. Is the night sky in the U.S. the same as in your country?

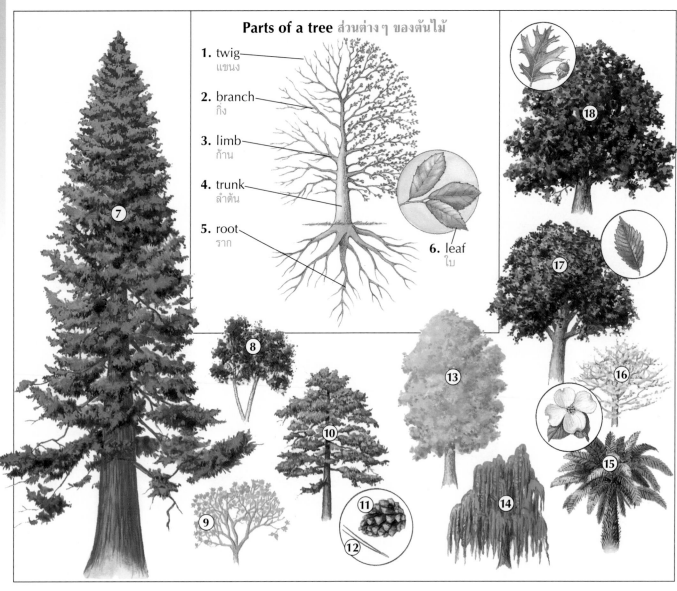

Parts of a tree ส่วนต่าง ๆ ของต้นไม้

1. twig
แขนง

2. branch
กิ่ง

3. limb
ก้าน

4. trunk
ลำต้น

5. root
ราก

6. leaf
ใบ

7. redwood
ต้นสนชนิดหนึ่ง/เร็ดวูด

8. birch
ต้นเบิช

9. magnolia
ต้นแมกโนเลีย

10. pine
ต้นสนชนิดหนึ่ง

11. pinecone
ลูกสน

12. needle
ใบสน

13. maple
ต้นเมเปิ้ล

14. willow
ต้นหลิวชนิดหนึ่ง

15. palm
ต้นปาล์ม

16. dogwood
ไม้ป่าทรงพุ่มมีดอกสีขาว

17. elm
ต้นเอ็ล์ม

18. oak
ต้นโอ๊ค

Plants พืชชนิดต่าง ๆ

19. holly
ต้นฮอลลี่

20. berries
ผลเบอรี่

21. cactus
ต้นกระบองเพชร

22. vine
ไม้เถาเลื้อย / ต้นองุ่น

23. poison oak
พืชลำต้นอ่อนมีพิษ

24. poison sumac
พืชลำต้นอ่อนมีพิษ

25. poison ivy
ไม้เลื้อยมีพิษ/ต้นตำแย

Parts of a flower ส่วนต่างๆ ของดอกไม้

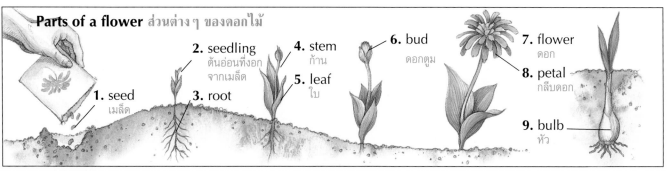

1. seed
เมล็ด

2. seedling
ต้นอ่อนที่งอก
จากเมล็ด

3. root
ราก

4. stem
ก้าน

5. leaf
ใบ

6. bud
ดอกตูม

7. flower
ดอก

8. petal
กลีบดอก

9. bulb
หัว

10. sunflower ดอกทานตะวัน	**15.** rose ดอกกุหลาบ	**20.** iris ดอกไอริส	**25.** crocus ดอกดิน
11. tulip ดอกทิวลิป	**16.** gardenia ดอกกาดีเนียร์	**21.** jasmine ดอกมะลิ	**26.** daffodil ดอกแดฟฟอดิล
12. hibiscus ดอกชบา	**17.** orchid ดอกกล้วยไม้	**22.** violet ดอกไวโอเล็ท	**27.** bouquet ช่อดอกไม้
13. marigold ดอกดาวเรือง	**18.** carnation ดอกคาร์เนชั่น	**23.** poinsettia ดอกคริสต์มาส	**28.** thorn หนาม
14. daisy ดอกเดซี่	**19.** chrysanthemum ดอกเบญจมาศ	**24.** lily ดอกลิลลี่/พลับพลึง	**29.** houseplant ไม้ประดับ

Marine Life, Amphibians, and Reptiles สัตว์น้ำ, สัตว์ครึ่งบกครึ่งน้ำ และสัตว์เลื้อยคลาน

Parts of a fish ส่วนต่างๆ ของปลา

Sea animals สัตว์ทะเล

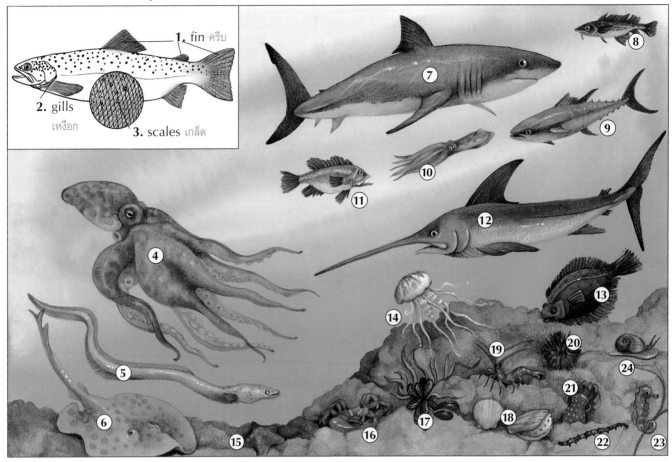

1. fin ครีบ
2. gills เหงือก
3. scales เกล็ด

4. octopus ปลาหมึกยักษ์	**11.** bass ปลากระพง	**18.** scallop หอยแครง
5. eel ปลาไหลทะเล	**12.** swordfish ปลาฉนาก	**19.** shrimp กุ้ง
6. ray ปลากระเบน	**13.** flounder ปลาลิ้นหมา	**20.** sea urchin เม่นทะเล
7. shark ปลาฉลาม	**14.** jellyfish แมงกะพรุน	**21.** sea anemone ดอกไม้ทะเลชนิดหนึ่งมีหนวด
8. cod ปลาค้อด	**15.** starfish ปลาดาว	**22.** worm หนอน
9. tuna ปลาทูน่า	**16.** crab ปู	**23.** sea horse ม้าน้ำ
10. squid ปลาหมึก	**17.** mussel หอยแมลงภู่	**24.** snail หอยทาก

Amphibians สัตว์ครึ่งบกครึ่งน้ำ

25. frog กบ	**26.** newt แย้	**27.** salamander สัตว์ชนิดหนึ่งคล้ายจิ้งเหลน ซาละมันเดอะ	**28.** toad คางคก

Sea mammals สัตว์ทะเลที่เลี้ยงลูกด้วยนม

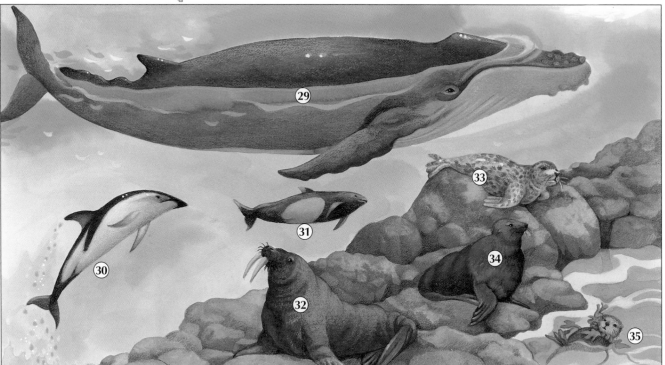

29. whale ปลาวาฬ	**31.** porpoise ปลาโลมาชนิดหนึ่ง	**33.** seal แมวน้ำ	**35.** otter นาก
30. dolphin ปลาโลมา	**32.** walrus ตัววอลรัช / ช้างน้ำ	**34.** sea lion สิงโตทะเล	

Reptiles สัตว์เลื้อยคลาน

36. alligator จระเข้ปากสั้น	**38.** rattlesnake งูหางกระดิ่ง	**40.** cobra งูเห่า	**42.** turtle เต่า
37. crocodile จระเข้ท้องเหลือง	**39.** garter snake งูไม่มีพิษ	**41.** lizard กิ้งก่า / จิ้งเหลน	

Birds, Insects, and Arachnids นก แมลง และแมง

Parts of a bird ส่วนต่างๆ ของนก

1. beak / bill
   จะงอยปาก
2. wing
   ปีก
3. nest รัง
4. claw
   อุ้งเล็บ
5. feather
   ขน

6. owl นกฮูก	**9.** woodpecker นกหัวขวาน	**12.** penguin นกเพนกวิน	**15.** peacock นกยูง
7. blue jay นกมีหงอนในอเมริกา	**10.** eagle นกอินทรี	**13.** duck เป็ด	**16.** pigeon นกพิราบ
8. sparrow นกกระจอก	**11.** hummingbird นกเล็กๆ ชนิดหนึ่งมีปากยาว ขนสดสวย	**14.** goose ห่าน	**17.** robin นกโรบิน

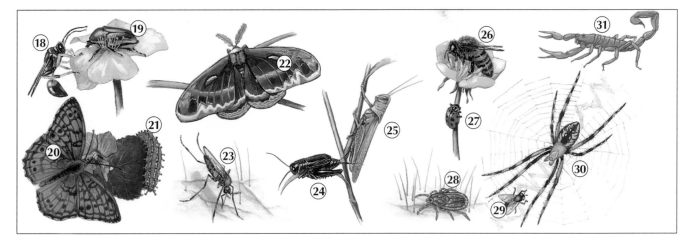

18. wasp ตัวต่อ	**22.** moth ผีเสื้อกลางคืน	**26.** honeybee ผึ้ง	**30.** spider แมงมุม
19. beetle แมลงปีกแข็ง	**23.** mosquito ยุง	**27.** ladybug เต่าทอง	**31.** scorpion แมลงป่อง
20. butterfly ผีเสื้อ	**24.** cricket จิ้งหรีด	**28.** tick หมัด, เห็บ	
21. caterpillar ดักแด้/บุ้ง	**25.** grasshopper ตั๊กแตน	**29.** fly แมลงวัน	

Farm animals สัตว์เลี้ยงในฟาร์ม

1. goat แพะ	**3.** cow วัว	**5.** hen ไก่ตัวเมีย	**7.** sheep แกะ
2. donkey ลา	**4.** horse ม้า	**6.** rooster ไก่ตัวผู้	**8.** pig หมู

Pets สัตว์เลี้ยง

9. cat แมว	**11.** dog สุนัข	**13.** rabbit กระต่าย	**15.** parakeet นกแก้วชนิดหนึ่ง
10. kitten ลูกแมว	**12.** puppy ลูกสุนัข	**14.** guinea pig หนูตะเภา	**16.** goldfish ปลาทอง

Rodents สัตว์จำพวกกัดแทะ

17. mouse หนู	**19.** gopher หนูขนาดใหญ่	**21.** squirrel กระรอก
18. rat หนู	**20.** chipmunk กระแต	**22.** prairie dog หนูชนิดหนึ่งเท่าเหมือนสุนัข

More vocabulary คำศัพท์เพิ่มเติม

Wild animals live, eat, and raise their young away from people, in the forests, mountains, plains, etc.

Domesticated animals work for people or live with them.

Share your answers. แลกเปลี่ยนคำตอบ

1. Do you have any pets? any farm animals?

2. Which of these animals are in your neighborhood? Which are not?

1. **moose**
   ตัวมูส / กวางขนาดใหญ่

2. **mountain lion**
   สิงโตภูเขา

3. **coyote**
   หมาป่าในอเมริกา

4. **opossum**
   สัตว์คล้ายหนูมีกระเป๋าหน้าท้อง

5. **wolf**
   หมาป่า

6. **buffalo/bison**
   ควายไบซัน

7. **bat**
   ค้างคาว

8. **armadillo**
   ตัวนิ่ม / ตัวนางอาย

9. **beaver**
   ตัวบีเวอร์

10. **porcupine**
    เม่น

11. **bear**
    หมี

12. **skunk**
    สกั๊งค์/ตัวเหม็น

13. **raccoon**
    ตัวแรคคูน

14. **deer**
    กวาง

15. **fox**
    สุนัขจิ้งจอก

16. **antler**
    เขากวาง

17. **hoof**
    กีบเท้าสัตว์

18. **whiskers**
    หนวด

19. **coat/fur**
    ขนสัตว์

20. **paw**
    เท้าสัตว์

21. **horn**
    เขาสัตว์

22. **tail**
    หาง

23. **quill**
    ขนเม่น

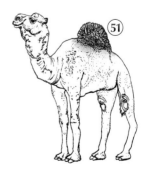

24. anteater ตัวกินมด	**30.** gorilla ลิงกอริลล่า	**36.** lion สิงโต	**42.** elephant ช้าง
25. leopard เสือดาว	**31.** hyena หมาป่าไฮอีน่าในอัฟริกา	**37.** tiger เสือ	**43.** hippopotamus ฮิปโปโปเตมัส
26. llama ตัวลามะ	**32.** baboon ลิงบาบูน	**38.** camel อูฐ	**44.** kangaroo จิงโจ้
27. monkey ลิง	**33.** giraffe ยีราฟ	**39.** panther เสือดำ	**45.** koala หมีโคล่า
28. chimpanzee ลิงชิมแพนซี	**34.** zebra ม้าลาย	**40.** orangutan ลิงอุรังอุตัง	**46.** platypus ตัวตุ่นปากเป็ด
29. rhinoceros แรด	**35.** antelope เลียงผา	**41.** panda หมีแพนด้า	

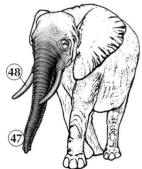

47. trunk งวงช้าง	**48.** tusk งาช้าง	**49.** mane แผงคอสิงโต	**50.** pouch กระเป๋าหน้าท้องจิงโจ้	**51.** hump โหนกบนหลังอูฐ

135

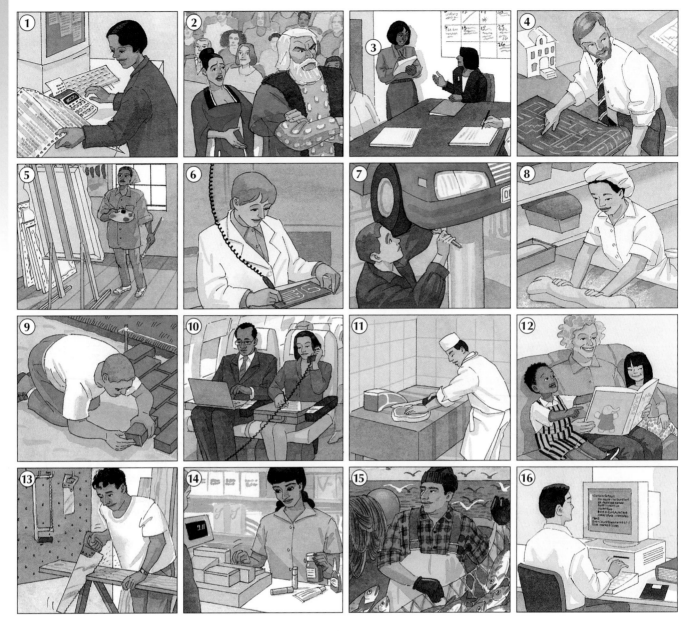

1. **accountant**
สมุหบัญชี

2. **actor**
นักแสดง

3. **administrative assistant**
ผู้ช่วยผู้บริหาร

4. **architect**
สถาปนิก

5. **artist**
จิตรกร

6. **assembler**
พนักงานประกอบชิ้นส่วน

7. **auto mechanic**
ช่างซ่อมรถยนต์

8. **baker**
คนทำขนมปัง

9. **bricklayer**
ช่างก่ออิฐ

10. **businessman/businesswoman**
นักธุรกิจชาย / นักธุรกิจหญิง

11. **butcher**
คนขายเนื้อ

12. **caregiver/baby-sitter**
ผู้มาอยู่เป็นเพื่อนเด็ก

13. **carpenter**
ช่างไม้

14. **cashier**
พนักงานเก็บเงิน

15. **commercial fisher**
ชาวประมง

16. **computer programmer**
นักเขียนโปรแกรมคอมพิวเตอร์

Use the new language. ใช้ภาษาใหม่

1. Who works outside?

2. Who works inside?

3. Who makes things?

4. Who uses a computer?

5. Who wears a uniform?

6. Who sells things?

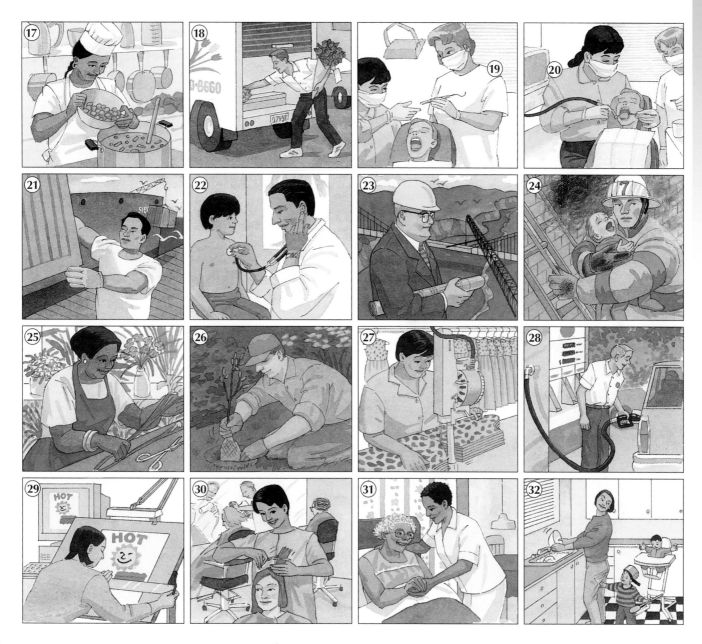

17. cook
พ่อครัว/แม่ครัว

18. delivery person
พนักงานส่งของ

19. dental assistant
ผู้ช่วยทันตแพทย์

20. dentist
ทันตแพทย์

21. dockworker
พนักงานท่าเรือ

22. doctor
แพทย์

23. engineer
วิศวกร

24. firefighter
พนักงานดับเพลิง

25. florist
คนจัดดอกไม้

26. gardener
คนสวน

27. garment worker
ช่างตัดเย็บเสื้อผ้า

28. gas station attendant
พนักงานบริการน้ำมัน

29. graphic artist
นักออกแบบ

30. hairdresser
ช่างแต่งผม

31. home attendant
ผู้ช่วยคนชรา

32. homemaker
แม่บ้าน

Share your answers. แลกเปลี่ยนคำตอบ

1. Do you know people who have some of these jobs?
What do they say about their work?

2. Which of these jobs are available in your city?

3. For which of these jobs do you need special training?

33. housekeeper ผู้ช่วยงาน/แม่บ้าน	**39.** model นางแบบ	**45.** postal worker พนักงานไปรษณีย์
34. interpreter/translator ล่าม	**40.** mover พนักงานขนย้าย	**46.** printer ช่างพิมพ์
35. janitor/custodian ภารโรง	**41.** musician นักดนตรี	**47.** receptionist พนักงานต้อนรับ
36. lawyer ทนายความ	**42.** nurse นางพยาบาล	**48.** repair person ช่างซ่อม
37. machine operator ผู้ใช้เครื่องจักร	**43.** painter ช่างทาสี	
38. messenger/courier พนักงานเดินหนังสือ	**44.** police officer เจ้าหน้าที่ตำรวจ	

Talk about each of the jobs or occupations. พูดคุยเกี่ยวกับงานและอาชีพต่าง ๆ

She's a housekeeper. She works in a hotel.   *She's a nurse. She works with patients.*

He's an interpreter. He works for the government.

49. reporter
ผู้สื่อข่าว

50. salesclerk / salesperson
พนักงานขาย

51. sanitation worker
พนักงานสุขาภิบาล

52. secretary
เลขานุการ

53. server
พนักงานเสิรฟ

54. serviceman / servicewoman
ทหารเกณฑ์

55. stock clerk
เจ้าหน้าที่คลังสินค้า

56. store owner
เจ้าของร้าน

57. student
นักศึกษา

58. teacher / instructor
ครู

59. telemarketer
นักเล่นหุ้นโดยใช้โทรศัพท์

60. travel agent
ตัวแทนบริษัทท่องเที่ยว

61. truck driver
คนขับรถบรรทุก

62. veterinarian
สัตวแพทย์

63. welder
ช่างเชื่อม

64. writer / author
นักเขียน/นักประพันธ์

Talk about your job or the job you want. พูดคุยเกี่ยวกับงานของคุณหรืองานที่คุณอยากทำ

What do you do?

　I'm a salesclerk. I work in a store.

What do you want to do?

　I want to be a veterinarian. I want to work with animals.

A. **assemble** components
ประกอบชิ้นส่วน

B. **assist** medical patients
ช่วยเหลือผู้ป่วย

C. **cook**
ปรุงอาหาร

D. **do** manual labor
ทำงานที่ใช้แรงงาน

E. **drive** a truck
ขับรถบรรทุก

F. **operate** heavy machinery
ปฏิบัติงานด้วยเครื่องจักรกลหนัก

G. **repair** appliances
ซ่อมเครื่องใช้ไฟฟ้า

H. **sell** cars
ขายรถยนต์

I. **sew** clothes
เย็บเสื้อผ้า

J. **speak** another language
พูดภาษาอื่น

K. **supervise** people
แนะนำการทำงาน

L. **take care** of children
ดูแลเด็กๆ

M. **type**
พิมพ์งาน

N. **use** a cash register
ใช้เครื่องคิดเงิน

O. **wait on** customers
บริการ / รับคำสั่งลูกค้า

P. **work on a computer**
ทำงานด้วยคอมพิวเตอร์

More vocabulary คำศัพท์เพิ่มเติม

act: to perform in a play, movie, or TV show

fly: to pilot an airplane

teach: to instruct, to show how to do something

Share your answers. แลกเปลี่ยนคำตอบ

1. What job skills do you have? Where did you learn them?

2. What job skills do you want to learn?

A. **talk** to friends
คุยกับเพื่อน

B. **look** at a job board
ดูที่แผ่นป้ายรับสมัครงาน

C. **look** for a help wanted sign
มองหาป้ายรับสมัครงาน

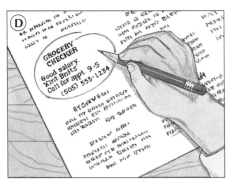

D. **look** in the classifieds
ดูในประกาศรับสมัครงาน

E. **call** for information
โทรศัพท์สอบถามข้อมูล

F. **ask** about the hours
ซักถามเกี่ยวกับเวลาทำงาน

G. **fill out** an application
กรอกใบสมัครงาน

H. **go** on an interview
ไปสัมภาษณ์

I. **talk** about your experience
พูดถึงประสบการณ์

J. **ask** about benefits
สอบถามเกี่ยวกับสวัสดิการ

K. **inquire** about the salary
สอบถามเกี่ยวกับเงินเดือน

L. **get hired**
ได้งานทำ

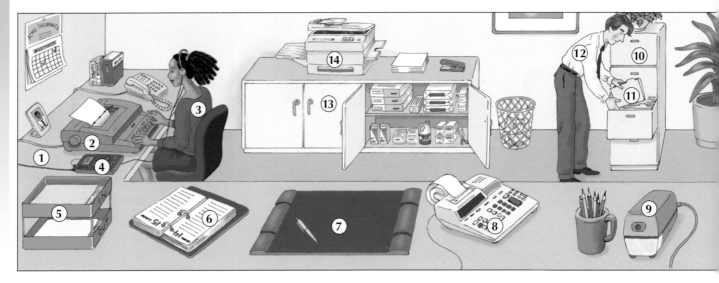

1. **desk**
   โต๊ะทำงาน

2. **typewriter**
   เครื่องพิมพ์ดีด

3. **secretary**
   เลขานุการ

4. **microcassette transcriber**
   เทปถ่ายข้อมูลสำหรับงานพิมพ์

5. **stacking tray**
   ชั้นใส่เอกสาร

6. **desk calendar**
   ปฏิทินตั้งโต๊ะ

7. **desk pad**
   แผ่นรองสำหรับเขียน

8. **calculator**
   เครื่องคิดเลข

9. **electric pencil sharpener**
   เครื่องเหลาดินสอไฟฟ้า

10. **file cabinet**
    ตู้เก็บแฟ้มเอกสาร

11. **file folder**
    แฟ้มเอกสาร

12. **file clerk**
    พนักงานจัดเก็บเอกสาร

13. **supply cabinet**
    ตู้เก็บพัสดุ

14. **photocopier**
    เครื่องถ่ายเอกสาร

A. **take** a message
   บันทึกข้อความ

B. **fax** a letter
   ส่งจดหมายทางโทรสาร

C. **transcribe** notes
   ถอดเทป

D. **type** a letter
   พิมพ์จดหมาย

E. **make** copies
   ถ่ายเอกสาร

F. **collate** papers
   ตรวจทานเอกสาร

G. **staple**
   เย็บกระดาษ

H. **file** papers
   เก็บเอกสารเข้าแฟ้ม

Practice taking messages. ฝึกการบันทึกข้อความ

Hello. My name is <u>Sara Scott</u>. Is <u>Mr. Lee</u> in?

   Not yet. Would you like to leave a message?

Yes. Please ask <u>him</u> to call me at <u>555-4859</u>.

Share your answers. แลกเปลี่ยนคำตอบ

1. Which office equipment do you know how to use?

2. Which jobs does a file clerk do?

3. Which jobs does a secretary do?

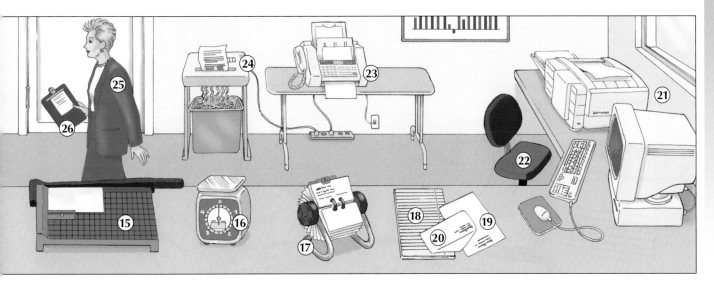

15. paper cutter
ที่ตัดกระดาษ

16. postal scale
ตาชั่งไปรษณียภัณฑ์

17. rotary card file
แฟ้มบัตรหมุนได้

18. legal pad
แผ่นรองเขียน

19. letterhead paper
กระดาษจดหมายที่พิมพ์หัวแล้ว

20. envelope
ซองจดหมาย

21. computer workstation
ที่ปฏิบัติการคอมพิวเตอร์

22. swivel chair
เก้าอี้หมุน

23. fax machine
เครื่องโทรสาร

24. paper shredder
เครื่องย่อยกระดาษ

25. office manager
ผู้จัดการสำนักงาน

26. clipboard
กระดานสำหรับหนีบเอกสาร

27. appointment book
สมุดนัดหมาย

28. stapler
เครื่องเย็บกระดาษ

29. staple
ลวดเย็บกระดาษ

30. organizer
สมุดบันทึกจัดเป็นหมวดหมู่

31. typewriter cartridge
กล่องหมึกพิมพ์ดีด

32. mailer
ซองพัสดุ

33. correction fluid
น้ำยาลบคำผิด

34. Post-it notes
กระดาษกาวเขียนข้อความ

35. label
ฉลาก

36. notepad
สมุดฉีก

37. glue
กาว

38. rubber cement
กาวยางน้ำ

39. clear tape
เทปใส

40. rubber stamp
ตรายาง

41. ink pad
แท่นหมึก

42. packing tape
กระดาษกาว

43. pushpin
หมุดกดกระดาษ

44. paper clip
ลวดเสียบกระดาษ

45. rubber band
ยางวง

Use the new language. ใช้ภาษาใหม่

1. Which items keep things together?

2. Which items are used to mail packages?

3. Which items are made of paper?

Share your answers. แลกเปลี่ยนคำตอบ

1. Which office supplies do students use?

2. Where can you buy them?

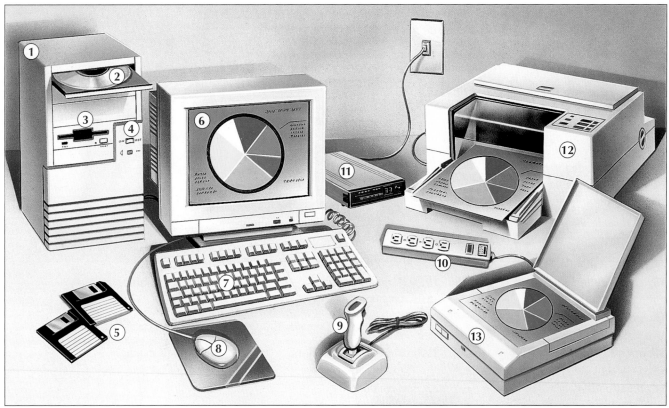

Hardware ฮาร์ดแวร์

1. CPU (central processing unit)
หน่วยประมวลข้อมูล / ซีพียู

2. CD-ROM disc
แผ่นซีดีรอม

3. disk drive
ช่องเล่นแผ่นดิสก์

4. power switch
ปุ่มเปิด - ปิด

5. disk/floppy
แผ่นดิสก์

6. monitor/screen
จอภาพ

7. keyboard
แท่นคีย์บอร์ด/แป้นพิมพ์

8. mouse
เมาส์

9. joystick
คันบังคับ

10. surge protector
ปลั๊กไฟป้องกันไฟเกิน

11. modem
โมเด็ม

12. printer
เครื่องพิมพ์

13. scanner
เครื่องอ่านเอกสาร / ภาพ

14. laptop
คอมพิวเตอร์กระเป๋าหิ้ว

15. trackball
ปุ่มควบคุม

16. cable
เคเบิ้ล

17. port
พอร์ต

18. motherboard
แผงวงจรหลัก

19. slot
ช่องสำหรับเสียบการ์ด

20. hard disk drive
ฮาร์ดดิสก์

Software ซอฟต์แวร์

21. program/application
โปรแกรม

22. user's manual
คู่มือการใช้

More vocabulary คำศัพท์เพิ่มเติม

data: information that a computer can read

memory: how much data a computer can hold

speed: how fast a computer can work with data

Share your answers. แลกเปลี่ยนคำตอบ

1. Can you use a computer?

2. How did you learn? in school? from a book? by yourself?

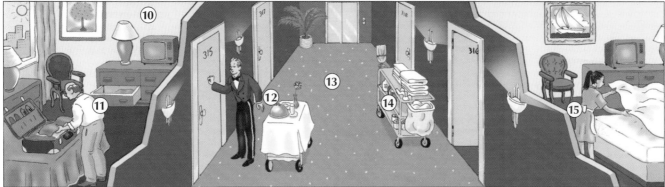

1. valet parking
บริการนำรถไปจอด

2. doorman
พนักงานเปิดประตู

3. lobby
ห้องโถงรับรองแขก

4. bell captain
หัวหน้าพนักงานขนกระเป๋า

5. bellhop
พนักงานขนกระเป๋า

6. luggage cart
รถเข็นกระเป๋า

7. gift shop
ร้านขายของที่ระลึก

8. front desk
โต๊ะบริการส่วนหน้า

9. desk clerk
พนักงานบริการส่วนหน้า

10. guest room
ห้องพักแขก

11. guest
แขกของโรงแรม

12. room service
บริการถึงห้องพัก

13. hall
ทางเดินหน้าห้องพัก

14. housekeeping cart
รถเข็นอุปกรณ์ทำความสะอาด

15. housekeeper
แม่บ้าน

16. pool
สระน้ำ

17. pool service
พนักงานดูแลสระน้ำ

18. ice machine
เครื่องทำน้ำแข็ง

19. meeting room
ห้องประชุม

20. ballroom
ห้องเต้นรำ / จัดงานเลี้ยง

More vocabulary คำศัพท์เพิ่มเติม

concierge: the hotel worker who helps guests find restaurants and interesting places to go

service elevator: an elevator for hotel workers

Share your answers. แลกเปลี่ยนคำตอบ

1. Does this look like a hotel in your city? Which one?

2. Which hotel job is the most difficult?

3. How much does it cost to stay in a hotel in your city?

1. front office
สำนักงานส่วนหน้า

2. factory owner
เจ้าของโรงงาน

3. designer
นักออกแบบ

4. time clock
เครื่องตอกบัตรลงเวลา

5. line supervisor
ผู้ตรวจงาน

6. factory worker
คนงานในโรงงาน

7. parts
อะไหล่

8. assembly line
สายพานประกอบเครื่องในโรงงาน

9. warehouse
โกดัง

10. order puller
คนเข็นของตามใบสั่ง

11. hand truck
รถเข็นของ

12. conveyor belt
สายพานเคลื่อนสินค้า

13. packer
พนักงานบรรจุหีบห่อ

14. forklift
รถยกของ

15. shipping clerk
พนักงานตรวจสอบการส่งของ

16. loading dock
ที่สำหรับขนถ่ายสินค้า

A. design
ออกแบบ

B. manufacture
ผลิต

C. ship
ขนส่ง

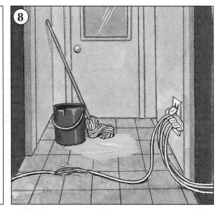

1. electrical hazard
อันตรายเกี่ยวกับไฟฟ้า

2. flammable
ไวไฟ

3. poison
สารพิษ

4. corrosive
เป็นกรด / กัดกร่อน

5. biohazard
เป็นอันตรายต่อสิ่งมีชีวิต

6. radioactive
มีกัมมันตภาพรังสี

7. hazardous materials
วัตถุอันตราย

8. dangerous situation
สถานการณ์ที่เป็นอันตราย

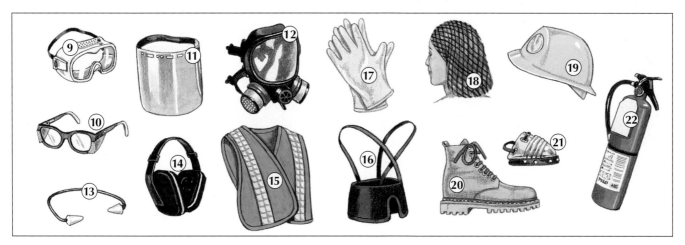

9. safety goggles
แว่นสำหรับกันเศษโลหะเข้าตา

10. safety glasses
แว่นตานิรภัย

11. safety visor
หน้ากากนิรภัย

12. respirator
หน้ากากกรองอากาศ

13. earplugs
ที่อุดหูป้องกันเสียงดัง

14. safety earmuffs
ที่ปิดหูนิรภัย

15. safety vest
เสื้อกั๊กนิรภัย

16. back support
เครื่องพยุงหลัง

17. latex gloves
ถุงมือยาง

18. hair net
ตาข่ายคลุมผม

19. hard hat
หมวกนิรภัย

20. safety boot
รองเท้านิรภัย

21. toe guard
ที่ครอบนิ้วเท้า

22. fire extinguisher
เครื่องดับเพลิง

23. careless สะเพร่า/ประมาท

24. careful ระมัดระวัง/รอบคอบ

Crops พืชผล

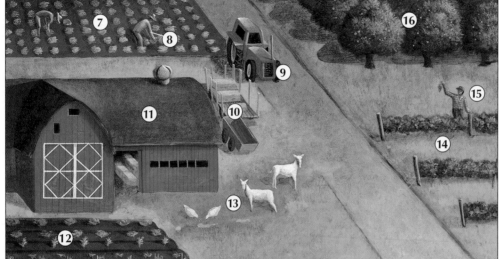

1. rice
ข้าว

2. wheat
ข้าวสาลี

3. soybeans
ถั่วเหลือง

4. corn
ข้าวโพด

5. alfalfa
หญ้าตระกูลถั่วเป็นอาหาร
สัตว์/แอลแฟลฟ่า

6. cotton
ฝ้าย

7. field
ไร่เพาะปลูก

8. farmworker
คนงานในไร่นา

9. tractor
รถแทรกเตอร์

10. farm equipment
เครื่องมือทำการเกษตร

11. barn
ยุ้งฉาง

12. vegetable garden
สวนผัก

13. livestock
ปศุสัตว์

14. vineyard
ไร่องุ่น

15. farmer/grower
ชาวนา / ชาวไร่

16. orchard
สวนผลไม้

17. corral
คอกสัตว์

18. hay
หญ้าแห้งใช้เลี้ยงสัตว์

19. fence
รั้ว

20. hired hand
ลูกจ้าง

21. steers/cattle
วัวควาย

22. rancher
คนเลี้ยงวัว/เจ้าของคอก

A. plant
ปลูกพืช

B. harvest
เก็บเกี่ยว

C. milk
รีดนมวัว

D. feed
ให้อาหาร

1. construction worker
คนงานก่อสร้าง

2. ladder
บันได

3. I beam / girder
คานเหล็กรูปตัว I

4. scaffolding
โครงเหล็กสำหรับนั่งร้าน

5. cherry picker
รถยก

6. bulldozer
รถตีนตะขาบ

7. crane
ปั้นจั่น

8. backhoe
รถตัก

9. jackhammer / pneumatic drill
เครื่องเจาะหิน

10. concrete
คอนกรีต / ปูนซีเมนต์ผสมแล้ว

11. bricks
อิฐ

12. trowel
เกรียงก่อ

13. insulation
แผ่นฉนวนกันความร้อน

14. stucco
ผนังสลัดปูน

15. window pane
บานกระจกหน้าต่าง

16. plywood
ไม้อัด

17. wood / lumber
ไม้ที่เลื่อยเป็นท่อนๆ แล้ว

18. drywall
แผ่นยิบซั่ม / กำแพงที่ยังไม่ฉาบปูน

19. shingles
แผ่นไม้มุงหลังคา

20. pickax
อีเต้อสำหรับขุด

21. shovel
พลั่ว

22. sledgehammer
ค้อนปอนด์

A. **paint**
ทาสี

B. **lay** bricks
ก่ออิฐ

C. **measure**
วัด

D. **hammer**
ตอกตะปู

149

Tools and Building Supplies เครื่องมือและอุปกรณ์ก่อสร้าง

1. hammer ค้อน	**4.** handsaw เลื่อยลันดา	**7.** pliers คีม	**10.** circular saw เลื่อยวงเดือน
2. mallet ตะลุมพุก / ค้อนหัวยาง	**5.** hacksaw เลื่อยตัดเหล็ก	**8.** electric drill สว่านไฟฟ้า	**11.** blade ใบเลื่อยวงเดือน
3. ax ขวาน	**6.** C-clamp ปากกาการูปตัวซี	**9.** power sander เครื่องขัดกระดาษทราย	**12.** router เครื่องเซาะร่อง

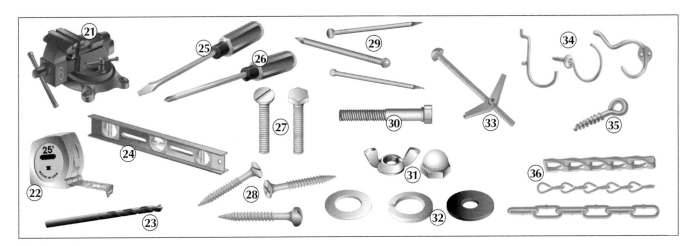

21. vise ปากกาตั้งโต๊ะ	**25.** screwdriver ไขควงปลายแบน	**29.** nail ตะปู	**33.** toggle bolt สลักเกลียวขยาย
22. tape measure ตลับเมตร	**26.** Phillips screwdriver ไขควงปลายแฉก	**30.** bolt สลักเกลียว	**34.** hook ตะขอ
23. drill bit ดอกสว่าน	**27.** machine screw น็อตสำหรับเครื่องจักร	**31.** nut น็อตตัวเมีย	**35.** eye hook ตะปูเกลียวห่วง
24. level ปรอทวัดระดับ	**28.** wood screw ตะปูเกลียวสำหรับไม้	**32.** washer แหวนรองน็อต	**36.** chain โซ่

Use the new language. ใช้ภาษาใหม่

1. Which tools are used for plumbing?

2. Which tools are used for painting?

3. Which tools are used for electrical work?

4. Which tools are used for working with wood?

13. wire
ลวด

14. extension cord
สายไฟต่อให้ยาว/สายไฟพ่วง

15. yardstick
ไม้หลา

16. pipe
ท่อ

17. fittings
ข้อต่อ

18. wood
ไม้

19. spray gun
กระบอกฉีด

20. paint
สี

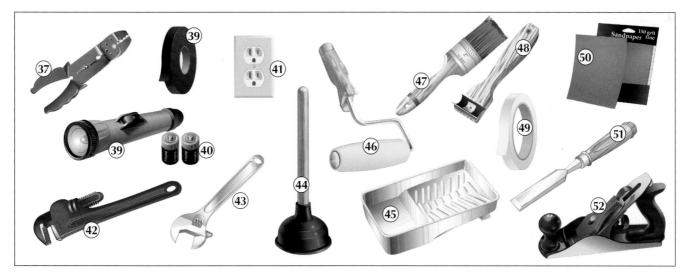

37. wire stripper
คีมปอกสายไฟ

38. electrical tape
เทปพันสายไฟ

39. flashlight
ไฟฉาย

40. battery
แบตเตอรี่/ถ่านไฟฉาย

41. outlet
เต้าเสียบ

42. pipe wrench
ประแจขันท่อ

43. wrench
ประแจเลื่อน

44. plunger
ปั๊มยางสำหรับท่อตัน

45. paint pan
ถาดสี

46. paint roller
ลูกกลิ้งทาสี

47. paintbrush
แปรงทาสี

48. scraper
ไม้ขูดสี

49. masking tape
กระดาษกาว

50. sandpaper
กระดาษทราย

51. chisel
สิ่ว

52. plane
กบไสไม้

Use the new language. ใช้ภาษาใหม่

Look at **Household Problems and Repairs,**
pages **48–49.**

Name the tools you use to fix the problems you see.

Share your answers. แลกเปลี่ยนคำตอบ

1. Which tools do you have in your home?

2. Which tools can be dangerous to use?

1. zoo
   สวนสัตว์

2. animals
   สัตว์

3. zookeeper
   คนดูแลสัตว์

4. botanical gardens
   สวนพฤกษศาสตร์

5. greenhouse
   เรือนเพาะชำ / เรือนกระจก

6. gardener
   คนดูแลสวน

7. art museum
   พิพิธภัณฑ์ศิลปะ

8. painting
   ภาพเขียน

9. sculpture
   ประติมากรรม

10. the movies
    ภาพยนตร์

11. seat
    ที่นั่ง

12. screen
    จอภาพยนตร์

13. amusement park
    สวนสนุก

14. puppet show
    การแสดงหุ่นมือ

15. roller coaster
    รถไฟเหาะตีลังกา

16. carnival
    การเล่นสนุกสนาน

17. rides
    ขี่ม้าหมุน / นั่งชิงช้าสวรรค์

18. game
    เล่มเกม

19. county fair
    งานออกร้านในชนบท

20. first place/first prize
    รางวัลที่ 1

21. exhibition
    นิทรรศการ

22. swap meet/flea market
    ตลาดนัดเล็กๆ

23. booth
    ร้านขายของเป็นล็อคๆ

24. merchandise
    สินค้า

25. baseball game
    การแข่งขันเบสบอล

26. stadium
    สนามกีฬา

27. announcer
    ผู้ประกาศ

Talk about the places you like to go.
พูดเกี่ยวกับสถานที่ที่คุณอยากไป
I like <u>animals</u>, so I go to <u>the zoo</u>.
I like <u>rides</u>, so I go to <u>carnivals</u>.

Share your answers. แลกเปลี่ยนคำตอบ
1. Which of these places is interesting to you?
2. Which rides do you like at an amusement park?
3. What are some famous places to go to in your country?

1. ball field
   สนามเบสบอล

2. bike path
   ทางสำหรับรถจักรยาน

3. cyclist
   คนขี่จักรยาน

4. bicycle/bike
   รถจักรยาน

5. jump rope
   เชือกกระโดด

6. duck pond
   สระเลี้ยงเป็ด

7. tennis court
   สนามเทนนิส

8. picnic table
   โต๊ะปิคนิค

9. tricycle
   รถสามล้อ

10. bench
    ม้านั่งยาว

11. water fountain
    น้ำพุสำหรับดื่ม

12. swings
    ชิงช้า

13. slide
    กระดานลื่น

14. climbing apparatus
    อุปกรณ์ช่วยปีนป่าย

15. sandbox
    บ่อทราย

16. seesaw
    กระดานหก

A. **pull** the wagon
   ลากรถเข็น

B. **push** the swing
   ผลักชิงช้า

C. **climb** on the bars
   ปีนป่ายโครงเหล็ก

D. **picnic/have** a picnic
   รับประทานอาหารกลางแจ้ง

1. camping
การตั้งค่ายพักแรม

2. boating
ขับเรือเล่น

3. canoeing
การพายเรือแคนนู

4. rafting
การล่องแพ / เรือยาง

5. fishing
การตกปลา

6. hiking
การเดินป่า

7. backpacking
ท่องเที่ยวแบบคำไหนนอนนั่น

8. mountain biking
การขี่จักรยานขึ้นเขา

9. horseback riding
การขี่ม้า

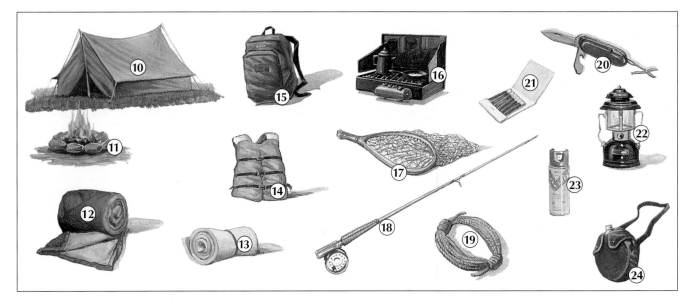

10. tent
กระโจมผ้าใบ / เต็นท์

11. campfire
กองไฟ

12. sleeping bag
ถุงนอน

13. foam pad
แผ่นโฟมสำหรับนอน

14. life vest
เสื้อชูชีพ

15. backpack
กระเป๋าสะพายหลัง

16. camping stove
เตาสำหรับออกค่าย

17. fishing net
สวิงจับปลา

18. fishing pole
คันเบ็ดตกปลา

19. rope
เชือก

20. multi-use knife
มีดพับเอนกประสงค์

21. matches
ไม้ขีดไฟ

22. lantern
ตะเกียงเจ้าพายุ

23. insect repellent
ยาฉีดไล่แมลง

24. canteen
กระติกน้ำ

1. ocean/water
มหาสมุทร / น้ำทะเล

2. fins
ตีนกบ

3. diving mask
หน้ากากดำน้ำ

4. sailboat
เรือใบ

5. surfboard
การดานโต้คลื่น

6. wave
คลื่น

7. wet suit
ชุดดำน้ำ

8. scuba tank
ถังอ๊อกซิเจน

9. beach umbrella
ร่มชายหาด

10. sand castle
ปราสาททราย

11. cooler
ถังน้ำแข็ง

12. shade
ร่มเงา

13. sunscreen/sunblock
ครีมกันแดด

14. beach chair
เก้าอี้ชายหาด

15. beach towel
ผ้าปูนอนบนชายหาด

16. pier
ท่าเรือ

17. sunbather
คนอาบแดด

18. lifeguard
ผู้ดูแลความปลอดภัย

19. lifesaving device
อุปกรณ์ช่วยชีวิต

20. lifeguard station
ที่ตั้งหน่วยรักษาความปลอดภัย

21. seashell
เปลือกหอยทะเล

22. pail/bucket
ถังน้ำ

23. sand
ทราย

24. rock
หิน

More vocabulary คำศัพท์เพิ่มเติม

seaweed: a plant that grows in the ocean

tide: the level of the ocean. The tide goes in and out every twelve hours.

Share your answers. แลกเปลี่ยนคำตอบ

1. Are there any beaches near your home?

2. Do you prefer to spend more time on the sand or in the water?

3. Where are some of the world's best beaches?

A. **walk**	E. **catch**	I. **shoot**	M. **tackle**
เดิน	รับ	ยิง	กระโดดจับคนถือบอล
B. **jog**	F. **pitch**	J. **jump**	
วิ่งเหยาะๆ	ขว้าง	กระโดด	
C. **run**	G. **hit**	K. **dribble / bounce**	
วิ่ง	ตี	เลี้ยงลูกบอล	
D. **throw**	H. **pass**	L. **kick**	
โยน	ส่ง	เตะ	

Practice talking about what you can do.

พูดเกี่ยวกับสิ่งที่คุณทำได้
I can <u>swim</u>, but I can't <u>dive</u>.
I can <u>pass the ball</u> well, but I can't <u>shoot</u> too well.

Use the new language. ใช้ภาษาใหม่
Look at **Individual Sports,** page **159.**
Name the actions you see people doing.
The man in number 18 is riding a horse.

N. **serve**
ส่งลูก

O. **swing**
ตีลูกวงกว้าง

P. **exercise / work out**
ออกกำลังกาย

Q. **stretch**
ยืด

R. **bend**
ก้ม

S. **dive**
ดำน้ำ/กระโดดน้ำ

T. **swim**
ว่ายน้ำ

U. **ski**
เล่นสกี

V. **skate**
เล่นสเก็ต

W. **ride**
ขี่

X. **start**
เริ่ม

Y. **race**
วิ่งแข่ง

Z. **finish**
เข้าเส้นชัย

Share your answers. แลกเปลี่ยนคำตอบ

1. What do you like to do?

2. What do you have difficulty doing?

3. How often do you exercise? Once a week? Two or three times a week? More? Never?

4. Which is more difficult, throwing a ball or catching it?

Team Sports กีฬาประเภททีม

1. score
คะแนน

2. coach
ผู้ฝึกสอน

3. team
ทีม

4. fan
ผู้ชม

5. player
ผู้เล่น

6. official / referee
ผู้ตัดสิน

7. basketball court
สนามบาสเก็ตบอล

8. basketball
บาสเก็ตบอล

9. baseball
เบสบอล

10. softball
ซอฟต์บอล

11. football
อเมริกันฟุตบอล

12. soccer
ฟุตบอล / ช้อคเกอร์

13. ice hockey
ฮอกกี้น้ำแข็ง

14. volleyball
วอลเลย์บอล

15. water polo
โปโลน้ำ

More vocabulary คำศัพท์เพิ่มเติม

captain: the team leader

umpire: in baseball, the name for the referee

Little League: a baseball league for children

win: to have the best score

lose: the opposite of win

tie: to have the same score as the other team

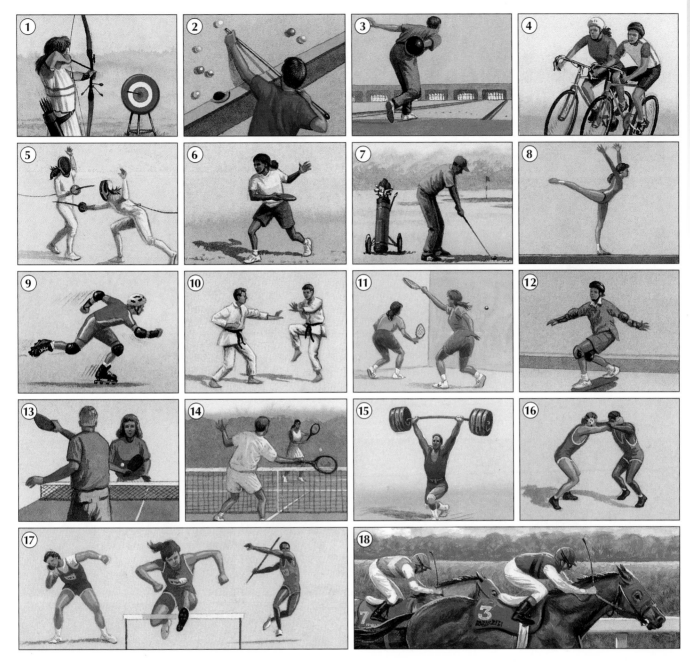

1. archery
ยิงธนู

2. billiards/pool
บิลเลียด

3. bowling
โบว์ลิ่ง

4. cycling/biking
การขี่จักรยาน

5. fencing
ฟันดาบ

6. flying disc*
ร่อนจาน / ฟริสบี้

7. golf
กอล์ฟ

8. gymnastics
ยิมนาสติก

9. inline skating
สเก็ตความเร็ว

10. martial arts
ศิลปะการต่อสู้

11. racquetball
แร็คเก็ตบอล

12. skateboarding
การเล่นสเก็ตบอร์ด

13. table tennis/
Ping-Pong™
ปิงปอง

14. tennis
เทนนิส

15. weightlifting
ยกน้ำหนัก

16. wrestling
มวยปล้ำ

17. track and field
กรีฑา / ลู่และลาน

18. horse racing
การแข่งม้า

*Note: one brand is Frisbee®
(Mattel, Inc.)

Talk about sports. พูดเกี่ยวกับกีฬา

Which sports do you like?

I like <u>tennis</u> but I don't like <u>golf</u>.

Share your answers. แลกเปลี่ยนคำตอบ

1. Which sports are good for children to learn? Why?

2. Which sport is the most difficult to learn? Why?

3. Which sport is the most dangerous? Why?

1. downhill skiing
การเล่นสกีลงจากเนินเขา

2. snowboarding
การเล่นกระดานหิมะ

3. cross-country skiing
การเล่นสกีทางไกล

4. ice skating
การเล่นสเก็ตน้ำแข็ง

5. figure skating
การเล่นสเก็ตลีลา

6. sledding
การเล่นเลื่อนบนหิมะ

7. waterskiing
การเล่นสกีน้ำ

8. sailing
การเล่นเรือใบ

9. surfing
การเล่นกระดานโต้คลื่น

10. sailboarding
การเล่นกระดานโต้ลม

11. snorkeling
การดำน้ำที่มีท่อต่อหายใจ

12. scuba diving
การดำน้ำโดยมีอุปกรณ์ช่วยการหายใจ

Use the new language. ใช้ภาษาใหม่

Look at **The Beach,** page **155.**

Name the sports you see.

Share your answers. แลกเปลี่ยนคำตอบ

1. Which sports are in the Winter Olympics?

2. Which sports do you think are the most exciting to watch?

1. golf club
ไม้กอล์ฟ

2. tennis racket
ไม้เทนนิส

3. volleyball
ลูกวอลเลย์บอล

4. basketball
ลูกบาสเกตบอล

5. bowling ball
ลูกโบว์ลิ่ง

6. bow
คันธนู

7. arrow
ลูกธนู/ลูกศร

8. target
เป้า

9. ice skates
รองเท้าสเก็ตน้ำแข็ง

10. inline skates
รองเท้าสเก็ต

11. hockey stick
ไม้ฮ็อกกี้

12. soccer ball
ลูกฟุตบอล

13. shin guards
สนับแข้ง

14. baseball bat
ไม้เบสบอล

15. catcher's mask
หน้ากากแคชเชอร์

16. uniform
ชุดกีฬา

17. glove
ถุงมือ

18. baseball
ลูกเบสบอล

19. weights
ลูกตุ้มยกน้ำหนัก

20. football helmet
หมวกสวมเล่นอเมริกันฟุตบอล

21. shoulder pads
เครื่องป้องกันไหล่ใน
กีฬาอเมริกันฟุตบอล

22. football
ลูกฟุตบอล (อเมริกันฟุตบอล)

23. snowboard
กระดานเล่นหิมะ

24. skis
สกี

25. ski poles
ไม้ค้ำเล่นสกี

26. ski boots
รองเท้าสกี

27. flying disc*
จานร่อน / ฟริสบี้

*Note: one brand is Frisbee®
(Mattel, Inc.)

Share your answers. แลกเปลี่ยนคำตอบ

1. Which sports equipment is used for safety reasons?

2. Which sports equipment is heavy?

3. What sports equipment do you have at home?

Use the new language. ใช้ภาษาใหม่

Look at **Individual Sports**, page **159**.

Name the sports equipment you see.

A. collect things
สะสมสิ่งของ

B. play games
เล่นเกมส์

C. build models
ประกอบแบบจำลอง

D. do crafts
ทำงานฝีมือ

1. video game system
ชุดเครื่องเล่นวีดีโอเกม

2. cartridge
ตลับวีดีโอเกมส์

3. board game
กระดานเล่นเกม

4. dice
ลูกเต๋า

5. checkers
กระดานหมากฮอส

6. chess
หมากรุก

7. model kit
ชุดแบบจำลอง

8. glue
กาว

9. acrylic paint
สีอาครีลิค

10. figurine
หุ่นประดับเล็กๆ

11. baseball card
บัตรดาราเบสบอล

12. stamp collection
การสะสมแสตมป์

13. coin collection
การสะสมเหรียญ

14. clay
ดินเหนียว

15. doll making kit
ชุดเครื่องมือทำตุ๊กตา

16. woodworking kit
ชุดเครื่องมือในการทำงานไม้

Talk about how much time you spend on your hobbies.
พูดเกี่ยวกับการใช้เวลาในงานอดิเรกของคุณ

I _do crafts_ all the time.

I _play chess_ sometimes.

I never _build models_.

Share your answers. แลกเปลี่ยนคำตอบ

1. How often do you play video games? Often?
Sometimes? Never?

2. What board games do you know?

3. Do you collect anything? What?

E. paint
ระบายสี

F. knit
ถักไหมพรม

G. pretend
เล่นบทบาทสมมุติ

H. play cards
เล่นไพ่

17. yarn
ด้าย / ไหมพรม

18. knitting needles
เข็มถักไหมพรม

19. embroidery
การเย็บปักถักร้อย

20. crochet
การถักโครเชท์

21. easel
ขาตั้งภาพ

22. canvas
ผ้าที่ใช้เขียนภาพสีน้ำมัน

23. paintbrush
พู่กัน

24. oil paint
สีน้ำมัน

25. watercolor
สีน้ำ

26. clubs
ดอกจิก

27. diamonds
ข้าวหลามตัด

28. spades
โพดำ

29. hearts
โพแดง

30. paper doll
ตุ๊กตากระดาษ

31. action figure
หุ่นยนต์

32. model trains
รถไฟจำลอง

Share your answers. แลกเปลี่ยนคำตอบ

1. Do you like to play cards? Which games?

2. Did you pretend a lot when you were a child? What did you pretend to be?

3. Is it important to have hobbies? Why or why not?

4. What's your favorite game?

5. What's your hobby?

1. clock radio
   วิทยุนาฬิกา

2. portable radio-cassette player
   เครื่องเล่นวิทยุเทปกระเป๋าหิ้ว

3. cassette recorder
   เครื่องบันทึกเทป

4. microphone
   ไมโครโฟน

5. shortwave radio
   วิทยุคลื่นสั้น

6. TV (television)
   โทรทัศน์

7. portable TV
   โทรทัศน์กระเป๋าหิ้ว

8. VCR (videocassette recorder)
   เครื่องบันทึก / เล่นวีดีโอเทป

9. remote control
   เครื่องควบคุมระยะไกล / รีโมท

10. videocassette
    วีดีโอเทป

11. speakers
    ลำโพง

12. turntable
    เครื่องเล่นแผ่นเสียง

13. tuner
    เครื่องรับวิทยุ

14. CD player
    เครื่องเล่นซีดี

15. personal radio-cassette player
    เครื่องเล่นวิทยุเทปแบบพกพา

16. headphones
    หูฟัง

17. adapter
    เครื่องแปลงไฟฟ้า

18. plug
    ปลั๊ก

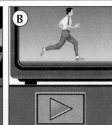
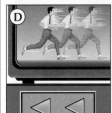
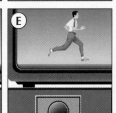
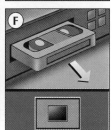

19. video camera
กล้องถ่ายวีดีโอ

20. tripod
ขาตั้งกล้อง

21. camcorder
กล้องถ่ายวีดีโอมือถือ

22. battery pack
ตลับใส่แบตเตอรี่

23. battery charger
เครื่องชาร์จแบตเตอรี่

24. 35 mm camera
กล้องถ่ายรูปขนาด 35 มม.

25. zoom lens
เลนส์ซูม

26. film
ฟิล์มถ่ายรูป

27. camera case
กระเป๋าใส่กล้องถ่ายรูป

28. screen
จอรับภาพ

29. carousel slide projector
เครื่องฉายสไลด์

30. slide tray
ถาดใส่แผ่นสไลด์

31. slides
แผ่นสไลด์

32. photo album
สมุดเก็บภาพถ่าย

33. out of focus
ภาพไม่ได้โฟกัส

34. overexposed
แสงสว่างมากไป

35. underexposed
แสงน้อยไป

A. **record**
บันทึกภาพ

B. **play**
เล่น / เปิดดูภาพ

C. **fast forward**
กรอขึ้นหน้า

D. **rewind**
กรอถอยหลัง

E. **pause**
หยุดชั่วคราว

F. **stop** and **eject**
หยุดและเอาเทปออก

Types of entertainment ประเภทของความบันเทิง

1. film/movie
ภาพยนตร์

2. play
ละคร

3. television program
รายการโทรทัศน์

4. radio program
รายการวิทยุ

5. stand-up comedy
การแสดงตลก

6. concert
การแสดงดนตรี

7. ballet
การแสดงบัลเล่ท์

8. opera
การแสดงอุปรากร

Types of stories ประเภทของเรื่อง

9. western
แนวตะวันตก / คาวบอย

10. comedy
แนวตลก

11. tragedy
โศกนาฏกรรม

12. science fiction story
แนววิทยาศาสตร์

13. action story/
adventure story
ตื่นเต้น / ผจญภัย

14. horror story
เรื่องสยองขวัญ

15. mystery
เรื่องลึกลับ

16. romance
แนวรักหวานซึ้ง

Types of TV programs ประเภทของรายการโทรทัศน์

17. news
ข่าว

18. sitcom (situation comedy)
ตลกที่เป็นเรื่องราว

19. cartoon
การ์ตูน

20. talk show
รายการพูดคุยสนทนา

21. soap opera
ละครสำหรับแม่บ้าน

22. nature program
รายการเกี่ยวกับธรรมชาติ

23. game show/quiz show
รายการเกมโชว์ / ทายปัญหา

24. children's program
รายการสำหรับเด็ก

25. shopping program
รายการขายสินค้า

26. serious book
หนังสือที่อ่านเป็นจริงเป็นจัง

27. funny book
หนังสือตลก

28. sad book
หนังสือเรื่องเศร้า

29. boring book
หนังสือที่น่าเบื่อ

30. interesting book
หนังสือที่น่าสนใจ

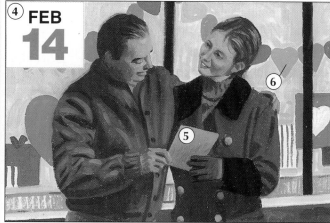

1. New Year's Day
วันขึ้นปีใหม่

2. parade
ขบวนพาเหรด

3. confetti
กระดาษสีโปรยในงาน

4. Valentine's Day
วันแห่งความรัก

5. card
บัตรอวยพร

6. heart
รูปหัวใจ

7. Independence Day / 4th of July
วันชาติ / วันประกาศอิสรภาพของ
สหรัฐอเมริกา

8. fireworks
พลุไฟ

9. flag
ธงชาติ

10. Halloween
วันปล่อยผี

11. jack-o'-lantern
โคมไฟทำด้วยฟักทอง

12. mask
หน้ากาก

13. costume
เสื้อผ้าเฉพาะงานเทศกาล

14. candy
ลูกวาด

15. Thanksgiving
วันเลี้ยงขอบคุณพระเจ้า

16. feast
งานเลี้ยง

17. turkey
ไก่งวง

18. Christmas
วันคริสต์มาส

19. ornament
เครื่องประดับ

20. Christmas tree
ต้นคริสต์มาส

A. **plan** a party
วางแผนจัดงานเลี้ยง

B. **invite** the guests
เชิญแขก

C. **decorate** the house
ตกแต่งบ้าน

D. **wrap** a gift
ห่อของขวัญ

E. **hide**
แอบ

F. **answer** the door
เปิดประตูรับ

G. **shout** "surprise!"
ตะโกนว่า "เซอไพรช์"

H. **light** the candles
จุดเทียน

I. **sing** "Happy Birthday"
ร้องเพลงสุขสันต์วันเกิด

J. **make** a wish
อธิษฐาน

K. **blow out** the candles
เป่าเทียน

L. **open** the presents
เปิดกล่องของขวัญ

Practice inviting friends to a party.
ฝึกการเชิญเพื่อนมางานเลี้ยง

I'd love for you to come to my party <u>next week</u>.
Could <u>you and your friend</u> come to my party?
Would <u>your friend</u> like to come to a party I'm giving?

Share your answers. แลกเปลี่ยนคำตอบ

1. Do you celebrate birthdays? What do you do?

2. Are there birthdays you celebrate in a special way?

3. Is there a special birthday song in your country?

Verb Guide

กริยาในภาษาอังกฤษจะเป็นแบบ Regular หรือ irregular เมื่อเป็น past tense และ past participle

Regular Verbs

กริยาต่อไปนี้จะมีเลข 1, 2, 3, หรือ 4 กำกับอยู่ท้ายคำตามลักษณะของการสะกดที่แตกต่างกัน

แบบแผนของการสะกดคำ		*ตัวอย่าง*		
1. Add **-ed** to the end of the verb.		ASK	→	**ASKED** เติม ED
2. Add **-d** to the end of the verb.		LIVE	→	**LIVED** เติม D
3. Double the final consonant and add **-ed** to the end of the verb.		DROP	→	**DROPPED** เพิ่มตัวสะกดตัวท้ายอีกหนึ่งตัว
4. Drop the final y and add **-ied** to the end of the verb.		CRY	→	**CRIED** ตัด Y แล้วเติม IED

The Oxford Picture Dictionary List of Regular Verbs
คำกริยาชนิด Regular ที่พบในพจนานุกรมเล่มนี้

act (1) แสดง
add (1) บวก, เติม
address (1) จ่าหน้าซอง
answer (1) ตอบ
apologize (2) ขอโทษ
appear (1) ปรากฏตัว
applaud (1) ปรบมือ
arrange (2) จัด
arrest (1) จับกุม
arrive (2) มาถึง
ask (1) สอบถาม
assemble (2) ประกอบ
assist (1) ช่วย
bake (2) อบ
barbecue (2) ย่าง, ปิ้ง
bathe (2) อาบน้ำ
board (1) ขึ้นเครื่อง
boil (1) ต้ม
borrow (1) ขอยืม
bounce (2) ทำให้เด้ง
brainstorm (1) ระดมพลังสมอง
breathe (2) หายใจ
broil (1) ย่าง, ปิ้ง
brush (1) แปรง
burn (1) เผา
call (1) เรียกโทรศัพท์
carry (4) ถือ, แบก
change (2) ทอนเงิน, เปลี่ยน
check (1) ตรวจตรา
choke (2) สำลัก, ติดคอ
chop (3) หั่น, สับ
circle (2) ทำวงกลม
claim (1) รับของ, รับกระเป๋า
clap (3) ปรบมือ
clean (1) ทำความสะอาด
clear (1) ทำให้โล่ง
climb (1) ปีนป่าย
close (2) ปิด
collate (2) ตรวจทาน

collect (1) สะสม
color (1) ระบายสี
comb (1) หวีผม
commit (3) กระทำ, ก่อการ
compliment (1) ชมเชย
conserve (2) อนุรักษ์
convert (1) แปลง, กลับไปมา
cook (1) ปรุงอาหาร
copy (4) คัดลอก
correct (1) แก้ไข
cough (1) ไอ
count (1) นับ
cross (1) ข้าม
cry (4) ร้องไห้
dance (2) เต้นรำ
design (1) ออกแบบ
deposit (1) ฝาก
deliver (1) ส่ง
dial (1) หมุนเลขโทรศัพท์
dictate (2) บอกให้เขียนตาม
die (2) ตาย
discuss (1) อภิปราย
dive (2) กระโดดน้ำ
dress (1) แต่งตัว
dribble (2) ไหลริน
drill (1) เจาะ, ฝึกฝน
drop (3) หยด-ทำตก
drown (1) จมน้ำ
dry (4) ทำให้แห้ง
dust (1) ปัดฝุ่น
dye (2) ย้อมสี
edit (1) แก้ไข, ตัดต่อ
eject (1) เด้งออกมา, ไล่ออกไป
empty (4) ทำให้ว่าง
end (1) จบลง, ลงเอย
enter (1) เข้า, เข้าร่วม
erase (2) ลบออก
examine (2) ตรวจ, พิจารณา
exchange (2) แลกเปลี่ยน

exercise (2) ออกกำลัง, ฝึกหัด
experience (2) ประสบ
exterminate (2) ทำลายล้าง
fasten (1) ผูกเชือก
fax (1) ส่งโทรสาร
file (2) เดินเรียงแถว, เก็บเอกสาร
fill (1) เติม, บรรจุ
finish (1) ทำเสร็จ
fix (1) ยึดติด, ซ่อม
floss (1) ขัดฟัน
fold (1) พับ, ปิด
fry (4) ทอด, ผัด
gargle (2) กลั้วคอ
graduate (2) สำเร็จการศึกษา
grate (2) ขูด, บดให้ละเอียด
grease (2) ทาน้ำมันหล่อลื่น
greet (1) ทักทาย
grill (1) ย่าง, ปิ้ง
hail (1) โห่ร้องอวยชัย
hammer (1) ตอกตะปู
harvest (1) เก็บเกี่ยว
help (1) ช่วยเหลือ
hire (2) จ้าง, ว่าจ้าง, ให้เช่า
hug (3) กอด, รัด
immigrate (2) อพยพ
inquire (2) ไต่ถาม, สอบถาม
insert (1) ใส่เข้า, สอด
introduce (2) แนะนำ
invite (2) เชื้อเชิญ
iron (1) รีดผ้า
jog (3) วิ่งเหยาะๆ
join (1) เชื่อม, ร่วมกัน
jump (1) กระโดด
kick (1) เตะ
kiss (1) จูบ, จุมพิต
knit (3) ถัก, ชุน
land (1) ขึ้นบก, เครื่องลงจอด
laugh (1) หัวเราะ
learn (1) เรียน, ศึกษา

lengthen (1) ทำให้ยาวขึ้น
listen (1) ฟัง, ตั้งใจฟัง
live (2) อยู่, อาศัย
load (1) บรรทุก
lock (1) ใส่กุญแจ, ปิดประตู
look (1) ดู, มอง
mail (1) ส่งทางไปรษณีย์
manufacture (2) ผลิต, สร้าง
mark (1) ทำเครื่องหมาย
match (1) จับคู่, เข้าคู่
measure (2) วัด, หาค่า
milk (1) รีดนม
miss (1) พลาด, พลาดโอกาส
mix (1) ผสม, ปนกัน
mop (3) ถูพื้นด้วยไม้ถูพื้น
move (2) เคลื่อนที่
mow (1) ตัดหญ้า
need (1) มีความจำเป็น
nurse (2) ดูแล, รักษา
obey (1) เชื่อฟัง
observe (2) สังเกต, คอยดู
open (1) เปิด
operate (2) ทำงาน, ปฏิบัติการ
order (1) ออกคำสั่ง, สั่งซื้อ
overdose (2) กินยาเกินขนาด
paint (1) ทาสี
park (1) จอดรถ
pass (1) ผ่าน, แซง
pause (2) หยุดชั่วคราว
peel (1) ปอกเปลือก
perm (1) ดัดผม
pick (1) หยิบ, จับ, เลือก
pitch (1) ขว้าง, โยน
plan (3) วางแผน
plant (1) ปลูก, เพาะปลูก
play (1) เล่น, ล้อเล่น
point (1) ชี้, ชี้ประเด็น
polish (1) ขัดให้เป็นเงาวาว
pour (1) ริน, ราด, หลั่ง
pretend (1) แสร้งทำ, เสแสร้ง
print (1) พิมพ์, อัดรูป
protect (1) ป้องกัน, พิทักษ์

pull (1) ดึง, ลาก, จูง
push (1) ผลัก, ดัน
race (2) แข่งขัน, แข่งม้า
raise (2) ยกขึ้น, เลื่อนขึ้น
rake (2) คราด, กวาด
receive (2) รับ, ต้อนรับ
record (1) บันทึก
recycle (2) นำกลับมาใช้ใหม่
register (1) บันทึก, ลงทะเบียน
relax (1) ผ่อนคลาย
remove (2) เอาออก, ปลดเปลื้อง
rent (1) ให้เช่า
repair (1) ซ่อมแซม, แก้ไข
repeat (1) ทำซ้ำ
report (1) รายงาน
request (1) ขอร้อง, เรียกร้อง
return (1) กลับคืน, ส่งคืน
rinse (2) ล้าง, ชะล้าง
roast (1) ย่าง, ปิ้ง, อบ
rock (1) โยก, เขย่า
sauté (2)
save (2) ช่วยเหลือ, ช่วย
scrub (3) ถู, ขัด
seat (1) นั่ง
sentence (2) ตัดสิน, พิพากษา
serve (2) บริการ, รับใช้
share (2) แบ่ง, แบ่งสรร, มีส่วนร่วม
shave (2) โกน, โกนด้วยมีดโกน
ship (3) เอาขึ้นเรือ, ขนส่งทางเรือ
shop (3) เดินดูหรือซื้อสินค้าตามร้าน
shorten (1) ทำให้สั้น, สั้นลง, เตี้ยลง
shout (1) ร้องตะโกน, ร้องเรียก
sign (1) ลงนาม, เซ็นชื่อ
simmer (1) เคี่ยว, ตุ๋น
skate (2) เล่นสเก็ต
ski (1) เล่นสกี
slice (2) เฉือน, แล่เป็นแผ่นบาง ๆ
smell (1) ดมกลิ่น, ได้กลิ่น
sneeze (2) จาม
sort (1) แยกประเภท
spell (1) สะกด
staple (2) เย็บด้วยลวดรูปตัวยู

start (1) เริ่มต้น, ลงมือทำ
stay (1) อยู่, พักอยู่
steam (1) นึ่ง, อบด้วยไอน้ำ
stir (3) กวน, คน
stir-fry (4) ผัด
stop (3) หยุด
stow (1) เก็บรักษา
stretch (1) ขึง, ยืดออก
supervise (2) ดูแล, ควบคุม
swallow (1) กลืน
tackle (2) รับมือ, เล่นงาน
talk (1) พูด, สนทนา
taste (2) ชิมรส
thank (1) ขอบคุณ, ขอบใจ
tie (2) ผูก, มัด
touch (1) สัมผัส, แตะ
transcribe (2) คัดลอก, ถอดความ
transfer (3) ย้าย, โอน , โยกย้าย
travel (1) เดินทาง
trim (3) เล็ม, ตัดแต่ง
turn (1) หัน, เลี้ยว
type (2) พิมพ์ดีด
underline (2) ขีดเส้นใต้
unload (1) เอาลง, ขนลง
unpack (1) แก้ห่อ, เอาออกจากห่อ
use (2) ใช้, ใช้ประโยชน์
vacuum (1) ใช้เครื่องดูดฝุ่น
vomit (1) อาเจียน
vote (2) ออกเสียง, ลงคะแนนเสียง
wait (1) คอย, รับใช้
walk (1) เดิน
wash (1) ล้าง, ซัก
watch (1) เฝ้าดู, ชม
water (1) พรมด้วยน้ำ, รดน้ำต้นไม้
weed (1) ถอนวัชพืชทิ้ง
weigh (1) ชั่งน้ำหนัก
wipe (2) เช็ด, ถู
work (1) ทำงาน
wrap (3) ห่อ
yield (1) ให้ผล, ผลิต

Verb Guide

Irregular Verbs

กริยาเหล่านี้เรียกว่า Irregular มีการเปลี่ยนแปลงเมื่อเป็น Past หรือ Past Participle

The Oxford Picture Dictionary List of Irregular Verbs

simple	past	past participle		simple	past	past participle	
be	was	been	เป็น, อยู่, คือ	leave	left	left	ออกจาก, ละทิ้ง
beat	beat	beaten	ตี	lend	lent	lent	ให้ยืม
become	became	become	กลายเป็น	let	let	let	ปล่อย
begin	began	begun	เริ่มต้น	light	lit	lit	จุดไฟ
bend	bent	bent	ก้ม, งอ	make	made	made	ทำ
bleed	bled	bled	เลือดออก	pay	paid	paid	จ่ายเงิน
blow	blew	blown	เป่า, พัด	picnic	picnicked	picnicked	ไปปิคนิค
break	broke	broken	แตก, หัก	put	put	put	ใส่, วาง
build	built	built	สร้าง	read	read	read	อ่าน
buy	bought	bought	ซื้อ	rewind	rewound	rewound	หมุนกลับ
catch	caught	caught	จับ	rewrite	rewrote	rewritten	เขียนใหม่
come	came	come	มา	ride	rode	ridden	ขี่
cut	cut	cut	ตัด	run	ran	run	วิ่ง
do	did	done	ทำ	say	said	said	พูด, กล่าว
draw	drew	drawn	วาด	see	saw	seen	เห็น
drink	drank	drunk	ดื่ม	sell	sold	sold	ขาย
drive	drove	driven	ขับรถ	send	sent	sent	ส่ง
eat	ate	eaten	กิน	set	set	set	จัด, ตะวันตกดิน
fall	fell	fallen	ล้ม, หล่น	sew	sewed	sewn	เย็บผ้า
feed	fed	fed	ให้อาหาร	shoot	shot	shot	ยิง
feel	felt	felt	รู้สึก	sing	sang	sung	ร้องเพลง
find	found	found	พบ	sit	sat	sat	นั่ง
fly	flew	flown	บิน	speak	spoke	spoken	พูด
get	got	gotten	เอา, ได้รับ	stand	stood	stood	ยืน
give	gave	given	ให้	sweep	swept	swept	กวาด
go	went	gone	ไป	swim	swam	swum	ว่ายน้ำ
hang	hung	hung	แขวน	swing	swung	swung	แกว่ง, โล้ชิงช้า
have	had	had	มี	take	took	taken	เอา, หยิบ
hear	heard	heard	ได้ยิน	teach	taught	taught	สอน
hide	hid	hidden	ซ่อน, แอบ	throw	threw	thrown	ขว้าง
hit	hit	hit	ตี	wake	woke	woken	ตื่น
hold	held	held	ถือ	wear	wore	worn	สวมใส่
keep	kept	kept	เก็บ	withdraw	withdrew	withdrawn	ถอน
lay	laid	laid	วางไข่	write	wrote	written	เขียน

Index (ดัชนี)

คำต่างๆ ที่อยู่ในดัชนีจะมีเลขอยู่ 2 ตัวข้างท้ายคำ เลขตัวแรกหมายถึงเลขหน้าของหนังสือที่มีคำนั้นๆ ปรากฏอยู่ ส่วนเลขตัวที่สองหมายถึง คำนั้นๆ โดยเฉพาะที่อยู่ในหน้านั้น ตัวอย่างเช่นคำว่า Cool [kōōl] 10-3 หมายความว่า คำว่า Cool เป็นคำที่ 3 ปรากฏอยู่ในหน้าที่10 ถ้าคำนั้น มีแต่ตัวเลขพิมพ์**ด้วยตัวหนา**บอกหน้าเท่านั้นแสดงว่า คำนั้นเป็นส่วนหนึ่งของหัวเรื่องหรือหัวเรื่องย่อยหรือมิฉะนั้นก็พบที่ใดที่หนึ่งในหน้านั้น ส่วนตัวเลขพิมพ์ตัวหนา **(bold)** และตามด้วยเครื่องหมาย ◆ แสดงว่าคำนั้นสามารถหาพบได้ในแบบฝึกหัดที่อยู่ข้างล่างของหน้านั้นๆ

คำหรือกลุ่มคำที่พิมพ์ด้วยตัวหนาจะเป็นรูปกริยา (Verbs) หรือกริยาวลี (Verb phrases) คำที่ใช้เป็นอย่างอื่นนอกจากคำกริยา จะ พิมพ์ด้วยตัวอักษรธรรมดา ตัวอย่างเช่นคำว่า file (ตัวหนา) คือใช้เป็นคำกริยา "file" ในขณะที่คำว่า "file" (ตัวพิมพ์ธรรมดา) จะใช้เป็นคำนาม (noun) ส่วนคำหรือวลีที่พิมพ์ด้วยตัวพิมพ์ใหญ่เช่น คำว่า HOLIDAYS จะใช้เป็นหัวเรื่องของบทนั้นๆ

วลีหรือคำอื่นๆ ที่นำมาร่วมใช้คู่กับคำหลักจะถูกนำไปบรรจุเอาไว้ใต้คำหลักนั้นๆ แทนที่จะเขียนคำหลักซ้ำๆ เวลาปรากฏแต่ละครั้งและแทน คำหลักคำนั้นด้วยจุดสามจุด (...) ตัวอย่างเช่นภายใต้คำว่า bus ท่านจะพบคำว่า ...driver และ ...stop นั่นหมายถึง bus driver และ bus stop ภายใต้คำว่า store จะพบคำว่า shoe... และ toy... หมายความถึง shoe store และ toy store

Pronunciation Guide (ข้อแนะนำการออกเสียง)

ดัชนีรวมถึงข้อแนะนำในการออกเสียงของคำทุกคำและทุกวลีที่มีอยู่ในหนังสือเล่มนี้ สัญลักษณ์ที่ใช้ในการแทนเสียงจะพบในพจนานุกรม สำหรับคนเจ้าของภาษาทั่วไป สัญลักษณ์ที่ใช้จะไม่เหมือนของระบบการออกเสียงของ International Phonetic Alphabet เพราะว่าเราจะใช้การ สะกดแบบใช้ตัวอักษร ภาษาอังกฤษช่วยการออกเสียงและจะช่วยให้ท่านมีความตระหนักถึงความสัมพันธ์ระหว่างภาษาเขียนและภาษาพูด

Consonants (พยัญชนะ)

[b] as in back [băk]	[k] as in key [kē]	[sh] as in shoe [shōō]
[ch] as in cheek [chēk]	[l] as in leaf [lēf]	[t] as in tape [tāp]
[d] as in date [dāt]	[m] as in match [măch]	[th] as in three [thrē]
[dh] as in this [dhĭs]	[n] as in neck [nĕk]	[v] as in vine [vīn]
[f] as in face [fās]	[ng] as in ring [rĭng]	[w] as in wait [wāt]
[g] as in gas [găs]	[p] as in park [pärk]	[y] as in yams [yămz]
[h] as in half [hăf]	[r] as in rice [rīs]	[z] as in zoo [zōō]
[j] as in jam [jăm]	[s] as in sand [sănd]	[zh] as in measure [mĕzh/ər]

Vowels (สระ)

[ā] as in bake [bāk]	[ĭ] as in lip [lĭp]	[ow] as in cow [kow]
[ă] as in back [băk]	[ï] as in near [nïr]	[oy] as in boy [boy]
[ä] as in car [kär] or box [bäks]	[ō] as in cold [kōld]	[ŭ] as in cut [kŭt]
[ē] as in beat [bēt]	[ö] as in short [shört]	[ü] as in curb [kürb]
[ĕ] as in bed [bĕd]	or claw [klö]	[ə] as in above [ə bŭv/]
[ë] as in bear [bër]	[ōō] as in cool [kōōl]	
[ī] as in line [līn]	[ŏŏ] as in cook [kŏŏk]	

สัญลักษณ์ที่ใช้ในการออกเสียงนั้นใช้ตัวอักษรภาษาอังกฤษทั้งหมด ยกเว้น schwa [ə] เสียง schwa เป็นเสียงสระในภาษาอังกฤษที่ใช้มาก ที่สุด ถ้าท่านใช้เสียง schwa อย่างถูกต้องและเหมาะสมในพยางค์ที่ไม่ได้รับน้ำหนัก (unstressed syllables) การออกเสียงของท่านจะฟังเป็น ธรรมชาติ

สระที่อยู่หน้าเสียง [r] จะมีเครื่องหมาย [¨] เพื่อให้ทราบถึงคุณสมบัติพิเศษที่เสียงสระนั้นเป็นอย่างไร เมื่ออยู่หน้าเสียง [r] (โปรดสังเกตว่า สัญลักษณ์ [ä] และ [ö] ใช้เป็นเสียงสระที่ไม่ตามด้วยเสียง [r] เช่นคำว่า box หรือ claw ท่านควรฟังคนที่เป็นเจ้าของภาษาเขาพูดจะทำให้ท่าน ทราบว่าเสียงสระที่ถูกต้องมีเสียงเป็นอย่างไร

Stress (การลงเสียงหนัก)

ดัชนีในเล่มนี้ใช้ระบบในการลงเสียงหนักที่พบได้ในพจนานุกรมสำหรับเจ้าของภาษาทั่วๆไป และมีข้อปฏิบัติดังนี้
1. เครื่องหมายลงเสียงหนัก (stress) จะไม่ใส่ให้ไว้ถ้าคำๆ นั้นมีเพียงพยางค์เดียว
2. ถ้าใช้เครื่องหมายลงเสียงหนัก เสียงที่ออกมาจะมี 2 ระดับอย่างชัดเจน

เครื่องหมายลงเสียงหนัก [/] จะอยู่หลังพยางค์ (syllable) ที่มีการลงเสียงหนักมาก (primary) ส่วนเครื่องหมายที่แสดงการลงเสียงเบา [/] จะอยู่หลังพยางค์ที่มีเสียงเบากว่าหรือดังน้อยกว่า คือ เป็นรองลงมา (secondary)

ในวลีหรือกลุ่มคำอื่นๆ เครื่องหมายลงเสียงหนัก (stress) จะอยู่ที่คำที่ออกเสียงหนักมากที่สุด ในวลีนั้นๆ หรือกลุ่มคำนั้นๆ ถ้าคำหนึ่งคำ ประกอบด้วยพยางค์เดียว และคำนั้นถูกนำมาผสมผสานกับคำที่อยู่ในบัญชีคำข้างใต้คำนั้นๆเครื่องหมายที่แสดงการลงเสียงหนักมากหรือน้อย (primary หรือ secondary) จะปรากฏอยู่ในวงเล็บเครื่องหมาย - (hyphen) จะใช้แทนส่วนของคำหรือ หรือวลีที่เว้นเอาไว้ตัวอย่างเช่นคำว่า bus [bŭs(/–)] แสดงว่าคำว่า bus จะมีเสียงหนักมาก เมื่อรวมกับคำที่อยู่ภายใต้คำว่า bus คำว่า ...driver [–drī/vər] อยู่ภายใต้คำว่า bus นั้นแสดงว่าคำว่า driver ได้รับการลงเสียงเบา (Secondary stress) ในการรวมคำเป็นวลี bus driver [bŭs/ drī/vər]

Syllable Boundaries (ขอบเขตของพยางค์)

พยางค์ต่างๆ จะมีขอบเขตของมันเองอย่างชัดเจนโดยใช้ช่องว่าง (space) 1 ช่องเป็นตัวแบ่งหรือโดยการใช้เครื่องหมายการลงเสียงหนัก (stress mark)

ข้อสังเกต การออกเสียงที่แสดงในดัชนีนั้นอาศัยหลักการออกเสียงที่เรียกว่า อังกฤษแบบอเมริกัน (American English) แต่ไม่ได้หมายความ ว่าจะเป็นการออกเสียง ที่เป็นตัวแทนของอังกฤษแบบอเมริกันที่มีมากมายทั่วสหรัฐอเมริกา นักเรียนควรจะฟังจากเจ้าของภาษาเพื่อให้ได้ยินว่า ภาษาแต่ละท้องถิ่นเขาออกเสียงกันอย่างไร

Index

Index

Index

184

Index

Index

Geographical Index

Continents ทวีป

Africa [ăf′rĭ kə] **125**–5 อัฟริกา
Antarctica [ănt ärk′tĭ kə, –är′tĭ–] **125**–7 แอนตาร์กติกา
Asia [ā′zhə] **125**–4 เอเชีย
Australia [ö strāl′yə] **125**–6 ออสเตรเลีย
Europe [yŏŏr′əp] **125**–3 ยุโรป
North America [nörth′ ə mĕr′ə kə] **124**–1 อเมริกาเหนือ
South America [sowth′ ə mĕr′ə kə] **124**–2 อเมริกาใต้

Countries and other locations ประเทศและดินแดนต่างๆ

Afghanistan [ăf găn′ə stăn′] **124–125** อัฟกานิสถาน
Albania [ăl bā′nē ə] **124–125** อัลเบเนีย
Algeria [ăl jir′ē ə] **124–125125** อัลจีเรีย
American Samoa [ə mĕr′ə kən sə mō′ə] **124–125** ซามัวอเมริกา
Andorra [ăn dör′ə] **124–125** แอนดอรา
Angola [ăng gō′lə] **124–125** แองโกลา
Argentina [är′jən tē′nə] **124–125** อาร์เจนตินา
Armenia [är mē′nē ə] **124–125** อาร์เมเนีย
Australia [ö strāl′yə] **124–125** ออสเตรเลีย
Austria [ö′strē ə] **124–125** ออสเตรีย
Azerbaijan [ăz′ər bī jän′] **124–125** อาเซอร์ไบจัน
Bahamas [bə hä′məz] **122–125** บาฮามาส
Bahrain [bä rān′] **124–125** บาห์เรน
Bangladesh [băng′glə dĕsh′, băng′–] **124–125** บังกลาเทศ
Barbados [bär bā′dōs] **124–125** บาร์บาโดส
Belarus [bē′lə rōōs′, byĕl′ə–] **124–125** เบลารุส
Belgium [bĕl′jəm] **124–125** เบลเยี่ยม
Belize [bə lēz′] **124–125** เบลิซ
Benin [bə nĭn′, –nēn′] **124–125** เบนิน
Bermuda [bər myōō′də] **122–125** เบอร์มิวด้า
Bhutan [bōō tän′] **124–125** ภูฏาน
Bolivia [bə lĭv′ē ə] **124–125** โบลิเวีย
Borneo [bör′nē ō] **124–125** บอร์เนียว
Bosnia-Herzegovina [băz′nē ə hër′tsə gō vē′nə] **124–125** บอสเนีย-เฮอเซอะโกวิเนอะ
Botswana [bät swä′nə] **124–125** บอสวานา
Brazil [brə zĭl′] **124–125** บราซิล
Brunei [brōō nī′] **124–125** บรูไน
Bulgaria [bŭl gër′ē ə] **124–125** บัลแกเรีย
Burkina Faso [bər kē′nə fä′sō] **124–125** เบอร์คินาฟาโซ
Burundi [bōō rōōn′dē] **124–125** บูรุนดี
Cambodia [kăm bō′dē ə] **124–125** กัมพูชา
Cameroon [kăm′ə rōōn′] **124–125** คาเมอรูน
Canada [kăn′ə də] **122–125** แคนาดา
Cape Verde [kāp′ vürd′] **124–125** เคพเวอร์ด
Central African Republic [sĕn′trəl ăf′rĭ kən rĭ pŭb′lĭk] **124–125** สาธารณรัฐอัฟริกากลาง
Chad [chăd] **124–125** แชด
Chile [chĭl′ē] **124–125** ชิลี
China [chī′nə] **124–125** จีน
Colombia [kə lŭm′bē ə] **124–125** โคลัมเบีย
Comoros [kăm′ə rōz] **124–125** คอมเมอร์โรช
Congo [käng′gō] **124–125** คองโก
Costa Rica [kōs′tə rē′kə, käs′–] **122–125** คอสตาริก้า
Croatia [krō ā′shə] **124–125** โครเอเชีย
Cuba [kyōō′bə] **122–125** คิวบา
Cyprus [sī′prəs] **124–125** ไซปรัส
Czech Republic [chĕk′ rĭ pŭb′lĭk] **124–125** สาธารณรัฐเช็ค
Democratic Republic of the Congo [dĕm′ə krăt′ĭk rĭ pŭb′lĭk əv dhə käng′gō] **124–125** สาธารณรัฐประชาธิปไตยคองโก
Denmark [dĕn′märk] **124–125** เดนมาร์ก
Djibouti [jĭ bōō′tē] **124–125** จิบูตี
Dominica [däm′ə nē′kə] **124–125** โดมินิก้า
Dominican Republic [də mĭn′ĭ kən rĭ pŭb′lĭk] **122–125** สาธารณรัฐโดมินิกัน
Ecuador [ĕk′wə dör′] **124–125** เอกวาดอร์
Egypt [ē′jĭpt] **124–125** อียิปต์

El Salvador [ĕl săl′və dör′] **122–125** เอล ซัลวาดอร์
Equatorial Guinea [ē′kwə tör′ē əl gĭn′ē, ĕk′wə–] **124–125** อีเควเทอเรียวกินี
Eritrea [ĕr′ə trē′ə] **124–125** เอริเทรีย
Estonia [ĕ stō′nē ə] **124–125** เอสโทเนีย
Ethiopia [ē′thē ō′pē ə] **124–125** เอธิโอเบีย
Fiji [fē′jē] **124–125** ฟิจิ
Finland [fĭn′lənd] **124–125** ฟินแลนด์
France [frăns] **124–125** ฝรั่งเศส
French Guiana [frĕnch′ gē ăn′ə, –ä′nə] **124–125** เฟรนชกิอานา
French Polynesia [frĕnch′ päl′ə nē′zhə] **124–125** เฟรนชโพลินีเซีย
Gabon [gä bōn′] **124–125** กาบอน
Georgia [jör′jə] **124–125** จอร์เจีย
Germany [jür′mə nē] **124–125** เยอรมันนี
Ghana [gä′nə] **124–125** กานา
Greece [grēs] **124–125** กรีซ
Greenland [grēn′lənd, –lănd′] **122–125** กรีนแลนด์
Grenada [grə nā′də] **124–125** เกรนาดา
Guatemala [gwä′tə mä′lə] **122–125** กัวเตมาลา
Guinea [gĭn′ē] **124–125** กินี
Guinea-Bissau [gĭn′ē bĭ sow′] **124–125** กินีบิสเชา
Guyana [gī ăn′ə] **124–125** กายอานา
Haiti [hā′tē] **122–125** ไฮติ
Honduras [hän dōōr′əs] **122–125** ฮอนดูรัส
Hong Kong [häng′ käng′] **124–125** ฮ่องกง
Hungary [hŭng′gə rē] **124–125** ฮังการี
Iceland [īs′lənd] **124–125** ไอซ์แลนด์
India [ĭn′dē ə] **124–125** อินเดีย
Indonesia [ĭn′də nē′zhə] **124–125** อินโดนีเซีย
Iran [ĭ rän′, ĭ răn′] **124–125** อิหร่าน
Iraq [ĭ räk′, ĭ răk′] **124–125** อิรัก
Ireland [īr′lənd] **124–125** ไอร์แลนด์
Israel [ĭz′rē əl, –rā–] **124–125** อิสราเอล
Italy [ĭt′l ē] **124–125** อิตาลี
Ivory Coast [īv′rē kōst′] **124–125** ไอวอรีโคสต์
Jamaica [jə mā′kə] **122–125** จาไมกา
Japan [jə păn′] **124–125** ญี่ปุ่น
Java [jä′və] **124–125** ชวา
Jordan [jör′dn] **124–125** จอร์แดน
Kazakhstan [kä′zăk stän′] **124–125** คาซัคสถาน
Kenya [kĕn′yə, kēn′–] **124–125** เคนยา
Kiribati [kïr′ə băs′] **124–125** เคียริบาต
Kuwait [kōō wāt′] **124–125** คูเวต
Kyrgyzstan [kïr′gĭ stän′, –stän′] **124–125** เคอร์กิสถาน
Laos [lows, lä′ōs] **124–125** ลาว
Latvia [lăt′vē ə] **124–125** แลธเวีย
Lebanon [lĕb′ə nən, –nän′] **124–125** เลบานอน
Lesotho [lə sō′tō, –sōō′tōō] **124–125** เลโซโฐ
Liberia [lī bïr′ē ə] **124–125** ไลเบอเรีย
Libya [lĭb′ē ə] **124–125** ลิเบีย
Liechtenstein [lĭk′tən stīn′] **124–125** ลิคเคนสไตน์
Lithuania [lĭth′ōō ā′nē ə] **124–125** ลิธัวเนีย
Luxembourg [lŭk′səm bürg′] **124–125** ลักเซมเบิร์ก
Macedonia [măs′ə dō′nē ə] **124–125** มาซีโกเนีย
Madagascar [măd′ə găs′kər] **124–125** มาดากัสการ์
Malawi [mə lä′wē] **124–125** มาลาวี
Malaysia [mə lā′zhə] **124–125** มาเลเซีย
Maldives [möl′dēvz, –dīvz] **124–125** มัลดีฟส์
Mali [mä′lē] **124–125** มาลี
Malta [möl′tə] **124–125** มอลตา
Marshall Islands [mär′shəl ī′ləndz] **124–125** หมู่เกาะมาร์แชล
Mauritania [mör′ə tā′nē ə] **124–125** มอริทาเนีย
Mauritius [mö rĭsh′əs] **124–125** มอริเชียส
Mexico [mĕk′sĭ kō′] **122–125** เม็กซิโก
Micronesia [mī′krə nē′zhə] **124–125** ไมโครนีเซีย
Moldova [mäl dō′və, möl–] **124–125** มอลโดวา

Bodies of water น่านน้ำ

The United States of America สหรัฐอเมริกา
Capital: Washington, D.C. (District Of Columbia)
[wä/shĭng tən dē/sē/, wö/–] เมืองหลวง : วอชิงตัน ดี.ซี.

Regions of the United States ภูมิภาคของสหรัฐ